THE
MYSTIC
HEART

ALSO BY WAYNE TEASDALE

The Community of Religions
Edited by Wayne Teasdale and George Cairns

More praise for *The Mystic Heart*

"My good friend Brother Wayne Teasdale has long been actively involved in the effort to bring our religious traditions together. In this book Brother Wayne explores what he calls interspirituality. He shares his deep respect for and knowledge of the world's religions, relates examples from the lives of many great spiritual practitioners, and illuminates the traditions' wonderful commonalities. *The Mystic Heart* is a work of great inspiration."   — His Holiness the Dalai Lama

"With loving clarity and understanding of all genuine mystical experience from the great traditions, Brother Wayne Teasdale illuminates the 'ecology of souls' so that each of us, no matter what our path, can be attuned and enriched by the others. A fine masterwork by a living embodiment of the mystic heart."
          — Barbara Marx Hubbard, author of *Conscious Evolution*

"Those who share Teasdale's optimistic vision of the coming age as fostering spiritual unity among diverse peoples will consider the book an inspirational guide."
          — *Publishers Weekly*

"This well-written and informative book will appeal both to scholars and informed lay readers. For academic libraries and public libraries with a strong religion collection."   — *Library Journal*

"This is a landmark book in the field of interreligious dialogue, written with sensitivity and deep respect for all the great traditions."   — *The Hartford Courant*

"*The Mystic Heart* is a visionary work that presents a bold and imaginative glimpse of the fruits of multifaith sharing and collaboration. Teasdale's yearning for a universal communal spirituality that cuts across all traditions is one that we can celebrate. On these pages, he has presented stirring blueprints of global mysticism."
          — *Spirituality & Health*

"Teasdale's interspiritulity is more than just developing tolerance: it opens the door to even greater truths."   — *Personal Transformation*

"Teasdale combines a Christian faith with an understanding of the world's religions, resulting in an excellent explanation of the principles and elements of universal spirituality."   — *The Bookwatch*

"*The Mystic Heart* is an excellent survey and overview of the present state of interfaith or multifaith spirituality at the end of the 20th century. Wayne Teasdale ... has put together a truly thought-provoking book — one that should prosper as a useful primer in the field of interreligious dialogue."
          — *America* magazine

"With a vast range of knowledge, Teasdale draws on the teachings, practices, and experiences of shamans, saints, and theologians of all ages and traditions, on his own experience, and on contemporary science, art, and poetry to provide an understanding of the goal of realizing ultimate reality as it appears under many names. . . . Hans Küng has said there will be no peace until there is understanding among world religions. This book is an informed and practical contribution to that understanding." — *CHOICE, Current Reviews for Academic Libraries*

"*The Mystic Heart* reminds us that the fruits of our personal spiritual journey also have their own reward in giving to ourselves a greater capacity for openness and awareness, for spontaneity and joy, to be really present for others, in compassion and without expectation." — *Conscious Choice*

"This book will appeal to a wide variety of readers, and especially those interested in mysticism, spirituality, and religion. . . . those who read *The Mystic Heart* will be inspired toward deep spiritual discovery." — *New Age Retailer*

" . . . For [those] just beginning to wonder what we all have in common, where to look for the one God underneath all the rich religious diversity of the human family, this may be just the right guide." — *National Catholic Reporter*

" . . . Teasdale has done us a service in synthesizing an enormous amount of material, and of presenting it to us in an eminently readable and digestible format. This book will create a great deal of soul-searching. . . . " — *Sisters Today*

"*The Mystic Heart* is a beautiful and profound meditation on the commonalities at the core of the world's great religions. In this age of extreme pluralism, which encourages us to all be different (and fragmented), Brother Teasdale reminds us that Spirit is common in and to us all, and thus in addition to cherishing differences we can embrace unity. A wise and wonderful wake-up call to a world in shattered pieces." — Ken Wilber, author of *The Marriage of Sense and Soul*

"This rare and wonderful book awakens its readers to their own mystic nature. We discover here how previously divided and distinguished spiritual traditions are converging into a new river of holiness, an interspirituality. What is unique in this work is the luminous guidance the author gives us for deepening one's personal faith while exploring the mystical genius of other traditions. It may well be, as Brother Teasdale so eloquently shows, that the mystical experience is perhaps the greatest accelerator of evolutionary enhancement. Through it, we tap into wider physical, mental, emotional and social systems and thus gain entrance into the next stage of our unfolding, both individually and collectively. Once the province of the few, the mystic path may now be the requirement of the many — a unique developmental path for self and world. *The Mystic Heart* goes to the heart of this matter." — Jean Houston, author of *A Mythic Life*

THE

MYSTIC
HEART

DISCOVERING A UNIVERSAL
SPIRITUALITY IN THE WORLD'S RELIGIONS

WAYNE TEASDALE

FOREWORD BY
HIS HOLINESS THE DALAI LAMA

PREFACE BY
BEATRICE BRUTEAU

NEW WORLD LIBRARY
NOVATO, CALIFORNIA

New World Library
14 Pamaron Way
Novato, CA 94949

Copyright © 1999 by Wayne Teasdale
Cover design: Big Fish
Cover photograph: Photonica
Text design: Mary Ann Casler

Library of Congress Cataloging-in-Publication Data
Teasdale, Wayne.
    The mystic heart : discovering a universal spirituality in the world's religions /
Wayne Teasedale ; foreword by His Holiness the Dalai Lama ; preface by Beatrice
Bruteau.
       p.   cm.
    Includes bibliographical references and index.
    ISBN 1-57731-102-7 (hardcover : alk. paper)
    ISBN 1-57731-140-x (paperback : alk. paper)
    1. Mysticism. 2. Religions. I. Title.
BL625.T43 1999
291.4'22 — dc21   99-41879
                                                                  CIP

First paperback printing, April 2001
ISBN 1-57731-140-x
Printed in Canada on acid-free, recycled paper
Distributed to the trade by Publishers Group West

10 9 8

*To my Uncle John Cosgrove
and my other teachers, spiritual and otherwise*

If the doors of perception were cleansed,
then everything would appear as it actually is, infinite.

— William Blake

CONTENTS

Part I: Finding What Unites Us

INTRODUCTION

The Mystic Heart: Our Common Heritage ✦ 3

The Interspiritual Age • The Parliament of the World's Religions •
The Turn to Spirituality • A Dot on a Blackboard

CHAPTER 1

A Bridge Across the Religions and Beyond ✦ 15

What Is Spirituality? • Spirituality in the Religions • The Nature of
Mysticism and Spirituality • What Is Interspirituality? •
The Treasure of Community

CHAPTER 2

Crossing Over: Pioneers of Interspiritual Wisdom ✦ 31

The Meeting of Christianity and Hinduism • Dialogue Between
Catholicism and the Other Religions • Buddhism Comes to the West •
Finding Your Place in the Interspiritual Movement

Foreword

BY HIS HOLINESS THE
DALAI LAMA

Forty years ago as a young man, I left my homeland and began a new life in India as a refugee. In general my departure from Tibet and the circumstances that led to it are causes for much regret. However, they have also inadvertently provided me personally with many reasons to rejoice. Among these are the many opportunities I have had to become better acquainted with the world's major religious traditions. I have been welcomed at places of worship throughout the world, and have visited and shared prayers at many sacred places of pilgrimage. But above all I have made friends with countless religious brothers and sisters. Some of these people occupy positions of religious authority, some are profound spiritual practitioners, and many are ordinary, kind-hearted women and men doing the best they can.

I have learned from these experiences that all the world's religious traditions have similar potential to help us become better human beings. For centuries, millions of people have found peace of mind in their own religious tradition. Today, the world over, we find followers of many faiths sacrificing their own welfare to help others. I believe that this wish to work for the happiness of others is the most important goal of all religious practice.

Human beings naturally possess different interests and inclinations. Therefore, it should come as no surprise that we have many different religious traditions with different ways of thinking and behaving. But this variety is a way for everyone to be happy. If we only have bread, people who eat rice are left out. With a great variety of food, we are able to satisfy everyone's different needs and tastes. And people eat rice because it grows best where they live, not because it is either any better or worse than bread.

Because all the world's religious traditions share the same essential purpose, we must maintain harmony and respect among them. This not only benefits the followers of each religion but makes our neighborhoods and countries more peaceful. To do this we need to understand something about the world's different religions. There are many ways to go about this, but I believe the most effective is face-to-face dialogue. Let religious and spiritual leaders meet together to discuss and share their experience and practice; let ordinary members of religious communities spend time with each other.

My good friend Brother Wayne Teasdale has long been actively involved in the effort to bring our religious traditions together. In this book Brother Wayne explores what he calls interspirituality. He shares his deep respect for and knowledge of the world's religions, relates examples from the lives of many great spiritual practitioners, and illuminates the traditions' great commonalities. *The Mystic Heart* is a work of great inspiration.

Religion, for most of us, depends on our family background — where we were born and grew up. I think it is usually better not to change that. The more we understand each other's ways, however, the more we can learn from each other. Our presentation of love and compassion may differ, but the concept of compassion remains the same. Once we realize this, and appreciate its deeper implications, it automatically brings genuine respect for other religions. And respect acts as a foundation for the development of harmony between different religious traditions.

On a personal level, I believe that we are all capable of improvement. We can transform ourselves. If, for example, as a reader of this book, you were to spend a few minutes every day thinking about and trying to develop compassion, eventually compassion, the essence of spiritual practice, will become part of your life. When that happens I am convinced that not only will your life be happier but you will also make a direct contribution to peace and happiness in the world as a whole.

— His Holiness the Dalai Lama

Preface

BY DR. BEATRICE BRUTEAU

Nothing is more practical for realizing our desire for a better world than mysticism. Better worlds have to be built on sure foundations; they must be able to withstand deep impediments to their development. What most of us now recognize as a "better" world is one in which we recognize that all people possess an incomparable value that we are morally obliged to respect. This respect originates in intelligence and feeling but eventually must be embodied in social, political, and economic terms. Honoring the humanity of your fellow beings means that if they are hungry, ill, or oppressed, you must exert yourself to help them. Doing so is not generosity beyond duty; failure to do so is culpable. But this view of moral obligation runs up against our inherited instincts of self-protection, greediness, and desire to dominate others. We can try, by various forms of legislation, to balance these two dynamisms, but they continue to conflict, causing tension and loss of energy. We are attempting to balance power *from the outside*. If we could rearrange energy *from within* — if we more often nurtured our companions and promoted their well-being, we would suffer much less. Rearranging energy *from within* is what mysticism does.

How does mysticism do this? Consider that domination, greed, cruelty, violence, and all our other ills arise from a sense of insufficient and insecure *being*. I need more power, more possessions, more respect and admiration. But it's never enough; the fear always remains. It comes from every side: from other people; from economic circumstances; from ideas, customs, and belief systems; from the natural environment; from our own bodies and minds. All these *others* intimidate us, threaten us, make us anxious. We can't control them. They are, to varying degrees, aliens. Our experience is: where I am "I," they are "not-I."

At least, this is our experience insofar as we are not mystics. But, fortunately, everyone is a mystic. At some deep level, we know that we are not mutually alienated from each other and that we do have sufficient being. Unfortunately, most of us have not raised that knowing to our explicit consciousness enough to transform our embodied life. When that knowledge does percolate up through the layers of our perceptions and behaviors, then our motives, feelings, and actions turn from withdrawal, suspicion, rejection, hostility, and domination to openness, trust, inclusion, nurturance, and communion. The practice of raising this knowledge is the process of becoming a mystic in experience as well as in potentiality.

Raising the hidden knowledge of unity, rearranging our interior dynamisms, is something we can practice. There are exercises for cultivating this transition in every culture and tradition. We can learn from any or all of them. This book is about that practice and about what we may experience along the way. And this comes at just the right moment in the world process. The planet is unified as never before and becoming more so every day. We used to say, "We must learn to live together." We can still say that, but the fact is that we *are* living together. We now have access to all the world's traditions, all the learning, all the customs and beliefs and expressions.

It turns out that we are not nearly so alien to one another as we had thought, and that our efforts to bring forth this mystic realization are happily consonant. In talking with one another, sharing experiences, teaching and encouraging one another, all the traditions are being enriched, individuals are growing, and mystical realization is rising. We are helping each other *know* that we are deeply related, that we are all precious and deserving, that the universe is our home, that we can feel safe on the deepest level of our being. In this mutual support, the sense of *oneness* that is the hallmark of the mystic is increasing. The very fact that all the traditions are trusting and sharing with one another is a powerful sign of the unity they all teach and honor. This oneness — freedom from alienation and insecurity — is the sure foundation for a better world. It means that we will try to help each other rather than hurt each other.

Of course, not everyone is seeing, feeling, and practicing this oneness. We are only at the beginning of this development. But the bellwethers — the mystics — are gathering and uniting. Our united insight and caring means that we can offer ways to overcome our impediments. At least we will be starting from the right principle, not from exclusion or supersession or domination of any sort. Mutual respect is the only possible foundation for a free, just, equal, and responsible society, and mystical experience is the ultimate ground for that respect. With freedom from the need to promote oneself — or one's nation, tradition, or religion — by devaluing others comes a great release of energy. What had been invested in protection is now available for caring for and rejoicing in others. Wayne Teasdale's instructive, inspiring, and beautiful book is a kind of interim report on this work in progress. This is where the world is in its journey toward unity, social justice, and happiness. This is how you can join in and contribute. Many people are devoted to this task all over the world. Now, more and more, they are consciously working *together.* This is a source of inspiration and a cause for celebration.

— Dr. Beatrice Bruteau
Author of *Radical Optimism, What We Can Learn from the East,* and
God's Ecstasy: The Creation of a Self-Creating World
Editor of *The Other Half of My Soul: Bede Griffiths and the
Hindu-Christian Dialogue*

Acknowledgments

I owe so much to so many people everywhere, particularly those who have influenced my spiritual growth. First I must thank my teachers who have contributed greatly to my formation, especially Bede Griffiths, Mary Sarah Muldowney, Mary Roman, Thomas Keating, Raimon Panikkar, Thomas Berry, Ewert Cousins, and the Dalai Lama. I want to thank all the monastic communities that have shown me unfailing hospitality over the years, especially St. Joseph's Abbey, Christ in the Desert, St. Benedict's Monastery, St. Procopius Abbey, Sacred Heart Monastery, Cardinal Stritch Retreat House, and the Cenacle. At Catholic Theological Union in Chicago I want to especially remember Ken O'Malley, Jim Barry, Don Senior, Gary Riebe-Estrella, John Pawlikowski, Mary Frohlich, Harrietta Holloway, Frances Hankins, Linda Mosley, Jim Doyle, Eleanor Holland, Zachary Hayes, Sean McEntee, Michael Tracy, Juventino Lagos, Ardis Cloutier, Eva Solomon, Anne McNamara, Al Poole, and Gerry Boberg.

Thanks to Jeff Carlson of DePaul University who has always been so kind to me, to Bill Hyashi of Columbia College, and the faculty of the

Senior Seminar. Jim and Cetta Kenney of Common Ground have always given me a forum to share my ideas and experience. I treasure every one of my friends in the Parliament of the World's Religions. Let me specially thank Howard Sulkin, Dirk Ficca, and again, the Kenneys, Haik Muradian, Daniel Gomez-Ibanez, Irfan Khan, Tom Baima, Joan MaGuire, Georgene Wilson, Rohinton Rivetna, Ma Jaya Sati Bhagavati, Jean Houston, Krishna Priya, Richard Rosancrantz (Brahmadas), Kevin Coval, Eboo Patel, Ravi Singh, and Travis Rejman. I am indebted to everyone in the Parliament, though I cannot mention them all by name.

Thank you to Beatrice Bruteau and her husband, Jim Somerville, both friends of many years. I am very grateful to Beatrice for her substantive preface, and to the Dalai Lama, another great friend, for his beautiful foreword. I also want to mention George and Nancy Cairns, Gary Shunk, Chuck Willis and all my friends at the Fetzer Institute, Lorene Wu and her family, Jeff Jaeger, Martha Howard, Gene Arbetter, and Tony Clifton.

Thank you to all my friends on the East and West Coasts, notably Jonathan and Lisanne LaCroix, Magdalena Gomez, Gary Mallalieu, Pam Delaney, Steve Delaronde, the Delarondes, Eric and Sarina Montenegro, Gene Gallogly, Luke O'Neill Jr., Marc and Jeanine Colbert-Boucher, and Tommy Sullivan. I must also mention Jim Connor, Pascaline Coff, Julian von Duerbeck, Johanna Becker, Kate Howard, Meg Funk, and Don Mitchell. I would like to thank in a special way Tenzin Choegyal, his wife, Rinchen Kando, and their children; Samdong Rinpoche; Lodi Gyari; Tenzin Geyche Tethong; and Dorjee Wandue.

Thank you to Theophane Boyd; my editor, Jason Gardner; my agent, Joe Durepos; Osa Sandlung; Preston Singletary; David Cox; Greg Belnap; Judy Walter; Robert Skall; Russill and Asha Paul D'Silva; Gregory Perron; David and Naomi Wilkinson; Robert Hopper; and Larry Korass — all of whom have encouraged my writing. My friends in Aikido also require mention: Tohei Sensei and his wife Joanne, Judy Leppert, Don and Joanne Wrona, Bernard Calma, Lor Siegel, Joe and Brenda Rosen, Joe McMahnn, and Darrell and Jeannie Jordan. I am indebted to T. J. McGovern for all he has done to facilitate my work, along with Bob and Jane McGuffey.

Thank you to Jim, Cheryl, Enid, Justin, and Lucy Keen; Arun and Sunanda Gandhi; Linda Groff; Robert Fastiggi; Hal and Betsy Edwards;

Diane Farah; Jose Pereira; Leo Lefebure; Laurence Freeman; Rose Isaacs; Paul Harris; Mark and Polly Schofield; Allen Harrison; Jon, Mary, and Sarah Derr; Hob, Olivia, Laura, Ethen, and Kanti Hoblitzelle; Jane B. Owen; Jackie Roemer; and Gordie and Pam Fellman.

Special thanks to Brian Muldoon, Barbara Fields Bernstein, and their children, Micky, Sean, Molly, and Sailer. Also special thanks to Joel and Gwen Beversluis, the Gustafsons, Joan McGlinchey, Patrick Hart, Astarius An, Nick and Carolyn Groves, Bill Epperley, Peggy Kay, and all the members of the Friends of Bede Griffiths. Thank you to the Jenung family; John Freeman; Tim and Barbara Cook; Mary Goens; Mimi Sullivan; Bob Rader; Lenny Coppenwrath; Ron Miller; Carol Henning; Dorothy and Karl Baughman; Ettore Di Filippo; Francis Tiso; Arlo and Jackie Guthrie; Rick Doblin; and Suzy, Chris, Gabriel, and Julia Happ-Shine. There are countless others I have not included here, but they all have a place in my heart.

PART I

FINDING WHAT UNITES US

Introduction

THE MYSTIC HEART:
OUR COMMON HERITAGE

Without opening your door,
you can open your heart to the world.
— Tao Te Ching

Physicist Stephen Hawking has remarked that mysticism is for those who can't do the math. In response to Hawking's remark, my friend George Cairns retorted, "Mystics are people who don't need to do the math. They have direct experience!"

One day, as a college sophomore in New Hampshire, I had an extraordinary encounter with one of my professors. "You have a mystical look to you," he observed out of the blue. "I've noticed it for some time. Your eyes seem to suggest a mystical place, and you are rooted there." I was just coming out of a terrible dark night of faith that had lasted some three years, and mystical experience had indeed been my doorway to release. His words, although a little bewildering at the time, were prophetic; they perceived the inner core of my being.

My case isn't unique. It's really the story of every person who awakens to himself or herself — to the mystery within, without, and beyond us. Every one of us is a mystic. We may or may not realize it; we may not even like it. But whether we know it or not, whether we accept it or not, mystical experience is always there, inviting us on a journey of ultimate discovery. We have been given the gift of life in this perplexing world to become who we ultimately are: creatures of boundless love, caring, compassion, and wisdom. Existence is a summons to the eternal journey of the sage — the sage we all are, if only we could see.

As a graduate student in the late 1970s, I studied and translated the *Itinerium Mentis in Deum* — *The Journey of the Soul to God* — a Latin work by St. Bonaventure, a great Franciscan mystic saint and theologian. This dense little book — barely fifty pages — is a treasury of all the trends in medieval mysticism. While reading this singularly profound, inspiring, but difficult work, I realized how much our modern culture needs the wisdom and direction housed in the pages of this little gem. I dreamed then of writing such a work for the widest possible audience. I'm glad I didn't rush into it; it certainly wouldn't be the book it is now. My experience needed to evolve, deepen, and expand in order to carry and reflect the spiritual nature each one of us has and quite simply *is*. In time, my inner life blossomed as I was exposed to India, other cultures, and precious people. More important, the human family is now much more open to receiving what I believe is so essential: a practical, mystical, and universal understanding of spirituality.

❖ The Interspiritual Age

We are at the dawn of a new consciousness, a radically fresh approach to our life as the human family in a fragile world. This birth into a new awareness, into a new set of historical circumstances, appears in a number of shifts in our understanding:

The emergence of ecological awareness and sensitivity to the natural, organic world, with an acknowledgment of the basic fragility of the earth.

A growing sense of the rights of other species.

A recognition of the interdependence of all domains of life and reality.

The ideal of abandoning a militant nationalism as a result of this tangible sense of our essential interdependence.

A deep, evolving experience of community between and among the religions through their individual members.

The growing receptivity to the inner treasures of the world's religions.

An openness to the cosmos, with the realization that the relationship between humans and the earth is part of the larger community of the universe.

Each of these shifts represents dramatic change; taken together, they will define the thought and culture of the third millennium. Fewer and fewer people are questioning the vital importance of the environmental issue. Its significance is so great that Thomas Berry — who refers to himself as a *geo-logian,* or a theologian for the earth — believes in naming this new period in history the *Ecological* or *Ecozoic Age.*[1] We could really name the age after any of these shifts in understanding. To encompass them all, however, perhaps the best name for this new segment of historical experience is the *Interspiritual Age.*

All of these awarenesses are interrelated, and each is indispensable to clearly grasping the greater shift taking place, a shift that will sink roots deep into our lives and culture. Taken together, they are preparing the way for a universal civilization: a civilization with a *heart.* Such a universal society will draw its inspiration from perennial spiritual and moral insights, intuitions, and experiences. These aspects of spirituality will shape how we conduct politics and education; how we envision our economies, media, and entertainment; and how we develop our relationship with the natural world, while pursuing our quality of life.

The awakening to our ecological interconnectedness, with its concomitant sense of the preciousness of all other species, raises the earth to where it becomes the center of our moral, aesthetic, economic, political, social, cultural, and spiritual activities. We have to learn to negotiate the balance between the individual and the totality, rather than erring too far to one side, as in the past. Negative forms of nationalism and tribalism are beyond redemption. They need to be firmly set aside. In their extreme expressions, they poison the earth's common good, as we have seen in Iraq, Iran, Yugoslavia, Rwanda, and elsewhere. As we become more aware of our intrinsic interdependence, destructive nationalism will pass away, and a more positive approach to nationhood as a cohesive force within a democratic system will take hold.

Interdependence is an inescapable fact of our contemporary world. Not only is it a prevailing condition that dominates international commerce, cultural exchange, and scientific collaboration, it is a value that promotes stable global peace. The more the bonds of interconnectedness define the shape and scope of the future, the less likely they will be ruptured. The more interdependent we are, the more we will safeguard the system of the universal society.

A *spiritual* interdependence also exists between and among the world's religions. This interdependence is more subtle, though the actual impact of traditions on each other is clearly discernable in history, particularly where cultural contiguity exists. Hinduism has directly influenced the rise of Buddhism, for example. Jainism, in its teaching of *ahimsa,* or nonharming, has influenced both Buddhism and Hinduism. Christianity would hardly be possible without Judaism, and Islam is inconceivable without these predecessors. Sikhism developed in North India in the sixteenth century as a reaction to Islamic persecution, but its religious life, beliefs, rituals, and spirituality were shaped by both Hindu and Muslim forms. Similarly, Confucianism and Taoism in China mutually influenced each other; and Taoism had a deep impact on Ch'an Buddhism, which became Zen in Japan. These are just a few examples. Endless studies demonstrate the impact of earlier, lesser-known traditions and myths on the development and doctrines of the historical faiths. The impact of myths and these other traditions on the biblical tradition alone is staggering.

This spiritual interdependence is often indirect and thus not clearly seen. But it is nonetheless real. Monasticism in the West, for instance, which arose in the third and fourth centuries of the Christian era in the deserts of Sinai, Palestine, and Syria, no doubt was affected by the *rishis,* the forest sages of Indian antiquity, and their monastic heirs, the *sannyasis* or renunciates. It is well known that Buddhist and Hindu monastic communities existed in Alexandria, Egypt, in the first century before Christ.

The younger religions also influence the older. Christianity's concept of the social gospel has profoundly influenced Buddhism and Hinduism, traditions that now encourage the growth of socially engaged religious life. And the *Christ event* has had an even more essential impact on the rise of the *bodhisattva* ideal, which sprang up in India five centuries after the death of the Buddha and became central to the Mahayana tradition. The bodhisattva is one who vows to selflessly place the liberation of all sentient beings before his or her own. Many scholars have recognized this influence, but one in particular, the anonymous author of *Meditations on the Tarot: A Journey into Christian Hermeticism,* does so within the context of spiritual interdependence, suggesting how the advent of Christ influenced the emergence of the bodhisattva:

> When the Gospel was preached by the light of day in the countries
> around the Mediterranean, the nocturnal rays of the Gospel effected a

profound transformation of Buddhism. There, the ideal of individual liberation by entering the state of nirvana gave way to the ideal of renouncing nirvana for the work of mercy towards suffering humanity. The ideal of mahayana, the great chariot, then had its resplendent ascent to the heaven of Asia's moral values.[2]

When we examine relations among the religions today, we find traditions increasingly discovering and pursuing a real experience of community, especially among individuals. This existential realization arises from actual encounters between people of differing traditions. Throughout history, members of different traditions have entered deep, meaningful dialogues, which arose out of amicable relations between communities. The third-century reign of the Buddhist Emperor Asoka of the Mauran Dynasty in India, for example, was enormously welcoming of other traditions. Asoka practiced tolerance and respect, stimulating interfaith encounters. India, alone, has many examples of interfaith encounter.

✦ The Parliament of the World's Religions

Most of recorded history, however, chronicles thousands of years of isolation. Cultures of separation have clung to an exclusivist perspective that has left no room for other traditions. The attitude of exclusivity is both distrustful of other faiths and disrespectful of their insights and experiences. There is no basis for dialogue, let alone a bond of community.

One of the special historical moments of breakthrough, however, occurred in 1893 when the World's Parliament of Religions was convoked in Chicago. The Parliament met for seventeen days in September as one of twenty-four congresses of the World Columbian Exposition, or world's fair. It brought the planet's religions together for the first time in the modern age. It wasn't completely inclusive: Native Americans, other indigenous peoples, and African Americans were excluded, and only one Muslim, an American convert, was present as a delegate. But it had a profound impact, capturing the imagination of the American people and the world press. It reinforced the study of comparative religion and helped make Catholicism and Judaism mainstream in America, while introducing the Asian religions to the West, especially Hinduism, Jainism, Buddhism, and Zen.[3]

Many early attempts to solidify the spirit of the Parliament in a permanent organization failed. But a number of organizations carried on the work, including the Fellowship of Reconciliation, the World Conference on Religion and Peace, the World Congress of Faiths, the Temple of Understanding, the Council for a Parliament of the World's Religions, and the United Religions Organization. Today, these groups collaborate on dialogue programs, and other projects of mutual concern. All the major cities of the world also have interfaith organizations: New York, Chicago, Los Angeles, San Francisco, Washington, Seattle, Denver, Austin, Toronto, Victoria, London, Paris, Madrid, Berlin, Tokyo, New Delhi, Madras, Bombay, Jerusalem, Ankara, and Moscow are all centers of interreligious encounter.

In August 1993, the Council for a Parliament of the World's Religions, founded in 1988, convened the Parliament of the World's Religions in Chicago.4 Initially designed to commemorate the centennial of the first great Parliament, the founders quickly realized that they had an opportunity to contribute something more substantial — to address the critical issues plaguing the planet: the environmental crisis, social injustice, poverty, malnutrition, disease, the plight of refugees — 80 percent of whom are women and children — the need for better education in developing nations, and numerous other threats to peace.

It soon became clear that a permanent organization could help educate the religions, and the world, about the need to work together on these critical issues. From August 28 to September 5, 1993, the Parliament met at Chicago's Palmer House Hilton and the Art Institute of Chicago — both sites of the first Parliament — and other venues throughout the city. Nine thousand people participated in the 1993 Parliament, and the registration had to be closed three weeks before the event; there simply was no more room. The closing event in Grant Park on Chicago's lakefront attracted seventy-five thousand people!

Sessions ranged from the colorful opening to explorations of the inner life, interreligious dialogue, memories of paradise, the next generation, the dispossessed, contributions of the imagination, seminars on all the religions, spiritual teachings by great masters, academic symposia, dance workshops, twice daily meditation sessions, lectures on virtually every aspect of religious knowledge, forums dedicated to ecology, and more than a thousand other programs involving spiritual practice. In a bow to tradition, the 250-member Assembly of Religious and Spiritual Leaders gathered for a three-day meeting at the Art Institute. These stormy sessions ended well when two hundred members signed the Parliament's document *Towards a Global Ethic (An Initial Declaration)*, the first consensus by the world's religions on basic standards of ethical behavior.

The Parliament represented the most diverse group of people ever to meet in one place in the history of humankind. Before the event's eight days, I assisted in the planning and served on four committees. During the Parliament itself, I participated in a number of forums, including the Buddhist-Christian Monastic Dialogue with the Dalai Lama and in the Assembly. I hoped, prayed, and even knew intuitively that it would represent a turning point. But it greatly exceeded everyone's expectations, certainly the planners'. For me, the opening morning held a sign of its special significance. I was having breakfast with Samdong Rinpoche, the chief of the Tibetan Delegation and an old friend, and Rolph Fernandes, a Franciscan brother from Montreal. As I returned with a cup of coffee for Rinpoche, somehow the cup, saucer, spoon, and coffee flew into Rinpoche's lap! To this day I don't know how it happened. Samdong looked up at me without the slightest irritation, and with perfect calm said, "This is an auspicious omen!" And indeed it proved to be so.

Something extraordinary happened during the Parliament's days. The divine showed up and opened everyone, inspiring enthusiasm, mutual trust, receptivity, and a wonderful sense of joy, spontaneity, community, and urgency. We were not of one mind but of one heart. For me as a Christian, the word that best describes this historic moment is *Pentecost:* the birth of the Christian church, when the Holy Spirit opened the minds and hearts of Jesus' disciples, uniting them in a corporate mystical knowing that illumined their path during the fledgling years of the apostolic age. The Parliament represented a second Pentecost because the spirit was tangibly present, prying hearts and minds open to receive the impulse of new vision. Community was born among the religions. The spirit gave us a whole new paradigm of relationship in the existential experience of community, replacing the old model of separation, mistrust, competition, hostility, and conflict. By supplanting the approach responsible for thousands of wars throughout human history, this new paradigm has enormous meaning. The advent of community between and among members of differing faiths is without parallel; its opportunity is extremely precious, not to be squandered but carefully cultivated and applied to the task of building a universal civilization.

Interspirituality and intermysticism are the terms I have coined to designate the increasingly familiar phenomenon of cross-religious sharing of interior resources, the spiritual treasures of each tradition. Of course everyone isn't participating; really it is only a minority, but its members are the more mystically developed in each tradition, and they each hold great influence. In the third millennium, interspirituality and intermysticism will become more and more the norm in humankind's inner evolution. Europeans often say a person isn't truly educated until they know more than one language. This can also be said of religions: a person is not really fully educated, or indeed "religious," unless they are intimately aware of more than their own faith and ways of prayer. Chapters 1 and 2 will examine the nature, scope, and value of interspirituality, a trend that is becoming ever more definitive of the coming age.

This new and fascinating time in history is finally characterized by the openness to the cosmos. For so many millennia we have been a curiously "geocentric" species in our unabashed anthropocentrism, or human-centeredness in thought, culture, and preoccupation. That is now changing as we gaze at the horizon and realize that our future, that of the earth itself, is tied up with what's out there and around us here. Our understanding of history has been enlarged to its proper cosmic dimensions. We are finally understanding that we belong to a vast community that is the universe in its totality. This realization will become more dominant in the coming century, and we will undoubtedly make new discoveries, perhaps even making contact with our nearest neighbors in our galaxy, if they exist.

❖ The Turn to Spirituality

Religion and spirituality are not mutually exclusive, but there is a real difference. The term spirituality refers to an individual's solitary search for and discovery of the absolute or the divine. It involves direct mystical experience of God, or realization of vast awareness, as in Buddhism. Spirituality carries with it a conviction that the transcendent is real, and it requires some sort of spiritual practice that acts as a catalyst to inner change and growth. It is primarily personal, but it also has a social dimension. Spirituality, like religion, derives from mysticism.

For thousands of years before the dawn of the world religions as social organisms working their way through history, the mystical life thrived. This mystical tradition, which underpins all genuine faith, is the living source of religion itself. It is the attempt to possess the inner reality of the spiritual life, with its mystical, or direct, access to the divine. Each great religion has a similar origin: the spiritual awakening of its founders to God, the divine, the absolute, the spirit, Tao, boundless awareness. We find it in the experience of the rishis in India; the Buddha in his experience of enlightenment; in Moses, the patriarchs, the prophets, and other holy souls of the biblical tradition. It is no less present in Jesus' inner realization of his relationship with his Father, who is also our Father. And it is clear in the Prophet Mohammed's revelation experience of Allah through the mediation of the Archangel Gabriel.

Everything stems from mysticism, or primary religious experience, whether it be revelation or a personal mystical state of consciousness. It is therefore quite natural and appropriate that spirituality should become more primary for people as they grow in their traditions and discover more substantial and ultimate nourishment in the living reality of the source. We need religion, yet we need direct contact with the divine, or ultimate mystery, even more. Religions are valuable carriers of the tradition within a community, but they must not be allowed to choke out the breath of the spirit, which breathes where it will.

For example, most Christian churches barely mention the mystical life, keeping the focus of prayer on the level of worship and devotion. The same is true in much of the Jewish and Islamic traditions, the Kabbalah and Sufism being exceptions. The religious life of the faithful is decidedly on the corporate, devotional level, while the contemplative and mystical are neglected.

By allowing inward change, while at the same time simplifying our external life, spirituality serves as our greatest single resource for changing our centuries-old trajectory of violence and division. Spirituality is profoundly transformative when it inspires in us the attitude of surrender to the mystery in which "we live, and move, and have our being," as the New Testament reminds us.5 The twentieth century has witnessed the rise and fall of so many bloody revolutions that have caused immense suffering in so many lives. The architects of these political movements defined the human in the abstract, which allowed them to destroy *living* human beings. These figures failed to see that people's hearts must change before structures can change. This change is the basis of genuine reform and renewal.

We need to understand, to really grasp at an elemental level, that the definitive revolution *is* the spiritual awakening of humankind. This revolution will be the task of the Interspiritual Age. The necessary shifts in consciousness require a new approach to spirituality that transcends past religious cultures of fragmentation and isolation. The direct experience of interspirituality paves the way for a universal view of mysticism — that is the common heart of the world.

The Mystic Heart attempts something new: to present a practical spirituality in a universal context; it is a work *in* interspirituality, or the intermystical experience. In this new age of interspirituality, all forms of spirituality are accessible to us, allowing creative crossover and borrowing among members of the world's religions. *The Mystic Heart* is a tool for everyone seriously committed to living the spiritual life, regardless of circumstance. We don't need to enter monasteries to become mystics or to cultivate our spirituality. We are all mystics! The mystic heart is the deepest part of who or what we really are. We need only to realize and activate that essential part of our being.

There is a desperate need for spirituality in our time, yet this spirituality must be in dialogue and communion with everything of value in our mystical and religious traditions. We require a spirituality that promotes the unity of the human family, not one that further divides us or maintains old antagonisms. At the same time, this interspiritual approach must not submerge our differences; it must see traditions in relationship to each other, and provide options. The truth itself is big enough to include our diversity of views. They are all based on authentic inner experience, and so are all valid.

Chapters 1 and 2 explores interspirituality in depth. Chapter 3 delves into a new understanding of divine and human identity by exploring them through consciousness itself. The routes of spirituality take us into an examination of the ways of extroversion and introversion in chapter 4. Here, we look at all the factors associated with the paths of the spiritual life, and the stages of human development that serve to give us a picture of the human in his or her spiritual environment. Chapters 5, 6, and 7 examine the shared practical elements of the spiritual life in all traditions: the universal components of mystical spirituality, the attitudes and practices essential to a substantive spiritual journey.

Chapter 8 considers the spiritual path through the natural world, or creation as the original form of spirituality and the basis of cosmic revelation. This form of the inner life can be called natural mysticism. As the experience of so many indigenous traditions, a primordial component of the historical religions, and a much-needed reconnection in this ecological age, it is a profoundly important part of interspirituality. Chapter 9 addresses the mystical, metaphysical, and theological core of a universal mysticism, how the summit or goal of the spiritual journey is understood in different traditions. Chapter 10 summarizes universal mysticism in the third millennium, which includes advice to youth in this crucial time. Words are defined at first usage, and you will also find a glossary to assist you in understanding new or unfamiliar terms. The bibliography will guide you to further reading and study.

Finally, this writing often has a deliberately personal tone. As a writer, teacher, and speaker, it is my custom to speak *from* my experience. Normally, however, I don't speak directly *about* my own experience — partially due to academic and monastic values. The difference is subtle. Here, because I hope to engender a deeply personal notion of mystical awareness, I will, at times, use a more direct, unambiguous approach. Jason Gardner, my editor at New World Library, has encouraged me to take this more personal tone, and share my own experience forthrightly. I hope this approach will provide some insight to the reader.

My own inner, or mystical, process has informed this text throughout, accounting for the passion with which I speak. While I explore the rich crossover of the world's religions, I am anchored in my Catholic tradition. I live as a lay monk, a Christian sannyasi, in a tiny apartment that serves as my hermitage at the Catholic Theological Union in Chicago. Father Bede Griffiths initiated me into sannyasa in India on January 5, 1989. *Sannyasa*, the way of the wandering Hindu ascetics, is the primordial manifestation of monastic life. Sannyasa is a medieval Sanskrit word that means renunciation, but it reflects a living reality of individual spiritual life whose roots go back thousands of years in India. The Catholic Church has yet to make provision for Christian sannyasis in its canon law; nonetheless, there have been Christian sannyasis since the seventeenth century. I have embraced a Christian form, but as a witness to the challenge of interspirituality and the intermystical life. From this vantage

I strive to integrate humankind's spiritual wisdom within the depths of my own mystic heart.

✦ A Dot on a Blackboard

It is essential for us to maintain a certain measure of perspective on human knowledge. Although science still enjoys enormous influence, we live in an age witnessing the decline of science's exclusive hold on the answers. A clear understanding of science's limitations is developing, and most scientists — especially the great ones — realize this truth. Mysticism invites us beyond all our human limitations and inadequate forms of knowing — inadequate because ultimately they don't go far enough.

As an exercise in perspective, let us imagine a blackboard. In the middle of this blackboard we place a dot that represents all human knowledge from the dawn of consciousness. Compare this little dot to the expanse of the blackboard, and then to the surrounding room; then step outside and look to the night sky. Take in the stars and realize that what there is to know lies in their immensity. Mystical wisdom allows us to extend our awareness far beyond the dot on the blackboard. It enlarges our understanding and gives us access to the experience of ultimate reality — to the principles governing existence. Mysticism grants us a picture of the totality; it is the most precious wisdom we have.

Chapter 1

A BRIDGE ACROSS THE
RELIGIONS AND BEYOND

*If your heart is truly open then all of nature, life and
experience is the mystery of interconnection and
opportunity for communion.*
— Anonymous

My own interspiritual journey began in earnest in 1973, when Bede Griffiths and I began to correspond. He was an English Benedictine monk, spiritual teacher, and writer who traveled to India in 1955, as he put it to a friend at the time, "to seek the other half of my soul" — meaning his mystical, intuitive side. His rational, analytical mind was already highly developed; he wanted to make room for the mystic to be born in him. Bede awakened in me a sense of the eternal value of India's spiritual traditions in the inner search and a powerful desire to discover the "other half" of my own soul. In the same year I met the Hindu master Swami Satchidananda in Hartford, Connecticut, where he'd come to give talks and lead retreats at his Integral Yoga Institute. My encounters with Swami Satchidananda reinforced my intuitions about the Hindu mystical culture as a living spiritual reality.

I was not alone in my discovery. Millions of other Westerners during the last century have shared this new appreciation of the East, an awakening that underscores the breakdown of isolation among all the spiritual traditions. Through these countless souls the *intermystical* life has become a reality, and through the agencies of easy travel, instant communication, and a spirit of openness, the *Interspiritual Age* has begun. A small but significant number of people in all the religions are transcending boundaries in search of enlightenment, salvation, or mystical realization.

Some cultures — India, Sri Lanka, Thailand, and certain indigenous societies, such as the native Australians, for example — arc organized to support and facilitate the inner search. Others, although not consciously structured to assist the spiritual life, are nonetheless conducive to contemplative experience. The Latin and Mediterranean countries, especially Italy and Spain, are nations in love with slowness, cultivation of the intellect, reflection, and quiet.

The United States, in this respect, is an anomaly. Every religion known to humanity exists in America — more than two hundred of them. Every form of spirituality is available, from Zen Buddhism to Centering Prayer, yoga to t'ai chi, Sufism to Tibetan *Dzogchen* practice.[1] Countless forms of meditation and self-realization programs are readily accessible to anyone willing to commit. Roshis, rinpoches, and gurus are providing American students with a virtual smorgasbord of disciplines for the inner life. Yet, with all this at our disposal, our culture often ignores our deepest longings. Although we enjoy unlimited freedom and endless opportunities to seek deeper experience, American culture — like the West in general — lacks a sense of the sacred and is indifferent to the mystical process of its citizens.

Many consider themselves to be religious. The vast majority of Americans believe in God and prayer; belong to a church, synagogue, or a temple; and have had a peak or mystical experience at some point in their life. Yet we are saturated with materialistic values that distract us, obscuring the things of the spirit. Wealth, consumerism, and entertainment have become the psychological fixations of the masses. Greed is widespread; consumerism and entertainment have assumed nearly religious significance. We proclaim ourselves "born to shop" or willing to "shop until we drop."

A friend of mine, a Catholic journalist, has made a religion of sports. "You know, Jim," I once said to him, "if you spent as much time in prayer as you do following baseball, you'd be a saint!" He didn't care for my observation, and I know I am in the minority. Others are completely absorbed by television and arrange their lives around its constant glow. Some years ago a Protestant theologian suggested, with tongue in cheek, that we replace the tabernacles in our churches with televisions! John Main, a

Benedictine monk and founder of the Christian meditation movement, once remarked to me, "Television was the absolute death of prayer!"

We have become spiritually illiterate: ignorant of the realization that life is a spiritual journey, that everything is sacred or a manifestation of the ultimate mystery. We are morally confused, precisely because of this illiteracy. And this illiteracy and confusion have led directly to psychological dysfunction: the breakdown of meaningful communication in the family, and the indifference and insensitivity with which we treat one another. We fear the intimacy inherent in the interactions of society itself. People regard one another as objects, rather than as the precious beings they are. Our addiction to violence — vicarious and otherwise — is nourished by a steady diet of irresponsible Hollywood images and stories that subtly, and not so subtly, insinuate that violence is fundamental to life. Psychological dysfunction also appears in our frenzied pace of life, with its inevitable fragmentation and tolerance of noise, and in the endless stimulation we require through news, sports, and other forms of excitement. We have become a nation of compulsive neurotics. No wonder the quiet spiritual life has difficulty being heard.

✦ What Is Spirituality?

Before we can really understand what interspirituality means in its depth, height, and breadth, we must consider briefly the meaning of the words religious, spiritual, and spirituality. With so many connotations, various contexts in which they are used, and meanings ascribed to them, they require clarification. What do they signify in their fullest sense?

Being *religious* connotes belonging to and practicing a religious tradition. Being *spiritual* suggests a personal commitment to a process of inner development that engages us in our totality. Religion, of course, is one way many people are spiritual. Often, when authentic faith embodies an individual's spirituality, the religious and the spiritual will coincide. Still, not every religious person is spiritual (although they ought to be!), and not every spiritual person is religious.

Spirituality is a way of life that affects and includes every moment of existence. It is at once a contemplative attitude, a disposition to a life of depth, and the search for ultimate meaning, direction, and belonging. The spiritual person is committed to growth as an essential, ongoing life goal. To be spiritual requires us to stand on our own two feet while being nurtured and supported by our tradition, if we are fortunate enough to have one.

Thomas Merton stressed this importance of individual strength on the last day of his life, in a talk to Christian and Buddhist monks and nuns in Bangkok. In regard to the Tibetans' desperate flight from Chinese persecution into exile, Merton told the story of Chögyam Trungpa Rinpoche's frightening experience of being cut off from his monastery. Staying in a village with a peasant family, and uncertain what to do, Merton said, "[Trungpa] sent a message to a nearby abbot friend of his saying: 'What do we do?' The abbot sent back a strange message, which [Merton thought] very significant: 'From now on, Brother, everybody stands on his own feet.' "[2]

Many religious people depend on institutions — their church, synagogue, temple, or mosque — to make their decisions. Rather than looking for inner direction, they shape their spiritual lives through conformity to external piety. They seem to lack the ability and desire to stand on their own two feet. Spirituality draws us into the depths of our being, where we come face to face with ourselves, our weaknesses, and with ultimate mystery. Many understandably prefer to avoid this frightening prospect by sinking into external religiosity and the safe routines of liturgy or ritual. A genuinely spiritual person passionately commits to this inner development. He or she knows that life is a spiritual journey, and that each one of us must take this journey alone, even while surrounded by loved ones.

How we make this journey is what spirituality is really about. No manual for the inner life fits the needs of all people. Finding our own path is part of what it means to have a measure of independence and inner directedness. There is a wonderfully practical saying in the English mystical tradition: "Pray as you can, not as you can't!" We must take responsibility for our spiritual lives. This means finding the right way to relate to the divine, and this is what prayer helps us to do.

The evolution of an individual's spirituality is a mysterious and intimate matter. It originates in the heart, in deep stirrings that may be only beginning to form. These stirrings represent an insatiable longing for fulfillment. St. Augustine identified the source of this stirring in his celebrated prayer at the beginning of his autobiographical *Confessions:* "You (O God) have made us for yourself, and our heart is restless until it rests in you."[3] We are created for the spiritual journey. To exist means that we share the task of perfecting self-transcendence through prayer, contemplation, meditation — the nitty-gritty of the spiritual quest. To be spiritual means essentially to take responsibility for our inner journey, while using all the resources from all the traditions available to us. They are our common heritage; they belong to each one of us. All we require to tap into them is the capacity to do so, the requisite generosity of spirit. These great treasures are part of a universal mystical tradition, and our growth in the future depends on our willingness to integrate them into our own experience.

❖ Spirituality in the Religions

The inner commitment to live the search for the divine — spirituality as the disciplined quest for enlightenment — is often lived out within a religious faith. Throughout many of the major religious traditions — in Hinduism, Buddhism, Jainism, Catholicism, and the Orthodox church — this search often unfolds within the context of monasticism.[4] The whole purpose of Christian monastic life, for example, is to activate inner experience, to intensify the search and cultivate spiritual practice through reading, reflection, meditation, and contemplation. Contemplation is the mystical process of cultivating union with God, or the inner realization of ultimate awareness. These experiences are further developed through study and discussion.

Monastics are, in a sense, "professionals" in spirituality, and monasticism has traditionally been the place where mysticism has flourished in the Church. Yet monastics often fall far short of realizing their ideal mandate of mystical contemplation. This is certainly true in most monasteries regardless of the tradition, though the Trappists in the Catholic tradition are very committed to contemplation. Thomas Merton, a Trappist or Cistercian, was almost single-handedly responsible for awakening a contemplative form of spirituality in the Catholic Church in America and Europe, and his influence extends far beyond Catholicism. To this end he wrote some fifty-one books and two thousand articles, all from his monastery!

Islam and Judaism lack a monastic system to cultivate the inner life of contemplation, but they have nonetheless reached a rich spiritual fruition in their own forms of mysticism. The Sufis, without rejecting their

Moslem identity, represent the heart of Islamic spirituality. In Judaism, the collection of esoteric wisdom known as Kabbalah, which means tradition, is the basis of Jewish mystical spirituality; as is the cultural and spiritual expression known as Hasidism, a form that came considerably later, in seventeenth-century Poland.

Countless souls throughout the world's religions live intensely focused mystical spiritualities, but most of them have taken responsibility for their spiritual journey. They relate to their religion in a healthy manner, avoiding overdependence, and thus remain able to grow into their full potential. Brother David Steindl-Rast is a Benedictine monk and leader of interfaith encounter, of learning from other cultures, and, so, of interspirituality. He has made the distinction between being *rooted* in your tradition and being *stuck* in it. The point is to have roots that nourish, rather than a desperate clinging that chokes off real spiritual vitality. Spirituality is always about what nourishes. Tradition is useful as long as it enhances and serves the inner life. When it becomes an obstacle, we need to rethink the hold our religion has on us.

Religion and spirituality are not antagonistic to each other; rather, they mutually enrich each other — if their relationship is based on openness and respect. Most mystics throughout history were part of a religious tradition. At the same time, anyone actually living an authentic spiritual path has assumed responsibility for their own development. Religious people without authentic spiritual paths often merely go through the motions of being part of a church, synagogue, mosque, or temple. They attend out of a sense of duty, tradition, or social expectation. Their observances are perfunctory rather than heartfelt; their minds and hearts are not in harmony with the spiritual quest. Of course, people grow as they move along in their earthly lives. Their desires and longings grow. Sooner or later something awakens in them, and they embark on their inner search of discovery and fulfillment.

✦ The Nature of Mysticism and Spirituality

Mysticism means direct, immediate experience of ultimate reality. For Christians, it is union and communion with God. For Buddhists, it is realization of enlightenment. Evelyn Underhill's classical definition is perennially true: "Mysticism, in its pure form, is the science of ultimates, the science of union with the Absolute, and nothing else, and that the mystic is the person who attains to this union, not the person who talks about it. Not to *know about,* but to *Be,* is the mark of the real initiate."5

Although all forms of mysticism are inherently part of spirituality, not all kinds of spirituality are intrinsically mystical. Because churchgoers usually don't experience ultimate perception during the mass, liturgical spirituality (forms associated with the rituals and public prayer of the churches) is not primarily mystical. But clearly the Eucharist, through participation in the rite itself, promises a mystical relationship with Christ and the Trinity. Although much of Christian spirituality is inspired by the Eucharist, and history has seen some eucharistic mystics, mystical spirituality goes beyond this mediated form to direct relationship with God.

The Types of Mystical Spirituality

Mystical spirituality has many types, each valid in its own way. *Natural mysticism* is found in every culture. *Theistic mysticism,* a mysticism focused on God is present everywhere except in Buddhism and Jainism. Intimately associated with many forms of theistic mysticism is the *mysticism of love,* a dominant, powerful spiritual orientation in Christian and Sufi contemplative literature. The mysticism of love is present throughout the Christian mystical tradition; it became deeply embedded in the culture of the Middle Ages through the *bridal mysticism* of the Victorine and Cistercian monks, with their emphasis on learning, withdrawal, and contemplation. The term "bridal" uses terms from human love to express intimacy with God and union. So profound was this monastic impulse that it inspired the courtly love tradition celebrated by the knights and troubadours of wider medieval society.

The *mysticism of knowledge* predominates among Buddhists. Unrelated to God or a divine being, it concerns the realization in consciousness itself of ultimate wisdom and compassion. This kind of mystical spirituality depends on actualization of awareness on an ultimate, nondual, or unitive level of mind.

The *mysticism of the soul* emphasizes the eternal nature of the self, the Atman as the vehicle for union with the divine. With its emphasis on the self, this form predominates in Indian mysticism. It is also found in some Christian mystics (notably Augustine, Meister Eckhart, and the Rhenish sage Jan van Ruysbroeck, who entered profound relationships with God through the depths of the self or soul), as well as Sufis like Rumi and Attar, and the many anonymous Jewish sages.

The Elements of Mystical Experience

We can also distinguish between mysticism as an *experience* and mysticism as a *process* of spiritual life. The former is very common, while the latter requires an ongoing commitment, regardless of the tradition.

Mysticism as a process — mystical or contemplative spirituality — has a number of characteristics, which are true of all its forms in the various traditions or schools. Mystical spirituality is practical, experiential, ineffable or nonconceptual, unitive or nondual, noetic, integrative, sapiential, giving certitude, and in possession of transcendent knowledge from direct experience.

All mystical experience, though involving the here and now, happens in the present moment of the eternal now, since time is contained in eternity. Mysticism is a revelation of the eternal in the midst of the temporal, and in that revelatory communication, it presents us with states of consciousness that possess the following elements.

Mystical spirituality is always *practical:* its experience is eminently beneficial to a person's life and well-being. Because it concerns one's ultimate situation, it is never abstract. It always contributes to one's inner landscape — the development of individual character.

Mysticism is also *experiential.* By stressing what can be known and experienced mysticism is similar to science's empiricism. Both are based on experience. Just as science is related to what actually is, so the mystical life is directly in contact with what is ultimately real.

Mystical spirituality, in its peak moments, is *ineffable.* In its infinite presence, it is incomprehensible to the mystic, who has infinite potential but only finite ability as a human to experience, at least in this mode of existence. The divine or ultimate mystery is infinitely actual with an infinite and eternal amount of time, and so the mystic always labors at a disadvantage in relation to the divine itself. Only the ultimate mystery, or the divine can compensate for us.

Mystical consciousness is *nonconceptual;* it transcends the need for concepts because it knows all things in its eternal now. It does not perceive successive events and individual objects but rather the totality, in every moment of eternity. It knows everything in knowing itself, and everything is always spontaneously present to it. Being infinitely aware in this manner it knows in a unitive fashion, which is also in an intuitive way. When we know or experience the reality of the divine, we know it through its own modes of knowing, and hence it is ineffable. We have nothing to which to compare it. Essentially ungraspable and incomprehensible, the source eludes us.

Mystical spirituality is also *unitive;* it seeks integration with the infinite. All theistic types of mysticism are interested in this integration, for the goal is to be invited into a permanent, divine union with God. This unity is the heart of all mysticisms. It is awareness of nonduality and non-separation, of no distance between ourselves, the ultimate mystery, and all other beings. The unitive level of consciousness is both integration with the divine and nondual awareness or perception. In Buddhism, this union describes nonduality of consciousness; it is through this quality of mind that the Buddhist tradition locates absolute truth. For Buddhists, all dualistic experience, thought, and consciousness yields only relative truth, which is impermanent, changing, and unsatisfactory. Theistic mysticism, however, is always about union. Thus there is a measure of the nondual in it, though it is dynamic and admits distinctions, as in the Christian understanding of the Trinity. This is how Christian mysticism can be unitive and yet contain real personal identities in the form of people. Union with the divine is just as absolute as Buddhist nondual awareness.

Mysticism is also supremely *noetic*. It grants us direct knowledge of the ultimate reality or the divine. Noetic means knowledge — actual, objectively real awareness of what is true through union with, or unmediated awareness of, what is ultimately real. To experience God, or ultimate states of consciousness, is to experience "that which is"; it is "that which is" that gives us the noetic quality. To this extent the noetic note is both practical and empirical. It suggests that mystical knowledge, based as it is on direct, unmediated experience, is in a certain sense, scientific, as both science and mysticism are empirical. The noetic dimension of spirituality is vast, organic, natural, and inevitable. Mysticism and mystical spirituality generate a *tasting* knowledge of God, or the ultimate realization — that is, enlightenment. Mystically, noetic knowledge is as unlimited as the source itself, which it mirrors. It is organic and natural because this precious knowledge grows out of the mystical experience. The Orthodox church has a beautifully apt aphorism: "The theologian is the one who prays!" Insights relevant to our spiritual life and journey arise organically, naturally, and inevitably from the practice of contemplative prayer.

The mystical path is also psychologically *integrative:* it unites the unconscious, the conscious, and the superconscious. It also integrates the memory, intellect, will, imagination, and emotions with the body and the spirit. Within them, it establishes the harmony of love, compassion, mercy, and kindness — the quieting of the emotions. All this surrenders to something much higher and more ultimate than the human. This surrender, and the integration that follows, puts order in the chaotic domain of the unconscious, and allows it to work with the other faculties in a person's spiritual life.

Mystical spirituality is *sapiential:* practical, spiritual wisdom. Mysticism's very essence — much more than mere knowledge or opinion — is wisdom itself. It grants a precious understanding of ultimate reality, the cosmos, and life itself. Part of sapiential awareness is metaphysical knowledge of the laws governing the universe, all that is involved in maintaining it, and insight into its nature, scope, and destiny. Sapiential awareness, which is a contemplative kind of consciousness, grants profound intuitive knowledge of the divine — and of others. Many saints and mystics of various ages and traditions had this extraordinary gift: the capacity to read hearts, to discern motives, to understand immediately a person's spiritual progress. In the Christian contemplative tradition, it is spoken of as *infused contemplation* or *passive contemplation* because God is doing the work in us. Whatever it may be called, it is a special grace that comes at an advanced stage of contemplation.

Mystical awareness confers an absolute *certitude* on the knower or experiencer. Every tradition makes the point that this certainty is total, undeniable, clear, and eternal. One cannot doubt the reality of the experience while in the midst of it. We all doubt all kinds of experiences we have in life — we doubt our fundamental subjectivity — but it is not possible to doubt mystical phenomena. The vividness, intensity, and immediacy are so profound, the magnitude of certainty so great, and the eternal so real, that the experiences are beyond doubt.

The mystical also gives us a glimpse of the *transcendent* mystery beyond this universe. When we encounter it, or it envelopes us, our capacities are enlarged, enhanced, and elevated into a higher, more ultimate way of knowing. We are then confronted by something more real than anything we have previously known. The mystical presents us with *more* reality and truth than we ordinarily experience in everyday life because it reveals a greater reality untouched by change, decay, and death. Cast in the light of the unchanging, boundless source, the mystical makes all things translucent with the eternal, transcendent being. Once touched — even for a brief moment — we are changed forever. Our inner life is transformed by the deifying radiance of the transcendent ground from which everything arises and to which everything returns.

The Goal of the Mystical Journey

Interspirituality points to the realization that although there are many spiritual paths, a universal commonality underlies them all. Nonetheless, the "object" of the mystical journey seems to differ depending on who embarks on it. To a Jew, a Christian, a Moslem, some Hindus, and the indigenous peoples of the world, the focus of the spiritual life is the personal God, or the Great Spirit — the mystery and reality known for tens of thousands of years by mystic sages, long before the time of the first religion's appearance in India some five thousand years ago. Of course, God is not an object, but the supreme *subject*. To a person in the Hindu Vedantic tradition who follows the teaching of *advaita* — the primal unity or nonduality of all being — we are all already divine, and we simply have to wake up and realize it. For them, the "object" of the mystical quest is an *impersonal* absolute discovered in meditation. And for Buddhists, the goal is the transpersonal awakening to boundless awareness, nondual experience, and infinite compassion.

The view of Advaita Vedanta and Buddhism on God amounts to a purely immanent approach, in which each person is divine. There is no transcendent other, only ourselves as potential god. Buddhism doesn't speak in terms of God; yet as one achieves absolute awareness, one realizes Buddha-mind, and so a kind of divine status. This potential to become god is actualized through intense spiritual practice, which allows us to realize our true nature. The spiritual life in these two traditions is the process of coming to terms with who we really are in an ultimate sense. If everything is God, and there is *only* the divine reality, then it makes no sense to talk about God as being out there, as objective, as the reality to which we relate ourselves in prayer or meditation. In Buddhist meditation we experience our true nature as mind or consciousness, and yet this consciousness is mysterious. While Buddhists don't speak of God, their understanding amounts to the view that we must take responsibility for our own development because we are divine ourselves. We all have Buddha nature, we all *are* Buddha nature — enlightened awareness. It's our job to claim it, and not depend on an outside force or God. Reclaiming who we actually are is a process of awakening into ultimate consciousness.

In resolving these seemingly conflicting views, I think we are going to discover in coming years that a more adequate view of the divine — something that can be verified in mystical experience — includes both personal and *trans*personal reality. God is both a loving presence, compassionate, wise, kind, and merciful, and an impersonal principle or ultimate condition of consciousness, the basis of karma, *shunyata* or emptiness, and *nirvana*. They represent two sides of the same source, two fundamental insights, two mystical realizations of the ultimate mystery. These two approaches to the question of our origin are recon-cilable, and I believe we will take this direction as we become more engaged in building the bonds of community among the religions, when we have more opportunities to achieve mutual understanding among members of the great spiritual traditions.

✦ What Is Interspirituality?

The real religion of humankind can be said to be spirituality itself, because mystical spirituality is the origin of the all the world religions. If this is so, and I believe it is, we might also say that *interspirituality* — the sharing of ultimate experiences across traditions — is the religion of the third millennium. Interspirituality is the foundation that can prepare the way for a planet-wide enlightened culture, and a continuing community among the religions that is substantial, vital, and creative.

Interspirituality is not about eliminating the world's rich diversity of religious expression. It is not about rejecting these traditions' individual-ity for a homogenous superspirituality. It is not an attempt to create a new form of spiritual culture. Rather, it is an attempt to make available to everyone all the forms the spiritual journey assumes. Interspirituality as a world-changing force is made possible by the openness of people who have a viable spiritual life, coupled with their determination, capacity, and commitment to the inner search across traditions.

The "Inter" in Interspirituality

The prefix *inter* in interspirituality expresses the ontological roots that tie the various traditions together and that are responsible for religions influencing each other throughout history. It conveys a fundamental truth: the essential spiritual interdependence of the religions. Spiritual interdependence among the religions exists because an essential interconnectedness in being and reality exists. The entire cosmos is one system in which all parts are interrelated. Everything is possible, and the religions themselves share in this one system of reality, life, and being.

Inter also indicates an eagerness to communicate with members of other faiths. This eagerness is particularly evident in people living their spiritual traditions with dedication and perseverance, individuals whose inner work has made them exquisitely whole human beings who are sensitive, wise, compassionate, and loving. *Inter* means an openness to learn from others, and the wisdom of their traditions; it is a trust in what will be found; it is the conscious assimilation of whatever is valuable to aid one's own journey. Interspirituality is not a one-way street, but an intermystical *intersection* where insights cross back and forth, intermingle, and find new habitats.

Inter conveys a sense of responsibility to humankind as a whole, and to all living beings, to contribute to a larger understanding of spirituality in our time and in times to come. It is an important aspect of what the Dalai Lama calls our universal responsibility to the global community of the earth, a responsibility that is both individual and collective.[6]

The curiously interspiritual metaphor of the blind men and the elephant — a story claimed by the Hindu, Jain, and Buddhist traditions — helps us understand the trajectory of interspirituality in terms of this larger universal responsibility. As the story has it, some blind men stumble across an elephant. Each tries to describe the elephant by touching it. One feels its trunk, and proclaims the elephant to be solid and wide. Another feels its tail, and describes it as thin and spindly. A third pats its ears, and assumes it is flat and floppy. A fourth touches its side, and concludes the elephant to be a rather nondescript, rough-textured being. On and on it goes. Each man knows one aspect, but none can comprehend the whole.

The religions find themselves in a similar predicament in attempting to describe the nature of ultimate reality. The Christians, Jews, and

Moslems say the elephant is a personal being with a head, eyes, ears, nose, mouth, and trunk. The Hindus say its nature is expressed in its feet, tail, size, and weight, thus a suitable beast of burden. The Jains and Buddhists chime in that the elephant is basically nondescript because they can only feel its sides and skin.

Interspirituality declares the elephant to be *all* these things. The elephant has a total being and reality; it is a personal creature with feelings and a capacity for love, friendship, and loyalty. The elephant as a metaphor for the absolute, the source, tells us that the ultimate mystery reflects all the attributes of the various traditions. Interspirituality recognizes that many paths lead to the summit, and each one of them is valid. Yet each has its unique perspective on the nature of the summit. Interspirituality is open to growth in perspective; it implies a commitment to always push forward toward a more adequate understanding of the source, the meaning of life, and the best methods of proceeding in our spiritual lives.

The *inter* in interspirituality also means that through all the diverse forms of spiritual experience and insight we can evolve a higher view. We need this higher view; its cultivation and attainment are the tasks before us.

Inter also recognizes a subtle, already existing and thriving community between and among members of the world's religions, persons who are in vital connection with one another in the pursuit of wisdom and spiritual depth. They are bound together in a common humanity and common aspiration for the truth. The Dalai Lama often remarks that interreligious dialogue must be based on friendship; the partners in dialogue must be friends for the conversation to be truly meaningful and life-giving. Community and the friendships that unfold are thus the basis on which interspirituality exists and develops in service to the planet.

✦ The Treasure of Community

The growth of interspiritual wisdom among the religions requires community. It is through community that the faith traditions pool their treasures of the spirit, culled through millennia of mystical inner realization. Sometimes community will take an intentional form: Different traditions may elect to share their lives together, experimenting with interspiritual prayer, meditation, and contemplation. Such communities can be monastic, or scholarly, as we find at Harvard's Center for the Study of the World Religions, a center whose building resembles a monastery. Other experiments in interspiritual living might involve families or friends bound together by a common search. The community's structure will play a major role in the outcome. A common orientation is not crucial — it may not even be possible, as it would be in a typical monastery. What is critically important is that the members share some kind of group prayer or spiritual practice to augment their private practice.

Most important for an interspiritual community is being committed to some part of a tripartite dialogue: the dialogue of the *head, heart,* and *hands.* The dialogue of the *head,* not surprisingly, represents the academic, intellectual level — the realm of conferences, symposia, seminars, debates, and panels. It is often textually oriented, and concerned with differences of doctrine, ritual, and symbol. It represents the careful work of striving to understand the specific, subtle meanings of religious concepts and how the traditions relate to each other.

While the dialogue of the head tends toward the abstract, concerned with principles and beliefs, the dialogue of the *heart* is engaged in shared spiritual practice, the most popular and rewarding being meditation. Something profoundly real occurs when people meditate together — a silent communication in the midst of the personal intimacy of prayer. There is a depth to meditation experiences among people of different traditions. Often practitioners achieve greater mutual understanding through a shared sitting than from endless hours of conversation, no matter how rich and meaningful. Important breakthroughs can occur, and these can carry into other areas of mutual discovery. For me, this is the most exciting level of encounter.

The third level of interfaith encounter, the dialogue of the *hands,* is in many ways the fruit of the preceding two, the dialogue of the heart in particular. Often performed without the others, such an approach is a way of building trust through a common goal, task, or concern: an issue of peace, justice, or perhaps simply a collaborative project. This dimension of dialogue is in many ways easier because participants can meet around common social interests and then discover further commonalities. If, for example, the partners are trying to save a building for the poor in their city, they will inevitably grow closer as their project progresses. This form of engagement not only brings people of different faiths together, it can

be the most profound form of spirituality and the most important contribution to interreligious encounter. It is an important way to encourage
the growth of interfaith community through concrete projects of mutual
concern and benefit.

Chapter 2

CROSSING OVER: PIONEERS
OF INTERSPIRITUAL WISDOM

As the river surrenders itself to the ocean,
what is inside me moves inside you.
— Kabir

Interspirituality is not a recent "invention." It has existed for centuries in India, China, and even Persia. Although usually expressed through individuals exploring other traditions, there have been important movements in the Middle East, and more recently in Europe and America. Our basic human curiosity about other cultures and mystical teachings inspires the continual growth of interspirituality. Many spiritual seekers, both exalted and unknown, have crossed over to other traditions while remaining firmly within their own. They may subscribe to certain doctrines or practices of their second faith, or they may simply find a preference for, or comfort in, this second religion.

Christians and Jews, for example, have often expressed a deep interest in each others' theology and practices; they study them, even becoming specialists in each others' tradition. Celebrating the Passover Seder has assumed an important place in recent Christian experience, particularly in the Catholic Church, and it is performed in parishes, monasteries, seminaries, and homes.

Eastern traditions are also in the mix. Many Christians and Jews follow Sufism or practice Zen meditation, while remaining Christians and Jews.[1]

The Jain notion of *ahimsa,* or nonviolence, as an ideal has spread to Buddhism, Hinduism, and now to Christianity. Eastern meditation has inspired Christian forms of contemplation like Thomas Keating's Centering Prayer and the Christian Meditation founded by John Main, an English-Irish Benedictine monk, though both remain rooted in the Christian mystical tradition. Reciprocally, some Hindus are passionately committed to the Sacred Heart of Jesus, a Catholic devotional practice, relating as it does to the primary Indian metaphor of the heart, the *guha,* to represent the spiritual life. Maseo Abe, a Japanese Buddhist thinker, is an expert in Christian theology, and the Dalai Lama has asked Tibetan Lamas to seriously study Christian theology and mysticism. The list goes on and on.

Although we will look at only a relatively small number of interspiritual figures here, they exist in every part of the world and in all the religions. Some belong to no religious tradition, while others have been part of many. Each has offered something to the process of turning this revolutionary page in world history. We will never return to the time when the religions lived in isolation and in ignorance of one another. Those times are happily a thing of the past. We can only go forward.

✦ The Meeting of Christianity and Hinduism

Let's begin by looking at the fertile meeting ground of Indian and Western spiritualities. This synthesis is exemplified in the lives of four men in particular: Roberto de Nobili, Brahmabandhab Upadhyay, Abhishiktananda, and Bede Griffiths.

Roberto de Nobili

One of the first pioneers of interspirituality, albeit unintentionally, was the great Italian Jesuit Roberto de Nobili, who lived from 1577 to 1656.[2] He traveled to India as a missionary; learned Sanskrit and Tamil; studied the Vedas, Upanishads, the Bhagavad Gita, and other works of the Hindu tradition; and finally adopted sannyasa, the life of the renunciate.

Initially, de Nobili became a sannyasi as a strategy to convert the Hindus to Christianity, but he gradually came to understand the authenticity of Hindu mysticism, and his life became a dialogue between the two traditions. As the first non-Hindu ever to read the Vedas and the Upanishads, he wrote original works in Sanskrit and Tamil, and was respected by the priestly caste of the Brahmins. His great contribution to an intermystical approach was his reverent adoption of sannyasa, which represented the giant step of breaking the centuries-old rejection of "pagan" religious forms, as well as his deep respect for the sacred texts of the Hindu tradition.

Brahmabandhab Upadhyay

De Nobili's experiment, though approved by Rome, was subverted by Indian conservative factions, and so no further interspiritual progress occurred until the late nineteenth century, with the appearance of Brahmabandhab Upadhyay, who lived from 1861 to 1907. He set out in the opposite cross-cultural direction as an Indian nationalist and Brahmin who converted to Catholicism. His great contribution to this interspiritual dialogue was to encourage inculturation, or the Indianization of the Catholic Church in liturgy, customs, symbols, and gestures. He advocated the development of an Indian Christian theology, which took its terms, concepts, and models from the Vedanta, the Hindu philosophical tradition. For instance, Upadhyay suggested the Sanskrit term Saccidananda for the Trinity. Saccidananda is the Hindu experience of the Godhead, the inner consciousness characterized as the absolute bliss of becoming completely aware of the fullness of existence.

Despite the fact that the British burned all his writings because he advocated Indian independence, he was immensely influential to those who followed him. Upadhyay succeeded in convincing countless missionaries to change their approach to Indians from outright conversion to that of listening to the subtleties of the Hindu religion. Hindu culture and spirituality, through his efforts, found fertile soil in Christianity.

Abhishiktananda

Again, the progress of interspirituality lagged until the arrival of two Frenchmen, who carried on the interspiritual work that de Nobili and Upadhyay began. The first to arrive was Jules Monchanin. In 1938 this French priest and intellectual founded Saccidananda Ashram, also called Shantivanam, or "forest of peace." It sits on the banks of the sacred river Kavery in Tamil Nadu, in southern India, 285 miles southwest of Madras. Monchanin began the ashram with the other Frenchman, Henri Le Saux, a Benedictine monk who later became known as Abhishiktananda, "the Bliss of the Anointed One," or "the Bliss of Christ."

Both Le Saux and Monchanin took sannyasa and wore the *kavi*, the saffron garb of the renunciate. Monchanin was convinced that the focus of their life at Shantivanam and in dialogue with their fellow Hindu sannyasis had to be *advaita*, the experience of nonduality, combined with the Christian notion of the trinity — the Godhead expressed as three identities united in one substance, in one actual being. If Hinduism and Christianity were to converge, he believed, it would be through these two approaches to God. His approach added clarity to the task of building common ground between Hindus and Christians by focusing on the two religions' statements of ultimate reality. Monchanin recognized that advaita and the trinity were both based on direct mystical experience.

Le Saux, or Abhishiktananda, was an extraordinary mystic who plunged into the acosmic life of the sannyasi. He lived for long periods of time in huts in the Himalayas or in caves at Arunachala, in Tamil Nadu in the south. It was at Arunachala that he met Ramana Maharshi, the silent sage, who awakened him to the depth, truth, and power of Indian mysticism. During these months-long retreats, Abhishiktananda would meditate for hours at a sitting. Once he was caught up in this vortex of mystical depth, this profound consciousness of nondual awareness or unity, he never returned from it. He wrote a number of important books, the chief of which is his interspiritual masterpiece, *Saccidananda: A Christian Approach to Advaitic Experience*.[3] Here Abhishiktananda described the point of convergence between Saccidananda and the Trinity with eloquence and power:

> Here there is no question of theologizing or of academic comparison between the terms of the Christian revelation and those in which India has expressed its own unique mystical experience. It is rather a matter of an awakening, an awareness far beyond the reach of intellect, an experience which springs up and erupts in the deepest recesses of the soul. The experience of Saccidananda carries the soul beyond all merely intellectual knowledge to her very center, to the source of her being. Only there is she able to hear the Word which reveals within the undivided unity and advaita of Saccidananda, the mystery of the Three divine Persons: in sat, the Father, the absolute Beginning and Source of being; in cit, the Son, the divine Word, the Father's Self-knowledge; in ananda, the Spirit of love, Fullness and Bliss without end.[4]

Abhishiktananda was a rare hybrid mystic spanning two traditions. His life of inner discovery cost him dearly; he suffered terrible doubt, anguish, and loneliness. As one of the first Christian mystics to enter the realm of advaitic mysticism, he had no one to whom to turn for advice and direction. In his own extraordinary accomplishment, he is a prophet of interspirituality, his life a living witness and symbol of a dynamic, open-ended dialogue of mystical experience between these two great traditions. He demonstrated the possibility of being a fully formed contemplative in both the Hindu and Christian traditions. In this way, he lived an intermystical life, an eloquent example for others.

Bede Griffiths

Abhishiktananda was a somewhat remote figure — certainly inaccessible to westerners during his years in India. Other pioneers, however, were more approachable. One of these figures, Bede Griffiths, has perhaps meant more to bringing these great traditions together than anyone else.

Bede Griffiths was an English Benedictine monk born in 1906, who lived in India from 1955 until his death in May 1993. A great contemplative, he also concerned himself with the practical task of running Shantivanam, the ashram founded by Monchanin and Abhishiktananda. There he built a viable monastic community following the Benedictine tradition in an Indian style: as sannyasis living a poor and simple life focused on the intense practice of contemplation and meditation. He became well known in his years at Shantivanam, writing fifteen books that all contributed in some way to furthering interspirituality.

Not content with just bridging the religions, Bede also added science to the equation.[5] He understood that scientific breakthroughs — notably discoveries in quantum mechanics and biology, Rupert Sheldrake's theory of morphogenic fields, and discoveries in transpersonal psychology — would transform the old antagonism between spirituality and science into a congenial relationship. He described in his later writings a new synthesis, a new vision of reality, built both on intellectual integration and direct experience. Three years before his death, he underwent a radical mystical process (brought on by an apparent stroke) which lasted for months. During this experience, he wrote: "I find myself in the Void, but the Void is totally saturated with Love."[6] This statement, like so many that came before it, grew out of his deep experience of uniting Christian,

Hindu, and Buddhist mysticism. In this sense, he was a prophet of inter-spirituality.

Sister Vandana Mataji and Sister Ishpriya

Many people are continuing the example of these great teachers. Sister Vandana Mataji, an Indian, and Sister Ishpriya, who is English, are Catholic nuns in the Sisters of the Sacred Heart who live in association with Sivananda Ashram in Rishikesh, which is dedicated to promoting Christian-Hindu dialogue and friendship. They follow Swami Chitananda, considered by many in contemporary India to be a great saint. Chitananda is renowned for his spiritual presence, his deep wisdom and warmth of personality, his acceptance of others, and his commitment to the Hindu-Christian dialogue. He has built a large following throughout India and abroad as president of the Divine Life Society. Sisters Vandana and Ishpriya travel the world giving retreats, lecturing, and teaching. They are always calling others to the inter-spiritual challenge through the simplicity of their lifestyle, their dedication to meditation, their renunciation, and their selfless service to the poor, which bridges both Christian and Hindu values. Their intense witness is to the common ground of interiority or mystical contemplation activated and culti-vated through regular meditation.

Raimundo Panikkar

Another influential figure in the marriage (in this case, literally) of East of West is the theologian Raimundo Panikkar. His mother was Spanish; his father was a Brahmin from Kerela in southern India.

Panikkar is a brilliant cross-cultural thinker who has managed to inte-grate three traditions in his own life and experience: Christian, Hindu, and Buddhist. In fact, he often calls himself "a Christian-Hindu-Buddhist"! Panikkar can make this claim because he understands that these traditions are not exclusive of one another but actually complementary; they com-plete one another. Through his writing and thinking, he has already helped the interspiritual age to emerge.7

Panikkar also had an amazing — amazing because it happened at all — friendship with and impact on Martin Heidegger. As close friends for the last fifteen years of Heidegger's life, Panikkar's influence awakened an interest in mysticism in the German philosopher, especially in Meister Eckhart.

Ignatius Hirudayam

One of the most fascinating Indian-Christian examples of interspiri-tuality is Ignatius Hirudayam, a Jesuit who founded Aikiya Alayam, or Temple of Unity, an *inculturation* center in Madras, India. In the Catholic Church, inculturation signifies the process of creating new Christian forms from the cultures in which missionaries find themselves. Within the Indian context, inculturation would mean expressing the gospel through Indian theology, ritual, and symbols.

Father Ignatius, who died in 1995, was an expert in Saiva Siddhanta, a Tamil or south Indian expression of Shaivism, a branch of Hinduism that looks to Shiva as its predominant deity. This school includes pro-found mystical literature reflecting the *personalist* school in the Hindu tradition, something very near the Western approach of Judaism, Christianity, and Islam. Personalism in these traditions refers to the expe-rience of intimacy with God, a personal divine reality. His Hindu follow-ers regarded him as they would a guru, with his kavi (religious habit or garb), his long white hair and beard, and his gentle, compassionate, and humorous eyes.

To watch Hirudayam in dialogue with his intimate group of Hindu and Christian scholars was to receive a lesson in interspiritual conversa-tion. He never argued, and he never dominated his gatherings. They were free of academic heaviness and its often tedious preoccupation with detail. He would focus on a theme, perhaps prayer or ascetical practice. Then he would introduce his topic as a kind of reflection or meditation, and open it to discussion. Instead of dissecting the topic, the scholars would each spontaneously add their comments, as if building some mar-velous new edifice of mutual understanding. In the calm of intimate friends who have nothing to prove to each other, their dialogues became a fascinating exercise in interspiritual communication. I witnessed this process twice in the 1980s, and both times thought to myself, "This is what true dialogue is all about." It embodied what Martin Buber, the Jewish existentialist philosopher, saw as the purpose of life itself: meeting others on a level of depth and creating new understanding.

Ma Jaya Sati Bhagavati

The "crazy wisdom" tradition of Hinduism gives voice to a type of spir-itual teacher who breaks the bounds of conformity to formal expectations of how masters should act and interact with their students. Some highly unconventional figures have followed this path. Ma Jaya Sati Bhagavati, formerly known as Joyce Green, is very much in this lineage.

Ma grew up in a Jewish family in Brooklyn, and associated with African-American homeless people from whom she learned much. She married an Italian-American man and raised five children. Looking into yoga as a way to lose weight, she began to have mystical experiences, including a vision of Christ in 1973, who told her "to teach all ways because all ways lead to God." She took spiritual guidance from deceased Hindu gurus Nityananda and Neem Karoli Baba, Ram Dass's teacher. Under the influence of these great masters and her own inner spiritual evolution, Ma blossomed as a spiritual teacher, attracting tens of thousands of followers around the world. Believed by many to be an incarnation of the goddess Kali, she exhibits psychic powers and *shakti* — divine energy.

Ma's spiritual practice relies heavily on humor and its shock value to awaken others to awareness. I was with Ma at the closing plenary of the Parliament of the World's Religions in Chicago on the evening of September 4, 1993, shortly after the Dalai Lama had spoken to a crowd of seventy thousand people. At the edge of Grant Park, where the event had taken place, a number of fundamentalist Christians picketed the proceedings and handed out leaflets attacking the Parliament as demonic. As we walked past a group of them, one man confronted Ma, pushing a brochure toward her and demanding, "Do you know Jesus Christ?" Calmly, and with a smile, Ma told him, "Know him? Honey, I'm his mother!" The poor fundamentalist was dumbfounded.

Ma Jaya is primarily a Hindu with an interfaith commitment that allows her to be equally at home in Jewish, Christian, Buddhist, Islamic, Jain, Sikh, and Native American settings. Kashi, her ashram or spiritual community, reflects her Hindu roots and serves as a home to roughly 250 students. Although Kashi features some Christian images on its walls, like Christ and Mary, most of the *murtis,* or divine images, are Hindu, such as Hanuman, the monkey god, and Ganesh, the son of Shiva. Ma's disciples bear Sanskrit names, speak Hindu prayers, and sing Hindu songs.

Perhaps most striking is Ma Jaya's unique and inspiring example of selfless service to all those who suffer and are marginalized by society. For years she has worked with AIDS sufferers, crack babies, and elderly shut-ins in nursing homes. Ma accepts everyone; like Mother Teresa, she provides uncompromising service to everyone she contacts, especially those who have no one. Ma overflows with love, and so, in this aspect, she is very Christian — a flamboyant manifestation of the social gospel. Her example of loving compassion, acceptance, and interfaith sensitivity continues to inspire all those who really know her.

✦ Dialogue Between Catholicism and the Other Religions

Since the Second Vatican Council opened the Catholic Church and other world religions to interreligious dialogue, monastics have carried the primary responsibility for this significant, mystical interfaith work. They have deeply assimilated Hinduism, Zen, Taoism and other forms of Buddhism, notably the Theravadan and Tibetan traditions. Thomas Merton and Thomas Keating, both Trappists, are two leading figures in this development.

Thomas Merton and Eastern Traditions

Thomas Merton was perhaps the greatest popularizer of interspirituality. Not only did he acquaint his readers with the rich and vast tradition of Christian contemplation (represented by fifty thousand volumes from the early church to the present), but he opened the door for Christians to explore other traditions, notably Taoism, Hinduism, and Buddhism. Among his many writings, several volumes explored Eastern traditions: *Zen and the Birds of Appetite, Mystics and Zen Masters, The Way of Chuang Tzu,* and *Contemplation in a World of Action.*

When Merton died in 1968, he was deeply engrossed in a study of Buddhism; his fascination was an honest attempt to integrate the East's mystical insights with the heart of Christian contemplative wisdom. His experience at Polonnaruwa, Sri Lanka, before the majestic statues of the reclining Buddha and Ananda, his beloved disciple, was a decidedly Buddhist moment in the inner landscape of this Christian monk. He relates his inner explosion of insight at Polonnaruwa in the *Asian Journal:*

> Looking at the figures I was suddenly, almost forcibly jerked clean out of the habitual, half-tied vision of things, and an inner clearness, clarity, as if exploding from the rocks themselves, became evident and obvious. The queer *evidence* of the reclining figure, the smile, the sad smile of Ananda standing with arms folded (much more "imperative" than Da

Vinci's Mona Lisa because completely simple and straightforward.) The thing about all this is that there is no puzzle, no problem, and really no "mystery." All problems are resolved and everything is clear, simply because what matters is clear. The rock and all matter, all life, is charged with *dharmakaya* (the body of reality, or the ultimate nature of the Buddha, identified with transcendental reality)...everything is emptiness and everything is compassion. I don't know when in my life I have ever had such a sense of beauty and spiritual insight running together in one aesthetic illumination. Surely, with Mahabalipuram (ancient site of Hindu temples on the southeastern coast of India) and Polonnaruwa my Asian pilgrimage has come clear and purified itself. I mean, I know and have seen what I was obscurely looking for.[8]

Merton was far ahead of his time. His spirit of openness, building on the work of countless others, guided the Catholic Church into new realms of interreligious understanding. The full realization of the Church's new view appeared in 1966 in a decree of the Second Vatican Council entitled *Nostra Aetate*.[9] In this document, the Church acknowledged the truth and moral values of the Eastern religions, and committed to a course of dialogue with them. The watershed document radically transformed — virtually overnight — a historically negative attitude into a dialogical one. By removing the obstacles to mutual exploration between Christianity and the other religions, particularly those of Asia, this change has greatly contributed to the emergence of interspirituality.

Indeed, the Vatican now has a department devoted to relations with non-Christian traditions. Formerly known as the Pontifical Council for Non-Christian Religions, it was renamed in the 1980s the Pontifical Council for Interreligious Dialogue, and is currently chaired by Francis Cardinal Arinze, a Nigerian. In the early 1970s, the department commissioned the Benedictines and Cistercians, or Trappists, to carry out the Church's dialogues and encounters with representatives of the Asian traditions, especially Hindus and Buddhists. The Church later formed an organization to implement this mandate, *Dialog inter Monasteres*, or simply DIM. A North America counterpoint was established in 1977, which is now called Monastic Interreligious Dialogue, or MID.[10] The founders of MID include, among others, Sister Pascaline Coff, OSB, a Benedictine nun from Osage Monastery in Sand Springs, Oklahoma, and Father Theophane Boyd, OSCO, a Trappist from St. Benedict's Monastery, in

Snowmass, Colorado. Both of these organizations actively promote dialogue and encounters with Buddhists and Hindus.

One of the most celebrated of these was the Gethsemani Encounter between Christian and Buddhist monastics at the Abbey of Gethsemani, Merton's monastery near Louisville, Kentucky, which took place for a week in July 1996.[11] The Gethsemani Encounter included dialogue on such issues as ultimate reality, prayer and meditation, monastic formation, work, and the role of the teacher. The warmth, openness, respect, and affection displayed among the participants made this event an important success. The Dalai Lama himself has told me that he felt it represented a great step forward in Catholic-Buddhist relations.

Thomas Keating and Centering Prayer

While institutions like these are doing wonderful work to foster communication among the religions, individuals like Merton and another Trappist monk, Thomas Keating, are responsible for many of the real breakthroughs. Few have contributed more to interspirituality in our time than Keating.

During his tenure as abbot of St. Joseph's Abbey in Spencer, Massachusetts, from 1961 to 1981, Keating welcomed Hindu gurus like Swami Satchidananda, Sufi masters, and rabbis representing mystical Judaism. He accompanied Zen roshis in *sesshins,* or intensive meditation retreats, including Joshu Sasaki-roshi of the Mount Baldey Zen Center near Los Angeles, who visited Spencer over ten years, giving two sesshins to the community. Many monks at Spencer refer to Keating's tenure as Spencer's golden age.

But Keating's most important contributions has been his development of Centering Prayer. Along with William Mennenger and Basil Pennington, also monks of Spencer, Keating revived this Christian form of contemplative meditation from *The Cloud of Unknowing,* a fourteenth-century Christian mystical manual of the inner life. Since its beginnings in the 1970s, Centering Prayer has spread throughout the world through Contemplative Outreach, an organization founded by Keating to promote the method and educate people about the mystical, or contemplative journey.[12] Keating saw Centering Prayer as a Christian answer to Hindu and Buddhist meditation, and an experiential platform for interspiritual experimentation and collaboration.

Keating participated for many years in this sort of collaboration at the Naropa Institute of Boulder, Colorado, the Tibetan Buddhist graduate school founded by Chögyam Trungpa Rinpoche that has spearheaded interspiritual dialogue and practice — mostly between Christians and Buddhists.[13] In the early 1980s, Abbot Thomas also established the Snowmass Conference to promote dialogue and explore spiritual practice across traditions. The group's fifteen members, each a teacher representing a different religious tradition, have all become great friends as they've faithfully met for a week each year. Through these conversations, the group has drafted a document called *The Guidelines for Interreligious Understanding* outlining eight common points describing interspirituality (we'll explore them in more detail later in this book).[14]

Abbot Thomas's contribution has been visionary, at once shedding light on the terrain to be traversed in the future, and engaging in a sensitive dialogue of the heart. The Snowmass Conference offers a paradigm of interspiritual sharing in which a comprehensive understanding of the major spiritual paths is gained through discussion and practice. The members consciously share their spiritual practices with one another, and discuss their differences and similarities. They have produced a holistic model of intermystical wisdom precisely because it is so inclusive of so many traditions.

Buddhists and Catholics Working Together

Closely akin to the work of Thomas Keating and the Snowmass Conference is the ongoing dialogue between Buddhists and Catholics. Significant interspiritual links have been forged between Buddhists and Catholic monastics. The Society for Buddhist-Christian Studies has encouraged a rich relationship between the two traditions on all three levels of dialogue — the *head, heart,* and *hands,* but primarily the head — through publications, regional conferences, and gatherings. Catholic monks and nuns have focused on the dialogue of the heart; and they have pursued common projects together under the category of the dialogue of the hands, or working together on social justice and the peace issue.

One example of the dialogue of the hands is the *Universal Declaration on Nonviolence,* an initiative Monastic Interreligious Dialogue took with the Dalai Lama.[15] Another one is the *Resolution on Tibet* introduced by MID at the 1993 Parliament of the World's Religions in Chicago.[16] This resolution advocated respect for the human rights of Tibetans, and the serious consideration of their plight in the United Nations and other international forums. There is a deeply held commitment among Catholic monastics to the Tibetans and their nonviolent struggle to regain their freedom and their rights in Tibet, although this commitment is not shared openly by the Vatican.

The Catholic Church Reaches out Toward Judaism

The Catholic Church today is confronting its relationship with Judaism, and is experiencing tremendous anguish over its role in history up to the time of the Nazis. Centuries of anti-Semitism cultivated in the bosom of Christendom contributed to the Nazi genocide. We must be clear on this painful matter: the Holocaust didn't happen in a vacuum. It arose out of the shadow side of Christianity, even though the Church completely rejected Nazism. Previous policies of the Church and the popes set in motion a hostility to the Jewish community that eventually culminated in the poisonous hatred of Hitler.

Despite this history, relations between two of the West's major religious traditions are growing warmer. The Church is steadily and systematically dismantling the cultural supports for anti-Semitism. This deeply sincere process has culminated in a recent Vatican document, We Remember: A Reflection on the Shoah, a brief statement that proclaims a special relationship between Jews and Catholics.[17] This new warmth has made possible a number of interspiritual sharings, such as the Passover Seder mentioned above; but the interest in each others' mystical tradition is very deep indeed. Many Christians interested in mysticism study the Kabbalah and the Hasidic writings.

✦ Buddhism Comes to the West

Much has been written about the growing relationship between Buddhism and the West, mostly about how Americans and Europeans are adopting Zen and Tibetan practices in ever-increasing numbers. But many are also working on the intersection of Buddhism and other faiths.

For example, there is the fascinating phenomenon of Buddhist Jews who call themselves "Bu-Jews" or "JUBUS." The work of Roger Kamenetz, poet, writer, and professor of English Literature at Louisiana State University, as detailed in his book The Jew in the Lotus: A Poet's

Rediscovery of Jewish Identity in Buddhist India is profoundly interspiritual.[18] He is someone who is being nourished by these two venerable springs of mystical insight. His attempt to relate these two traditions, and his deep appreciation of Buddhism within his Jewish identity, makes his work noteworthy. He explores Buddhism *as a Jew;* he hasn't left his faith behind. The Jewish community and the Buddhists have come along way in their dialogical process.

Thich Nhat Hanh, the saintly Vietnamese Zen Buddhist monk, has also become a leading proponent of an interspiritual approach. Again, his approach arises from contemplative awareness. His bestseller *Living Buddha, Living Christ* is a compelling gem of interspiritual wisdom replacing an immature, even spiritually narcissistic view.[19] His gentle presence has opened hearts and minds in virtually every part of the planet, and his works are invitations to dialogue and mutual sharing of our spiritual resources. His long-standing commitment to peace — even when it meant being exiled from Vietnam during the war — is a direct result of his deep discipline of meditation, and his dedication to all sentient life. Thich Nhat Hanh is a reminder of what we can become if we surrender to inner change, that we can open ourselves to the depth of other faiths, even as we remain firmly rooted in our own.

The Christian/Buddhist Encounter as Model for the Interspiritual Age

The British historian Arnold Toynbee once remarked to the Buddhist thinker Daisaku Ikeda that the meeting of Buddhism and Christianity would be the most significant event of our period in history. These prophetic words are often quoted in various encounters between the two venerable traditions — two traditions so different that a working relationship is, indeed, momentous news. No doubt Toynbee suspected that if Christianity, taken as representative of all theistic traditions, and Buddhism, a nontheistic religion or, as some call it, a psychology, can somehow reconcile their differences, then perhaps all the faiths can similarly be brought into harmony.

Buddhism and Christianity have a historic mission to create, together, a new vision for the world. By maintaining mutual openness, trust, and respect in the dialogue of the decades ahead, such a breakthrough can become reality.

Truth abhors a contradiction; it compels us to resolve the contradiction between the two views. The basic contradiction lies between the Buddhist concept of no god, and the Christian commitment *to* God. In the resolution of this contradiction, something new will be born that moves beyond both while including each. When religions and cultures meet in openness and willingness to learn, they change each other. They are living organisms that grow. The two worldviews of Buddhism and Christianity will carry humankind's awareness forward precisely because they have the capacity to do so.

For this to happen, however, the conversation must be between equals. Dialogue presupposes genuine equality, free of hidden agendas. The old exclusivity of Christianity, especially of Catholics, on one side and the unacknowledged spiritual imperialism of some Western Buddhists on the other, must give way to a symbiotic understanding that transcends dominance. Some Americans have made a fetish of Zen and Tibetan Buddhism, and smugly think everything else relative, false, or naive. Many of these Western Buddhists, as former Jews and Catholics, look down their noses at their erstwhile faiths — especially the idea of believing in God. It's important to transcend this polemical attitude if we are to proceed with the work of generating a more universal vision.

Of course, it isn't just these new Buddhists who hold strong views. Some Christians regard Buddhism with suspicion, and even contempt, among them Joseph Cardinal Ratzinger, the prefect of the Vatican's Congregation for the Doctrine of the Faith, the department that maintains orthodoxy. In "off-the-cuff" remarks during an interview with the French weekly *L'Express* in March 1997, Ratzinger astoundingly called Buddhism "spiritual, mental autoeroticism," or mental masturbation. He quoted an unnamed writer who had said in the 1950s that Buddhism would be the undoing of the Catholic Church. Vatican officials don't usually make "off-the-cuff" statements without calculating their impact. Unfortunately, these views appear to be based in fear and ignorance, not genuine understanding. Far from promoting mutual respect and trust, they reveal a fear of Buddhism's intellectual challenge in some officials of the Holy See, perhaps even including the pontiff himself. They appear worried about inroads Buddhism is making among certain influential Western populations, principally in America, Europe, and Australia.

I am convinced that Christianity and Buddhism each have a unique opportunity — and responsibility — to enter a sustained dialogue. Both sides must avoid the poison of negative caricatures, remarks, and misunderstandings. If the two traditions work together on resolving the critical issues facing the planet, committing themselves to an open-ended dialogue on matters of belief, prayer, and social engagement, they will make a precious contribution toward the evolution and communication of a new consciousness all around the world.

My own work in this area of interfaith encounter has led me to the terrifying realization of how easily we fall into confusion, especially if two traditions are at odds within one's own heart. I have culled the depths of my heart trying to integrate the paths of Christianity and Buddhism, two traditions whose authenticity are beyond question for me. This has been a long and painful process; periods of confusion, doubt, and uncertainty were very difficult. Such integration is the nitty-gritty work of interspirituality.

Understanding Toynbee's Remark

I have puzzled for years over Arnold Toynbee's observation that the meeting of Buddhism and Christianity would be the most significant event of our period in history, trying to understand its meaning and implications. One resource we can enlist in helping us unpack Toynbee's statement is the much maligned and misunderstood German philosopher G. W. F. Hegel.

Hegel made an important discovery about how human understanding develops. After reading Plato's *Dialogues* with great attention, he perceived in them just how our awareness grows. As he watched Socrates converse and debate, meeting others' certainties with objections or questions, Hegel slowly saw the first position shift as it took objections into account. He realized that understanding is a dynamic operation of thought that requires the tension of opposites to unfold. Insight develops out of this conflict of opposites.

If we examine our own views over time, we can easily recognize this principle at work. It is called *dialectic*. Hegel not only discovered its operation in human understanding — in all human beings — but in history as well. History is dialectical; it advances through a series of polar tensions that are resolved in a higher view. For example, the tension between the Roman Empire and the Christian Church led to a synthesis in which the church as the new establishment became the empire. Later, the struggle between the medieval church and the state led eventually to the emergence of the modern secular state, which in turn led to democracy. Throughout it all, an inner struggle waged between the logic and consistency of the positions.

Toynbee's point becomes concrete in the actual relationship of Christianity and Buddhism, especially in the light of Hegel. It is clear to me that these two traditions are in a dialectical historical process. If Christianity can represent, in this relationship, the position that God exists, while Buddhism negates this view or is silent about the existence of God, then up the road of history, the honest, open, patient, and generous dialogue over this and other matters — such as arguments over the existence of the soul, karma, reincarnation, grace, free will, and eternal life — will lead to a breakthrough that will carry humankind to a higher level of awareness. The dialectic must progress because truth cannot tolerate a contradiction, and the Christian-Buddhist relationship is a historical contradiction awaiting resolution.

What eventually does emerge will go beyond both Buddhism and Christianity in their present views. It will be a new view that both can embrace, a subtle refinement of what they have both known. It is difficult to predict the precise shape of this forthcoming breakthrough, but I think it will have something to do with a process understanding of the divine — even though this process may occur in human reason and understanding, rather than in the divine itself. Process theology or thought assumes an incomplete quality to God's knowledge and being, that somehow the divine needs us to complete itself. I think it is more accurate to say that human understanding of the divine is in process, or development, and this is suggested by the differences between Buddhism, Christianity, and other faith traditions.

The implications for the human family are far-reaching. A change in view that takes us beyond the impasse between the positions of God or no God can introduce a vehicle to higher consciousness into world culture. Discovering a way to reconcile this supreme contradiction is not unrealistic when we consider that religions are not static systems but living social organisms capable of unlimited growth. To journey toward this enlarged vision, we must experience the truth found in the meeting — and dialogue — of opposites.

In dialogue, these opposites open a way for the truth to reveal itself. I have often felt that Buddhist mysticism begins and ends where Christian mysticism ends: in unitive consciousness. Buddhism declares nondual awareness as the truth, the ultimate level of reality. Christian mystics refer to the same thing. Meister Eckhart, for instance, tells us of the soul's return to the Godhead, the God beyond God. "When I go back to the divine ground," he wrote, "back to the Godhead, nobody asks me where I've been, and God passes away."[20] How can we speak of God when there is only God? This God is the absolute reality of ultimate awareness. Ultimate awareness, the vast unlimited consciousness of the divine, is also the nature of mature enlightenment. Thus Christian mysticism ends where Buddhist mysticism begins, and ends — its goal. This starting point and goal is what the Buddha himself understood through his awakening to enlightenment.

Followers of Christ and the Buddha are engaged in deep, meaningful, vital, exciting, ongoing conversations. With their openness, awareness, and sense of responsibility to humankind and the planet, they will serve as a platform to launch humanity to a new understanding of life, reality, nature, and the cosmos — an interspiritual understanding. History clearly demonstrates that spiritual vision sustains civilization. Without such a vitalizing spirituality, the ultimate heart of religion, civilizations inevitably decline, and are taken over by other systems.

The Buddhist-Christian relationship is a bridge to a new, universal civilization. If Christians and Buddhists enter the relationship with genuine openness and trust, free of hidden agendas and expectations, these meetings will change both paths. The relationship will mutually expand the horizon of their understanding of faith, reality, and truth. The fruit of their conversation will be a new vision of the divine, one that embraces all sentient beings. Combining the powerful social engagement of Christianity — in particular Catholicism — with Buddhism's all-encompassing, nondiscriminating awareness of all life forms will create a deeper, more meaningful practice of justice. The resulting spirituality or mystical practice will embrace the totality available from the vast deposit of humankind's inner experience. This is one of the primary goals of interspirituality.

✦ Finding Your Place in the Interspiritual Movement

I have only offered a few examples from tens of thousands, but it should be clear that a permanent, growing interspiritual movement is on the rise everywhere! You can do many things to participate in this great outpouring of spiritual vitality. You can read interspiritual books — works on meditation and prayer and other spiritual experience — like those listed in the recommended reading section. You can join the interfaith groups that exist in most cities, and are becoming increasingly common in churches, temples, synagogues, and mosques. You can participate in retreats in other traditions, and encourage the study of the world's religions in our schools — beyond the universities to high schools and grade schools, cultivating religious tolerance and curiosity in our children. Ultimately, through these actions, you can enlarge their vision and heart to include all the traditions.

Back in the 1970s in Hartford, Connecticut, where I grew up, I attended a talk by Rabbi Gliberman, an Orthodox rabbi from New York City who was speaking at the local Integral Yoga center, an enthusiastic venue for interfaith understanding. In addressing the then-new phenomenon of people from one faith crossing into another, Rabbi Gliberman beautifully defined the task of interspirituality in our lives: "In exploring other traditions and in embracing them, remember, it isn't a question of *instead of* — Buddhism instead of Christianity, or Christianity instead of Islam — but rather of *in addition to,* that is, in addition to Buddhism, Christianity, in addition to Christianity, Islam." We don't reject our own tradition, but build on it. I have never forgotten these precious words. They are prophetic, defining in clear, simple terms how we must view our future. Basically, Rabbi Gliberman was teaching the necessity of an open heart, the attitude of openness in the face of the monumental changes that is required of us in this universal, interspiritual age.

Chapter 3

THE MIRROR OF THE HEART: CONSCIOUSNESS AS THE ROOT OF IDENTITY

If you could get rid of yourself just once,
the secret of secrets would open to you.
The face of the unknown, hidden beyond the universe
would appear on the mirror of your perception.
— Rumi

We've all looked into the mirror and been confounded by the strange combination of body and identity reflected back at us. We've all asked, as we stare into our own eyes, "Who am I?" and perhaps, *"What am I?"* Sometimes, in a fleeting moment, we receive an answer, a glimpse of our true identity. It is real but intangible, indefinable. Although we might attain a momentary peek, the locus of individual identity remains a mystery, a source of reflection and speculation for as long as we've been conscious.

The major world religions have come to complex understandings of this identity. The Hindu approach has been dominated by the mystical understanding of the *Atman:* the eternal self immanent in all beings, the essence of life — spirit itself. Western understanding has been formed by the Greeks, particularly Plato and Aristotle, and then fixed by Thomas Aquinas in the thirteenth century. The religions of the West — Judaism, Christianity, and Islam — inherited these early Greek and Semitic (that is, Middle Eastern) influences in their conceptions of God, self, soul, and spirit. The dissent from both Western and other Eastern views is the Buddhist, a curious anomaly in the history of humankind's spiritual evolution. By precluding the acceptance of a creator of the universe, it stands virtually alone. But as we've seen, the Buddhist view converges with the theistic in the remote regions of mystical consciousness.

This chapter is ultimately concerned with the *who* of life, the subject of experience and awareness — that is, *us*. We'll first examine all of these notions of identity, and then explore an approach that incorporates all the traditions: an understanding of human nature as consciousness, and consciousness as the source of self-identity.

✦ Hinduism: Supreme Identity in the Mahavakyas

Hinduism provides one of the most profound views of the nature of the person of any tradition. In some ways, it is unmatched; it encompasses an expansive understanding of how everything fits together — an understanding that springs directly from mystical experience.

The Hindu tradition's mysticism issues from its sustained contemplation of the absolute, which Hindus name *Brahman*. Through higher states of meditation, mystic seers contact Brahman, which then opens the way to inner awareness of the self, or *Atman,* the immanent presence of the Brahman within all beings and every particle of reality. Atman is Brahman, and Brahman is Atman. They aren't concepts but pure mystical realization.

The Hindus call their tradition the *Sanatana Dharma,* the Eternal Religion, because it was revealed to the rishis, the mystic saints of Indian antiquity, and thus has no origin in this world. Hindu mysticism, or the *Vedanta* — the end goal of the Vedas, the first and most sacred Hindu text — is communicated in the four *mahavakyas*. These are the four great utterances, sentences, statements, or experiences of the Vedas and the *Upanishads*. The Upanishads are metaphysical reflections on the content of the Vedas, or their essential mystical insights. The mahavakyas really summarize *upanishadic mysticism* and the contemplative wisdom of the Sanatana Dharma.

The first mahavakya, found in the Taittiriya Upanishad, addresses the nature of the Brahman. *"Brahman* is Consciousness," it states, and consciousness is Brahman. Brahman can also be translated as perception or intelligence.[1] This great utterance was made thousands of years ago, but its experiential reality was known in India for several millennia preceding. How did the rishis discover this truth?

The answer lies in their practice of meditation. Their meditative practice and ascetical discipline brought profound breakthroughs into ultimate levels of awareness. Although there are clearly mythological dimensions to Hinduism, the understanding of Brahman and Atman comes directly from mystical experience. Rather than an old man in the sky, or some mythological being, Hinduism sees consciousness itself as the full divine mystery. Brahman pervades the entire cosmos, and it exists within its own consciousness. The Mundaka Upanishad reads: "What is smaller than the smallest and intensely bright, in which rest these worlds and those who live therein — it is the imperishable *Brahman;* it is the breath, it is the immortal."[2]

The rishic seers, the mystic founders of Hinduism, also experienced continuity between the divine presence encompassing the entire cosmos and the inner depths of their own hearts, the *guha* or cave of the heart, the deepest point of human subjectivity and freedom, a "place" uncorrupted by time and external actions. In India, the guha is a metaphor for that hidden, transcendent place within us that is totally transparent to the divine. These early mystic sages of India's forests, mountains, and rivers inwardly realized the presence of the divine in their own deepest experience. They encountered, and were encountered, by this presence within, the immanent presence of God as the eternal self, the Atman.

The second mahavakya, found in the Mandukya Upanishad, is actually the second most important discovery of upanishadic mysticism: *"Atman* is Brahman," and Brahman is Atman.[3] The inner reality of the self in us *is* Brahman, and vice versa. This great unitive, or nondual, correlation between Atman and Brahman proclaims that the deepest center of ourselves is one with the deepest center of the universe. All beings and reality are united with the Brahman. The second mahavakya really tells us that the Atman, the self in us, is also consciousness. Consciousness is thus regarded as the central truth in human existence.

The third mahavakya, or great utterance, which appears in the Chandogya Upanishad, concerns ultimate human identity. A conversation between Uddalaka and his son Svetaketu — the foundation of the guru-disciple relationship — illustrates how spiritual wisdom and mystical insight are transmitted in the Hindu tradition down through the ages. In teaching his son about the subtle essence of the Atman in all things, Uddalaka says, "The finest essence here — *that* constitutes the self

(Atman) of the whole world; that is the truth; that is the self (Atman). And that's how you are, Svetaketu."4 The upanishadic seers were teaching that the human person is divine, just as the Atman and the Brahman are. No less than they, we simply haven't yet realized the fullness of our potential through inner transformation. The outer, transcendent source, and the immanent divine presence are the one ground of our human identity as eternal selves, or Atmans. Each one of us is an eternal Atman.

The fourth mahavakya develops the identification further by identifying an ultimate, supreme divine nature in the human person. The Brhadaranyaka Upanishad boldly states: "I am Brahman."5 This daring assertion falls in the context of the Brahman reflecting on itself, but the implication is that each one of us can arrive at this same self-knowledge about our ultimate identity in God and *as* God — as Brahman. This upanishad reveals the Brahman's own self-awareness, which becomes the sage's own self-awareness when, through deep meditation, he or she accesses, or "tunes into" the Brahman. The mystic "hears" and "feels" God's self-awareness, and shares in it to the level of declaring, with Brahman, "I am Brahman."

The *Purusha* — the cosmic person, or lord — appears in several places in the Vedas, the Upanishads, and the Bhagavad Gita. The Svetasvatara Upanishad states that we need to pass through him in order to achieve or activate our immortality. "Who is higher than ... Brahman," it reads, "the immense one hidden in all beings, in each according to his kind, and who alone encompasses the whole universe — when people know him as the Lord, they become immortal. I know that immense Person, having the colour of the sun and beyond darkness. Only when a man (a person) knows him does he pass beyond death; there is no other path for getting there."6

This Hindu understanding of a separate God evolved alongside Hinduism's earlier nondual view of the divine. The latter approach emphasized advaita, or nonduality. Advaita means "not-two" and yet "not-one": that is, in the relationship between the divine reality and the human being there is a subtle distinction, but yet not a separation, and so, they say, the relationship is nondual. This system of thinking sees human beings as essentially divine — we are the Atman and the Brahman in our ultimate nature.

Extreme forms of advaita have existed since Shankara, who lived from

788 to 820. He systematized advaita from the Vedas and the Upanishads. Advaita has its origin in the Vedas themselves, and is further unfolded in the Upanishads. Basically, advaita, or nonduality teaches that there is a unity, or nondifference between the person and Brahman, and that the world has only a relative existence. Saccidananda, the absolute's consciousness as infinite existence *(sat)*, infinite awareness *(chit)*, and infinite bliss *(ananda)*, or the infinite bliss of being totally, infinitely aware of being, is the content of advaita, or nondual consciousness. This is at once God's inner awareness and the mystic's. We will have occasion to return to a consideration of Saccidananda when taking up views of the divine reality.7 The Purusha, however, allows a distinction between divine reality and the human sphere.

In Hinduism, the *who*, the person who passes through this life, is an immortal, divine being who slowly awakens from self-ignorance to remember his or her true identity and finally return to the Brahman. This process often takes many lifetimes. Because the world is *maya* — completely or relatively unreal — one must avoid getting bogged down in the world's temptations, the cause of further illusion and self-forgetting. Essentially, the Atman, or self, is an immortal *using* a body, which is likened to a piece of clothing that when worn out is discarded for a new one. The person, as an individual Atman united with the Brahman, is consciousness, and consciousness is the medium in and through which the self exists. Just as Brahman is infinite consciousness, and the Atman is boundless mind, so the human Atman, through awareness, is a potentially infinite being. This potentially infinite being is the subject and goal of the spiritual journey.

✦ Buddhism: Enlightenment, Shunyata, Nirvana, and the Doctrine of No-Self

The Buddhist way, what is called the *Dharma* or teaching, rests on the inner experience of Siddhartha Gautama Sakyamuni, who became the Buddha, or the Enlightened One. His awakening to enlightenment became a model for all those who would follow him. His life, inner process, and direct teachings are lost in the remote past where fact and fiction mix, creating a superhuman image of a mythic, almost divine being. Between the Buddha's life twenty-five centuries ago and the first written Buddhist texts came four centuries of oral tradition.[8] Given shaky human memory — an issue rarely addressed by Buddhist scholars — determining what the Buddha actually said and what was attributed to him by tradition is difficult. It is even more difficult, if not impossible, to reconstruct the Buddha's inner experience of enlightenment.9 We know, rather, what Buddhists believe. The question of whether or not the Buddha, if he were here today, would be a Buddhist has no easy answer.

Enlightenment

Buddhists do agree on the inner reality of enlightenment. This experience and awareness is central to the Buddhist outlook, its view of existence, and its concept of personal identity. Our word enlightenment derives from the Sanskrit word *bodhi,* or in Japanese, *satori* and *kensho.* All three words refer to the experience of being awakened — aware of the nature of reality, being, and life as essential emptiness. This emptiness *(shunyata,* in Sanskrit), however, is not negation of being, reality, or life. In actuality, it is the opposite of its apparent nihilism: It concerns the intrinsic interconnectedness of all beings, total reality, and life itself. The Sanskrit term for this metaphysical condition is *pratitya samutpada,* and it is the heart of the Buddhist view.

Shunyata

All beings in moment-to-moment life are conditioned by every other being. Everyone and everything arises together, and so are inherently interdependent. Emptiness means the experience and fact of impermanence, an essential Buddhist insight. Everything here is transient, and so empty — *shunya.* The reality of individual beings is relative and impermanent. They exist only in relationship with everyone and everything else. Individuals are not isolated selves, souls, or egos doing their own thing or following their own projects for happiness. They will, of course, continually attempt them; but the results will be, at best, impermanent and empty, and at worst, frustrating and painful.

But there is another way. If we conceive of happiness in relation to the totality of other beings or to our essential interconnectedness with all other beings, then a higher happiness is possible.

Emptiness also refers to the lack of a permanent self or soul. We are empty of genuine selfhood in the Hindu and Western senses. With enlightenment comes a keen understanding of reality, being, and life as this emptiness. Enlightenment also means understanding our tendency to crave what is not ultimately good for us — how desire, craving, and longing are the root causes of our suffering. Enlightenment shows the basic emptiness of our desires and thus the necessity of leaving them behind by quieting our desires, especially selfish desire or *tanha*.

In the Mahayanan doctrine of perfect wisdom found in the *Heart Sutra* — the *Prajnaparamita Sutra* — emptiness is the central insight: "Form is emptiness and the very emptiness is form; emptiness does not differ from form, nor does form differ from emptiness; whatever is form, that is emptiness, whatever is emptiness, that is form."[10] Form is what appears, manifests, sustains existence, and constantly changes — in flux because impermanent, and, so, empty.

Emptiness holds both an immanent and a transcendent truth. As described above, its immanent nature is impermanence and the interrelatedness of all beings, reality, and life. Its "other" side, transcendent shunyata, is a pure, nondual awareness, free of any form. This emptiness is absolute and unconditioned; nothing arises or passes away. It is eternal, unchanging, ineffable, blissful, and secure, like nirvana itself. Transcendent emptiness, like immanent emptiness, is also not a negative but a positive, ultimate threshold of consciousness. It is the ground and source of immanent emptiness, and the inner principle of shunya, or conditioned being and reality affecting all sentient beings. Ultimate, or transcendent emptiness is equivalent to *parinirvana*, or the goal of existence as boundless consciousness beyond desire and personal identity as we understand it in this world through our notions of self, soul and ego.

Nirvana

In the West we frequently use the word nirvana as a synonym for bliss, or heaven, but this is a misunderstanding. The Buddhist concept of nirvana has complex moral, psychological, metaphysical, and spiritual levels.

Morally, nirvana is the decision to abandon desire, or selfish craving; it means embracing the Dharma and thus following the Eight-Fold Path that leads to nirvana. Psychologically, nirvana is the experience of actually being free of selfish desire. It is the peaceful letting go and the letting be, found by freeing ourselves from the emotional turmoil of our desires. These desires inevitably rule us when we give them center stage in our lives. Metaphysically, nirvana is the absolute condition beyond the transient nature of human existence; it is the conditionless, immutable, eternal reality of awareness. It is the transcendent side of shunyata, the absolute reality that contains all the fullness and emptiness implicit in all things. Finally, we achieve nirvana *spiritually* when we personally appropriate its nature in our lives. It is our experience of enlightenment beyond desire, of the emptiness of individual being, of the impermanence of phenomena, of everything.

The Buddha is said to have achieved all these levels of nirvana. By abandoning the world, withdrawing from its seductive influence, he made the decision *morally* to liberate himself from craving's control. Here the Buddha's inner process is similar to that of any other saint who has let go of selfishness in the depths of the will — a pattern found in all traditions. Then, through wandering and intense asceticism, he disciplined himself and freed himself *psychologically* from the hold of desire. He sought the middle way, the essential path to liberation, what later tradition would call the Dharma. He learned from other ascetics he encountered, those like him who had renounced the world, but he also realized that asceticism alone wasn't enough. The Buddha discovered an unlimited freedom beyond emotion's flux. By liberating himself within and without, and by complete commitment to meditation, he entered infinite awareness, the metaphysical summit of nirvana, in which he understood the nature of existence, its roots or cause, and its eventual destiny. Spiritually, the Buddha lived his enlightenment experience in the world, and shared its fruits with others, attempting to awaken them to what he had discovered, the revelation of our ultimate nature as this vast awareness.

Nirvana is directly related to *samsara,* the seemingly endless cycle of rebirths. After enlightenment, in the view of the Mahayana, the Great Vehicle School, samsara and nirvana are the same: nirvana is samsara, and samsara is nirvana. If we perceive the world, nature, all beings, and our existence in their actual nature — their emptiness — then no difference exists between samsara and nirvana. Our purely rational mind obscures our perception of the deeper nature of reality, and traps us in relative understanding. Here Buddhism distinguishes between relative and absolute truth. All relative truths are the product of dualistic perceiving and thinking, while all absolute truths are the fruit of nondual perception and thought. Enlightenment, shunyata, and nirvana are absolute truths; they do not change. Samsara in the human condition is an absolute truth because it names the real situation of existence for us in this world of becoming before awakening. Cultures, with their language, customs, music, art, clothing, and food, are relative.

Nirvana has many similarities to the Christian understanding of the Godhead as described by mystics like Pseudo-Dionysius and Meister Eckhart. They are, indeed, almost identical, according to Edward Conze:

> Nirvana is permanent, stable, imperishable, immovable, ageless, deathless, unborn, and unbecome, that it is power, bliss, and happiness, the secure refuge, the shelter, and the place of unassailable safety, that it is the real Truth and the supreme Reality; that it is the *Good,* the supreme goal and the one and only consummation of our life, the eternal, hidden and incomprehensible Peace.[11]

Like the Godhead of the Western mystics and Hinduism, absolute nirvana is incomprehensible. It cannot be understood rationally. It is best approached through an *apophatic* method — a Greek term for a suprarational way of reflecting on ultimate reality. It is a way of knowing God by *not* knowing. The mystic has direct experience of the divine but cannot adequately express this experience through intellectual concepts and so must use the negative form of mystical language that exists in most traditions. Some Hindu mystics, when referring to the absolute, will use an apophatic approach by referring to *neti, neti:* God is "not this (neti), and not that (neti)."[12] If you examine all of the terms used in the above description of nirvana, not one of them actually conveys the infinite content of nirvana itself. It must be approached with subtlety; it cannot be grasped directly. These same terms are used by Western mystics to characterize the Godhead. The terms' similarity leads to the question of whether or not the differences are more semantical than real. I have often encountered this possibility, or suspicion, in my dialogues with Buddhists about shunyata, nirvana, and the Godhead.

No-Self

In Buddhism the personal self, soul, or ego has no real meaning because it doesn't really exist; it is finite and passes away like everything else. Any self, soul, or ego that does exist is destined to disappear, since they are just as impermanent as everything else. This leads the Buddha and his followers to reject a personal self, soul, or ego as the basis of identity.

The Buddha rejected these ideas of human identity for two reasons: because of the problem of impermanence, and because of the way in which selfhood can be used socially to benefit some while enslaving others. Tradition holds that the Buddha's teaching was a critique of bramanical Hinduism, with its dominant priestly caste's oppression of the lower castes and misuse of God and the self to control others. Thus the Buddha's silence about God and his rejection of the self is as much political and social as philosophical. In Buddhism, the only thing that survives death, change, and impermanence is consciousness: our real identity of ultimate awareness — our Buddha-nature. This is the eternal nature of the mind.

The Buddhist notion of no-self, with the insight of emptiness as the matrix of interconnectedness of all beings, suggests that although no individual self exists, there is a greater self called Buddha-mind or Buddha-nature — what exists beyond appearances. Coming back to our Buddha-nature is the object of the spiritual journey, of all our efforts at meditation and other means of transformation. Each person has a capacity to awaken this higher awareness of Buddha-nature. In the end, this is the key to the human mystery. Understanding the inner reality of the Buddha-nature, this vast consciousness or awareness, takes a lifetime of practice, nurtured by the growth of insight and compassion to the sufferings of others, a response based in attitude and action.

✦ The Greeks: Plato and Aristotle

The Semitic biblical tradition, from which the three Western faiths descend, contends that people — both men and women — are created in the divine image and likeness of God.[13] Thus a person, at least subtly, is a reflection of divine reality. Although the Bible has a lot to say about the *heart* as the center of depth and openness to God, it doesn't elaborate much on human identity beyond that we reflect the image and likeness of God. But since God has no physical form, this likeness refers to something more refined. We are most like God, and wrought in the divine's radiance, in our capacity for consciousness and love. The Bible speaks of the human "soul" as the "breath of life." St. Paul and other New Testament writers describe the nature of the person as the union of body, mind, and spirit. They never elaborate, however, and it is left to the Greeks to fill in the conceptual void.

When the Fathers of the Church were developing Christian theology, they turned to Greek speculation, to Plato and Aristotle. These two thinkers gave Christian philosophy the basic questions, solutions, and terminology. They profoundly influenced the Christian understanding of the person, on the formation of the West's understanding of the soul, self, and spirit. Together they provided two alternatives, and Christian thought absorbed both of them, with some writers, like Augustine, Origen, and Pseudo-Dionysius, siding with Plato, and others, like Thomas Aquinas, with Aristotle.

Plato

Plato's view of the nature of the person resembles a more dramatic Hindu notion. For him, the soul is primary and the body dispensable — an extreme form of dualism. Indeed, for Plato, the soul is a "prisoner" of the body. The immortal soul has always existed, or at least it has been around for countless ages. Plato interprets all knowledge as a remembering of what the soul knew previously from other lives, or from its origin in the realm of divine reality. In an important passage of the *Meno*, which explores transmigration, immortality, and recollection, Plato records Socrates' and his own views: "The soul, since it is immortal and has been born many times, and has seen all things both here and in the other world, has learned everything that is...for seeking and learning are in fact nothing but recollection."[14] Human identity thus comes through the soul: the self is this soul.

Aristotle

Aristotle, who wrote an entire treatise on the nature of the soul, or the *psyche,* presents a slightly tempered dualism. Plato considered the soul estranged from the temporal vehicle of the body, which inevitably passes away. Aristotle has a more positive attitude toward the body and its role.

In his *hylomorphic theory,* he distinguishes between what he calls *primary matter* and *substantial form,* or simply matter and form. The soul is the substantial form of the body. It is the principle of life in the body as well as the seat of knowing in us. Matter is only potential until form actualizes it by giving it a certain order. Here is what Aristotle says: "The soul must be a substance in the sense of the form of a natural body having potentiality within it. But substance is actuality, and thus soul is the actuality of the body...."¹⁵ The soul has a higher part called the active and passive reason. This is what is meant by mind. The soul as active reason, as actual mind, is what is separable from the body, and so, capable of perpetual existence in a disincarnated state, and it has always existed. Aristotle emphasizes this point: "When mind (soul as active reason) is set free from its present conditions it appears as just what it is and nothing more; this alone is immortal and eternal...."¹⁶ It has neither a beginning nor an end.

✦ The Christian Understanding

Both the Platonic and Aristotelian notions of the person — the knower or the subject of experience — stress the soul as the locus of identity. These two views have been immensely influential in the formation of the West's understanding of selfhood. St. Augustine, who lived from 354 to 430, adopted Plato's philosophy as the basis of his psychology to such an extent that he is called the "Christian Plato." He brought Plato's understanding to the Church, while modifying it in relation to the place and value of the body, especially in light of the Resurrection doctrine, the Christian doctrine that the human body will rise at the end of the world and live eternally just as Jesus is said to have risen from the dead after his crucifixion. Augustine's view prevailed until St. Thomas Aquinas introduced Aristotle's thought to the West via Arabic translations in the thirteenth century.

St. Thomas, as he is called, achieved the brilliant philosophical synthesis of integrating Neoplatonic and Aristotelian insights with Christianity. His synthesis was so consistent and persuasive that it lasted in the Catholic Church for centuries — until the Second Vatican Council, which met from 1962 to 1965. Thomas accepted much of the Aristotelian understanding of the soul as the vivifying principle in all living beings: the principle of life, of movement and activity, and as an intellectual substance with the higher function of contemplating God. For St. Thomas, the soul is immortal, though not eternal; it was created by God to participate in the inner life of the divine. The soul's vocation is intimacy with God. And knowing God directly and permanently is eternal life.

The early Greek Church Fathers called this process *theosis*, or *deification:* becoming divine by participation in God, in infinite love. In the *Summa Contra Gentiles*, Thomas argues that knowing God in this way is the purpose of every soul with an intellectual substance, meaning human beings and angels.[17] As an intellectual substance, a being capable of contemplative or mystical wisdom, the soul achieves, with the aid of grace, its fulfillment. Thomas tells us that in this way of knowing God in paradise (heaven) all our desires to know are also fulfilled, but primarily our desire to know him, who is the truth: "There is a desire in man, an intellectual being, to *know the truth,* and men pursue this desire by the pursuit of the contemplative life. And this will be most clearly fulfilled in that vision, when the intellect, by gazing on the First Truth, will know all that it naturally desires to know...."[18]

Selfhood, for Thomas, arrives by knowledge of God through direct contemplation, though the human person is a composite of body and soul, or matter and form. A person's ultimate happiness is in God, and so, self-identity lies in our relationship with the divine. All our relationships — with other people or the larger community — aim at God, whether we realize it or not.

In his notion of *intellectual substance,* Thomas also emphasized the mind as expressing the essence of soul or selfhood. Contemplation of God is total enjoyment in love, the maturity of a selfless intimacy with the divine in which the person transcends selfishness. It is love. The intellect and the heart are united in knowing the absolute directly. For Thomas, the person fulfills his or her human nature in the contemplation of God, the whole point of life: "Intellectual substances by seeing God attain true beatitude, when their every desire is satisfied...."[19] Many of us — maybe all of us, whether we realize it or not — glimpse this ultimate satisfaction, this blending of the intellect and the heart, in the creative act: a work of art, a poem, a piece of music, or the act of truly understanding something. The philosopher Spinoza was suggesting this experience when he spoke of the intellectual love of God. The highest kind of knowing unites love and knowledge: It is more than love, because vivified by the intellect, and more than reason, because expanded by love.

This vision is the Christian insight. It is the larger Western ideal toward which the three religions of the Book strive. It is the end and beginning of the spiritual journey to the ultimate source of love. The self, the soul, or human identity means returning to the ground of infinite life in the divine through mystical elevation in contemplation. Selfhood is rooted in God; it is the mystic who finally understands this nature and meaning of selfhood. The Rhenish mystic Jan van Ruysbroeck reveals how deep these roots go, uncovering the eternal nature of the self in God as an abiding presence:

> All those men who are raised up above their created being into a contemplative life are one with this divine brightness and are that brightness itself. And they see, feel, and find, even by means of this Divine Light, that as regards their uncreated nature, they are that same simple ground from which the brightness without limit shines forth in a godlike manner, and which according to the simplicity of the essence remains in everlasting, mode-less simplicity.[20]

✦ Who We Are Is Where We're Going

In all the instances of human identity we have seen in this chapter — the soul, self, no-self/soul, intellectual substance — who we are relates directly with the goal of life itself. Thus the self is intimately related to the task of realization. Identity is dynamic, not fixed or static. It is an evolving program of inner development.

In popular, everyday culture, people often conceive the soul in Platonic terms: maybe not a prisoner of the body but certainly a tenant of a temporary host! We commonly disassociate the body from the long-term identity of the person. People see themselves, at death, *leaving* their bodies, discarding them for something better. Despite 2,000 years of Christianity, with its emphasis on the resurrection of the body, most people are reluctant to believe that their ultimate identity has anything to do with a body, and hence with the notion of resurrection. The vast majority have no difficulty envisioning eternal life as a discarnate being, a self, soul, or mind. Even among Christians, the idea of reincarnation is common — another example of interspirituality. The Greeks have had a lasting impact on our understanding!

✦ A New Paradigm of Identity: We Are Consciousness

We can integrate all of these insights into human identity, into the *who* of experience, into a reconciling understanding that more deeply comprehends the nature of the human within the matrix of divine, cosmic, and earthly reality. For this, we need a new paradigm. Yet as our knowledge continues to advance by leaps and bounds, our old cultural and religious paradigms of human identity (with the exception, thanks to Abraham Maslow, of transpersonal psychology) remain virtually unchanged.

This new paradigm must be able to accommodate all human experiences, knowledge, and capacities. It must be based on the recognition that we are intimately connected with the earth, other species, and the cosmos. Although Western cosmology from the Greeks to the present ignores the interrelatedness of all beings and dimensions of reality, mystics and certain philosophers have known this truth for millennia.[21] It is what philosopher Ken Wilber calls the Great Chain of Being, the basis of the primordial tradition, the *perennial philosophy*, terms referring to the nature of reality underlying all the ancient civilizations.[22] To be fair, we've come a long way in a relatively short time. We only discovered the existence of other galaxies in the twentieth century; the universe was previously seen as heavenly bodies that only related to each other externally through physical law. Today's science has exploded these ideas and forced us into a new way of thinking that shares in the mystic vision. According to quantum physics, the universe is *one* system. The new cosmology explores this system, which directly affects our understanding of the human.[23]

Everything Depends on Consciousness

This new understanding must begin and end at the point of real human experience, the point of inner life: consciousness itself.[25] It simply is unknowable if anything exists in its own right beyond or outside of consciousness or mind. We have no such experience to which we can point, and which can then prove a philosophical view like realism (which holds that the world, the universe, and everything else is here whether we are aware of it or not). As we have become more self-aware as a species, we are outgrowing realism, and leaving it behind as inadequate.

All that we experience — or know, think, imagine, remember, feel, and dream — we experience because we are first *aware*. For us, everything requires and depends on consciousness to be. The perception of an external world, the existence of others, even the fact of our own bodies, are presented and represented to us through the agency of our consciousness. Consciousness is the inside, outside, nearside, and farside of reality; it is the height, breadth, and transcendent beyond. Consciousness is the locus of all reality. Even the fact that we have a brain is mediated to us through our awareness of it; our perception of the brain, as of all other perceptions, occurs in our thought and awareness.

We are unable to get outside the "skin" of our consciousness to experience what might be there. Even if it were possible we would still have to be aware to perceive what might be outside or beyond. A fundamental contradiction thus prevents us from even entertaining the possibility. It is simply not meaningful to speak of a world or cosmos independent of mind. That which makes perception possible is the basis of reality. Reality, cosmos, life, and being all rest on mind. Consciousness makes perception and everything else happen. Every system of thought that exists — every theory, science, art, literature, culture, religion, spirituality, family life, our own personal existence, all experience — requires consciousness. It is the most fundamental insight in human life, and nothing is beyond its truth.

The experience of selfhood, the soul, the Atman, no-self, emptiness, and all the rest demand consciousness. They cannot exist without self-awareness, or even awareness. If we are aware that we *are*, it is precisely because we are *aware*. The weight of being is on awareness, not on external phenomena. All the concepts we have of human identity depend on this principal insight, and it is capable of reconciling all of them. A shift to consciousness as the locus of identity will harmonize the various views as it also gives us an insight into human identity that is consonant with the way the cosmos is. It is consistent with the new physics, cosmology, biology, psychology, and most importantly for us, with mysticism.

The Community of Consciousness

To understand the nature of human identity we must abandon the notion of ownership in relation to ourselves, especially our sense of "I-ness." We don't own our consciousness, we *inhabit* it — we *are* it. The idea of ownership is a legal, social, political, and economic category. It is not an existential; it has no validity in relation to nature, which recognizes no such right. The fiction of ownership doesn't exist outside human society and culture. When nature vents its fury on us as tornado or earthquake or volcano, it ignores our legal rights and place in society.

The consciousness we inhabit is that ultimate community of interconnected being to which we all belong, and from which we have no escape.[24] We inhabit consciousness, and so we *are* this awareness; but we cannot own it for ourselves alone. It belongs to the community of consciousness itself. Reality, cosmos, life, and being are one vast system created by and sustained *in* consciousness or mind. Here's the breakdown:

A human being is a *local awareness* within our species.

The human species — perhaps all species — are *regional awareness*. Each one of us is a local consciousness within a regional consciousness. We look out onto the world, others, nature, and the universe through our unique perspective, but we exist within a regional awareness: the human race, with its highly developed and various forms of culture.

Beyond us, but experienced in and through our awareness, is the earth, or *planetary awareness.*[25]

Beyond our planet is our solar system, and it has its own kind of awareness. Our sun and all stars have a *stellar awareness.*

The galaxy has a *galactic consciousness.*

The entire universe has a *transcendental cosmic awareness.*

Beyond the universe awareness there may be other universes with their respective consciousnesses, perhaps even a *multiverse,* or many universes.

Higher and outside the manifested universe(s) is the totality: infinite consciousness, without form — what is often meant by the term spirit and the spiritual realm, that which is unmixed with manifested reality or form.

The totality is the divine consciousness in which all things, all levels of awareness, are held in ultimate awareness. Within the totality are realms of consciousness, domains of awareness that have special functions. There are kinds of awareness situated in beings that are higher than anything in the universe itself. There are regions of consciousness that are purely realms of light, forms, essences, natures, principles, mathematical ideas, angelic intelligences, areas of simultaneity in which all events occur in an eternal now. There are types of consciousness for which there are no appropriate terms because these experiences transcend our reach, at least until we graduate to those levels of pure thought and intuition. There are subtle realms of consciousness that require a certain amount of training in order to know them. Then there are parapsychological experiences that take us beyond the limitations of the sensory realm.

The Stages of Awareness

Here I want to briefly outline the different levels of awareness that each person normally passes through on the way to boundless mind. I am not concerned with the evolution of consciousness (covered so well by Ken Wilber in his books), but with what is possible for everyone right now. Some of these stages of awareness are beyond the human, and yet may also admit us into their range. These stages include: infancy; childhood; adolescence; self-conscious awareness; other-centered consciousness; partial, complete, and total enlightenment; transpersonal, angelic, and divine consciousness. There are also many subtle and elusive intermediate realms of awareness.

In infancy we experience little self-consciousness, and certainly no actual reflection — only moments of partial awareness and illumination. Such moments are few and fleeting, with hardly any connection with what precedes and follows them. The infant perceives everything as undifferentiated, only gradually distinguishing loved ones. As the child develops, it becomes aware of itself, but the inner life of the child is dominated by the pull of external reality and relationships with its parents, siblings, and the larger extended family. The adolescent becomes increasingly self-aware. But it is a self-awareness always in relation to a peer group that governs how the person should act or be.

As the young adult leaves adolescence behind, there is a turn inward and a more profound discovery of the knower that he or she is. The whole inner world opens up as a possibility, and the realization dawns that we are capable of living on a more subtle level of life: within the depths of ourselves. This period of life can be wonderfully philosophical; but one must avoid a temptation to solipsism, to mistakenly regard oneself as the center of existence.

Other-centered life or consciousness begins, hopefully, when one enters adult awareness. One becomes more self-aware but also aware of others. One reaches out beyond oneself in concern and love, balancing self-interest with genuine care for others. But the person's love tends to remain confined to family and friends with selective compassion on occasion. This stage is the ordinary level of awareness in which consciousness is immersed in the immediacy of experience, half aware and half asleep. In this period, knowledge, compassion and love are limited by egoic fixation. Until that hold is broken, the person is in a kind of mental straightjacket.

Some people access a state of consciousness where infinite creativity is available. This level is the source of all genius and inspiration, the source of poetry, music, art, literature, science, and philosophy. In that realm of awareness, consciousness is receptive to the pure flow of intuition. Intuition is itself the faculty of integration with infinite consciousness. It is always related to interconnection. Even states of metaphysical awareness and intellectual illumination are intuitive forms of knowing. Although one may not be aware of the unity of everything, it is nevertheless the background perception in every act of intuition.

Next are the three degrees of enlightened awareness: partial, complete, and total. In partial enlightenment, individual awareness expands. This expansion of awareness includes transcendental experience, but what makes this form of enlightenment only partial is that it doesn't include an integration with the heart. The heart is not transformed, and selfish desire may remain intact. Real surrender hasn't occurred, only a greater knowledge of the mysteries surrounding human existence. While there is a larger understanding of life, reality, and being, the heart's transformation hasn't met the depth of the mind's enlightenment, and so, the enlightenment is only partial.

Complete enlightenment, however, is the fruit of an expanded integration of the mind and the heart. Wisdom, love, and compassion join together in animating consciousness. Self-interest is transcended in a larger identity beyond ordinary life and perception. Consciousness and will conform to love through surrender. Self-interest is abandoned in the will's surrender to this love and wisdom. Although this stage of enlightenment is complete it is not total. It is complete only in the sense of its spiritual maturity.

Beyond complete or integrated form, there is total enlightenment. While it includes the previous levels, it is infinitely greater because it enjoys a vast or cosmic consciousness wedded to an equal degree of heart or sensitivity. The quality of its sensitivity is such that it embraces in its compassion all sentient beings. It flows from a natural sense of solidarity with them and its concomitant expressions of compassion and love. This degree of enlightenment is actually a state of total sensitivity, of total intelligence and awareness, a vast range of perception. This precious sensitivity is characteristic of Christ, the Buddha, bodhisattvas, mystic sages, and saints. This kind of sensitivity is the fullness of awareness. Consciousness knows reality through pure intuition and affirms it through pure compassion. Desire no longer operates, and such beings can read hearts without effort, since everything is open to the glance of intuition.

Beyond these levels of awareness are further degrees of consciousness with their defining natures. There is transpersonal consciousness, which is again a vast state of awareness; it is characterized by *impersonal* infinite mind. This realm is the goal of Buddhist enlightenment. There are also angelic domains of awareness with numerous degrees of perfection and qualities in their consciousness. The awareness of angelic entities is quite vast, combining the personal and transpersonal modes of awareness.

Beyond all the realms of knowing is the divine itself. Divine consciousness is the totality; it is infinite awareness, compassion, love, and sensitivity known in an eternal now. It is the mystery of eternity in an infinite awareness of the present moment, the eternal now that has always been and always will be. More will be said of this reality near the end of the chapter.

Experiences of the Totality

Now, as human beings, our identity is this consciousness that we inhabit and are; but our identity is vaster than local awareness. We are potentially already coextensive with the totality, realms of which we can access in special experiences and perceptions.

For example, when we feel a particularly deep experience of unity with nature, or when we are aware of an enormous presence binding us together with it, we break out of our local and regional awareness. This experience, seemingly rare, is actually quite common; most of us are inspired by nature at some point. When we have an aesthetic awakening through contact with an art work, or are touched by a profound piece of music, we traverse other dimensions of consciousness. In experiences of tragedy, of the death of a loved one, we leave our local awareness for a while and are brought into a higher realization. In love and intimacy we discover still another realm of consciousness that is greater than local and regional awareness. It takes us beyond ourselves, suggesting a far vaster

awareness that envelopes us and those we love. Finally, in mystical experiences, we are touched by something ultimate, by a mystery that takes us
to transcendental realms, perhaps, to the sphere of the divine itself, the
"place" of the totality, the source.

All the different types of mystical consciousness constitute further
subtle realms not normally accessible to us in our local awareness. These
may be gentle encounters, or fully developed unitive envelopings by the
divine that take us completely out of ourselves and into the cosmic mystery. We may be awakened into the experience of *spiration,* in which we
are aware of the divine breathing, a type of awareness attested to in most
ancient traditions. There are all kinds of transformative contemplative,
mystical stages of awareness, and these are also subtle forms of consciousness. And on and on it goes; there is no end to the dimensions of
awareness available to us.

Each one of us is conscious, self-conscious, unconscious, and superconscious. Most, however, choose not to be aware, or simply to remain in
local awareness, where it is comfortable, perhaps even delightful, because
it is free of the spiritual effort necessary to inhabit other regions of
awareness. We often also fear growth and change, or simply sit in ignorance and stasis. Our usual awareness is basically the level of sense
perception without self-awareness. We slip into it in our activities when
we are so involved in them that we are unaware of ourselves and perhaps
of others as well. The unconscious gives us access to all the other realms,
and is a source of unlimited wisdom. It is also free of time-space
constraints, and is often a meeting place with deceased loved ones who
are now free of our phenomenal, relative world. As every culture has
known, our dreams are often doorways to higher realms of perception.
Our ego-awareness, or I-ness, is situated within our local consciousness;
it seems so substantial and real, but if it merges into the divine orbit of
consciousness, it becomes overwhelmed by the totality, in which the
I-ness passes like a shadow in the night.

Mystical consciousness carries us into the vastness of supercon-
sciousness, into the realms of the divine, free of our human limitations
but completely dependent on the divine to experience and know its infinite reality and truth. The mystic, contemplative seer is someone — no
matter what tradition he or she comes from — who lives in the presence
of the superconscious, in the reality of the ultimate, the divine mystery,

but who has also integrated the conscious, self-conscious, unconscious, and superconscious levels in the depths of his or her being.

All these levels of awareness, all the realms of consciousness are available to each and every one of us. All that we require to enter them is the willingness and capacity to embrace them.

✦ Quantum Physics Shows Us Reality and Self-Identity

The mystics and some enlightened philosophers (such as Plotinus, Spinoza, and Hegel in the West, and Shankara and Nargarjuna in the East) have known and proclaimed the essential interconnectedness of all things. Western cosmology, however, has been dominated by a crassly materialistic view that reduced all reality, matter, and energy to the lowest level of manifested being. Even Kepler and Newton embraced this kind of view, though they were themselves theists.

The thinkers who shaped the Western scientific approach locked it into a mechanistic straightjacket without room for the divine. They saw the cosmos as a vast space occupied by heavenly bodies in motion. These bodies related in an external way, mindlessly and without purpose. But like an immense machine, it worked perfectly. This view lasted about three hundred years and was shattered in the twentieth century by the advent of quantum mechanics and relativity theory.[26]

What Einstein Saw

When Albert Einstein looked to the stars, he saw a radically different vision than what came before. In 1916, his general theory of relativity demonstrated that space and time are directly related and work together. He discovered the speed of light as a constant in his understanding of space-time. His theory is a way of studying and measuring the space-time phenomenon. Focusing on gravity, the general theory predicted that gravity was a curved field in the space-time continuum. The implication is that the universe is a single system that possesses an internal order, and the space-time continuum is a substantial part of that ordered system.

Einstein and other physicists and cosmologists have searched for a *unified field theory,* which would prove the unity of the cosmos as a system by integrating, or discovering the point of integration of the four forces: gravity, electromagnicism, and the strong and weak nuclear forces. Mystics would say the reason why the unified field has eluded the grasp of Einstein and others is that it is not something outside or beyond, not some other force, but consciousness itself! Consciousness is the unified field that brings everything together in itself, in the cosmic totality that grounds all creation. They didn't see it because they were inside it.

The New World of Quantum Mechanics

Quantum mechanics verifies the primacy of consciousness as the basis of reality and existence, and so sheds light on human identity. A difficult subject that cannot be put into simple terms, quantum mechanics developed in the 1920s. It was greatly influenced by Max Planck's quantum theory, which he conceived in 1900. This system of mechanics, emanating from quantum theory, and developed by Louis de Broglie and Erwin Schrödinger, is applied to explaining and describing the properties of molecules, atoms, and subatomic particles. It took traditional scientific thought into another realm altogether.

Starting with quantum energy, it drew on Heisenberg's uncertainty principle and the de Broglie wavelength to demonstrate the particle-wave ossilation, complementarity or duality of nature. The de Broglie wavelength concerns the length of waves related to moving particles, while Heisenberg's uncertainty principle concerns the impossibility of knowing certain variables, such as the location of particles in space. Schrödinger's celebrated equation presupposes complementarity. His equation describing the wave function of a particle is based on the uncertainty principle and the de Broglie wavelength. The activity of the particle-wave function, or alternation, defies the classical model of mechanics — Newton's mechanical model — which works when studying large-scale phenomena whose relative motion is slower than in the quantum situation.

Light is composed of photons, and photons are energy *quanta*. Photons act in a wavelike fashion, and then assume the nature of the particle. The particle-wave function suggests how something is and is not at the same time — now it's this particle, now it's that wave, and now it's a particle again. Particles can be in two different places at the same time, and the wave-like function means that it is more subtle than mere matter. Essentially, when describing quantum realities we are not doing so in terms of space and time, but something much more elusive and ineffable.

Physicists have discovered, in the quantum situation, that there is no such thing as pure objectivity, and this may account for why the

uncertainty principle holds true: because the mediating role of consciousness negates precise prediction. The objective ideal of science is
just not possible. Inherent limitations on objectivity are imposed by our
subjective, or conscious-bound identity. Subjectivity is intimately part of
the theoretical and experimental phases of quantum research. The
researcher is part of the quantum phenomena observed or predicted by
probability. The observer affects the results of what is observed, and
intentionality appears to be at work in particles, waves, and atomic structures. They are perhaps as conscious as we are, and make decisions as
we do, but in and through their mode and degree of thought. It is more
and more evident that consciousness is at work even on every level of
phenomena.

More New Physics: Consciousness Is the Basis of All Reality

Amit Goswami is one of the most eloquent voices in physics today. In
his seminal book *The Self-Aware Universe: How Consciousness Creates the
Material World,* he addresses this issue and offers a familiar new paradigm: that consciousness is the basis of all reality.[27] He calls his theory
monistic idealism. On the basis of his approach — through consciousness
itself — science and spirituality can be integrated, and the paradoxes of
quantum mechanics can be reconciled. He is convinced that only through
an emphasis on consciousness can we present a coherent picture of reality and heal the old antagonism between science and religion.[28]

Nonlocal Communication

One of the most intriguing discoveries in quantum physics is the
phenomenon of *quantum nonlocality.* It has far-reaching implications for
our understanding of the nature of reality and human identity. Particles,
atoms, waves, and larger entities have nonlocal communication. A particle — say an electron in the air above Seattle's Space Needle — can communicate with an electron in the entrance to Chicago's Art Institute
instantaneously: without a physical signal or any direct medium. Particle
accelerator experiments demonstrate that this phenomenon of nonlocality is universal throughout the cosmos. An electron in our galaxy can
instantaneously communicate with an electron in a galaxy fifteen billion
light years away without having to go through any physical medium.

This is possible because matter and energy alone are not the "stuff" of the universe, of life, nature, and being. Rather, consciousness serves as the foundation of everything. Everything is happening again in consciousness, not outside of it in a merely material cosmos. Everything is mind-dependent. In consciousness there is no separation and no actual distance, and, so, they are not limiting factors. The unity of consciousness, of cosmos and reality, mean that the seeming limitations of space-time are transcended in consciousness itself.

Amit Goswami feels that nonlocality is at work on all levels of the universe and reality; it is at work in the human sphere, and is what makes paranormal phenomena possible. It is present in all parapsychological experiences.[29] It is certainly a factor in mystical awareness, in which we have a direct relationship with ultimate reality. Since we are all participating in that one vast system of mind, there is no separation among any of the infinite number of members.

On the basis of all of this, we can give a definition of human identity that bridges the gap not only between Buddhism and the other traditions, but between science and Western religion: *The self, the soul, the human identity is a community of consciousness individually appropriated and known.* We are all united in a corporate self. Eventually, each one of us achieves the divine totality of consciousness. The spiritual journey is essentially one of discovering the roots of our identity; it is a process of returning to that totality of consciousness from which we have arisen.

A Child's View of the Universe

The metaphor of the child's view of the universe gives some idea of this reality of the divine as boundless consciousness. When they want to represent the cosmos, with its numberless stars, children will construct a homemade planetarium by punching holes in a box. Then they darken the room, put a flashlight inside the box, and turn it on. Light emanates gloriously from all the holes.

I think this is a wonderful symbol of the reality of divine and human identity. Human identity is similar to the little apertures of light coming through, and God is the light. All is really light, but the many *holes* of light obscure the source. In the same way, God is this infinite light that shines in the depths of our being as its origin. The many beacons of this light — ourselves and the infinite forms of creation — tend to obscure that origin. We need to arrive at the realization that there is really only this one vast light, or God. There is no leaving of consciousness because there is *only* consciousness, this infinite light of awareness, like the flashlight shining through the holes of the box. Outside the box there is only light, not the holes through which the light has shone. That light is our ultimate and permanent identity, and so death is simply a return to a more total awareness.

❖ The Nature of the Divine

The divine, as we have seen above, is infinite consciousness: the totality, the source, the spirit, the Tao, God, the ground of being, the ultimate reality, the ultimate mystery, the nameless one, Yahweh, Allah....there are countless other names for this being. This infinite awareness has a nature, an inner reality that expresses the unlimited mystery of the divine. The divine is boundless compassion in itself, and this quality governs its relations with all other beings. This compassion is pure sensitivity, an eternal and total capacity to understand. Divine consciousness possesses complete understanding.

The divine, in its knowing, is not confined to successive acts of cognition, as human beings are. It knows everything, always, in one simple cognitive act. To God, everything is present in the eternal now. All things are simultaneous to the divine consciousness, and nothing escapes its awareness. Everything is part of an undivided wholeness where each being, or each conscious spirit, reflects the totality. The divine knows the totality in each part, much like a hologram. God knows the totality in Himself, and we can glimpse it in and through His awareness.

Eternity and time are one; they are not distinct or different. Time happens in eternity, and is part of its reality: a manifested mode of the eternal in the space-time continuum. There is no past or future to God, only the unlimited reaches of the present in its eternity. The divine is the everlasting light of awareness that is in all, behind all, beyond all, and intimate to all. As the totality, it encompasses everything; nothing is beyond it and all are *within* it.

This totality is boundless, self-subsistent love. This insight and experience is fundamental to the Christian tradition, verified again and again by its mystics, and those of other traditions, notably by the Sufis. This self-subsistent love thrives in its vitality in the communal matrix of the Trinity. The Trinity names this inner community at the core reality of the divine nature. This love is beyond the comprehension of the human. It is ineffable, ungraspable, nameless and formless, perfect, and free of all limitations. Divine love reveals itself to us by its care for the natural world, the cosmos, all creatures, and ourselves, principally by its close attention to the vast details of the universe. It mothers us, encourages us, challenges us, and consoles us in times of trial. Divine love is personal and intimate. It gives itself to us in complete freedom. It is what makes us whole, or complete, what heals us from the scars or wounds of the human condition.

The divine calls us all into being out of itself. We are meant for it: That is the point of the spiritual journey. The journey puts us on the road to realizing and actualizing who we really are in our ultimate being. Enlightenment is the awakening to our identity as boundless awareness, but it is incomplete unless our compassion, sensitivity, and love are similarly awakened and actualized in our lives and relationships. Awakening to and developing compassion, sensitivity, and love is thus also part of the spiritual journey. In the next chapter we will explore together what is involved in the nature and direction of this spiritual journey.

Chapter 4

"THE PATHS ARE MANY BUT THE GOAL IS THE SAME": DISCOVERING THE WAY

The heart is a sanctuary at the center of which there is a little space wherein the Great Spirit dwells, and this is the Eye. This is the Eye of the Great Spirit by which He sees all things, and through which we see Him. If the heart is not pure, the Great Spirit cannot be seen.
— Black Elk

Bede Griffiths was fond of telling a story that illustrates how differently East and West approach the spiritual journey. During his life in India, he would often ask Hindus from all walks of life, "Where is God?" They immediately pointed to their heart because they knew that Atman dwells within the depths of their inner being. In contrast, when Bede questioned Jews, Christians, or Moslems, they would invariably point upward or outward because they conceived of God as external to themselves. Clearly, Hindus also understand that the divine is beyond us and around us, just as Christians, Jews, and Moslems know that God dwells in their heart. The East and West simply have a different emphasis. This difference points to the two paths we can take on the spiritual journey: the inner path of contemplation and the outer path of action. That they do not have to be mutually exclusive is the basis of this chapter.

A wonderful aphorism in the Hindu tradition extols the rich variety of spiritual approaches: "The paths are many but the goal is the same." Every tradition offers multiple paths for the spiritual life, and we take the one that resonates with our temperament, capacity, understanding, and maturity. No hard and fast rules determine the best path; no how-to manuals apply to everyone's situation — or even one person's. Each of us is unique. If there were a manual, we would each need our own personal version. Books and teachers can be wonderful aids at certain stages in our inner development, but our own nature must determine the best path for us. Yet, whichever path proves best for us, we can be sure that it will involve either the inner way or the outer way.

The tension between the inner and outer journey, between introversion and extroversion (not to be confused with the psychological constructs), can be understood as the relationship between the demands of contemplation and action — perhaps the strongest dichotomy of spiritual life. Ultimately, however, in the blazing light of higher awareness this tension is resolved when the two ways converge in their goal: in unitive awareness.

✦ The Inner Path: The Way of Contemplation

The inner path is the road of radical interiority, the path through the lonely wilderness deep within one's own being. This placeless "place" lies beyond the world and all the influences of human culture, with its endless distractions, noise, and confusion, and its addiction to hurry, worry, excitement, and inertia. The inner way leaves all this behind, finding safe refuge in the depths of subjectivity — in the cave of the heart, the guha, the locus of encounter with the eternal self, the Atman.

This is the spiritual path emphasized and celebrated throughout the millennia of India's history, and long before. India has always looked within for one simple reason: God can be found there! Only by this experiential discovery can we attain the final goal of liberation and union with the divine. In laying out interiority as the way to God and eternal life, Hinduism's Svetasvatara Upanishad promises the fulfillment of our ultimate longing: "The wise who perceive him (God) as abiding within themselves (Atman), they alone, not others, enjoy eternal happiness."[1] To know God directly in this life is *brahmavidya* (experiential, mystical knowledge of Brahman) and *atmavidya* (mystical, experiential knowledge of Atman). Both of these represent God-realization and self-realization. They lead to liberation from the samsaric cycle, from the seemingly endless round of births. This liberation is *moksha,* the goal of life.

The way of introversion opens the reality and mystery of interiority. India has always counseled meditation as the essential method of the inner way. In the Katha Upanishad, the narrator explains how God gave us the five senses in order to experience the world, and yet to discover the self, the Atman, we need to look within. The Katha says: "The Self-existent One pierced the apertures outward, therefore, one looks out, and not into oneself. A certain wise man in search of immortality, turned his sight inward and saw the self within."[2]

India has always sought immortality through its search for the self. To know the self, we must withdraw attention from the senses, from the outward realm. In passing into the interior life, we must leave reason behind as well, reaching the inner stillness beyond the phenomenal world. The spiritual journey only begins in earnest when we can still our senses and mind. The Katha Upanishad puts it clearly: "When the five perceptions are stilled, together with the mind, and not even reason bestirs itself, they call it the highest state. When [the] senses are firmly reined in, that is Yoga.... From distractions a man is then free...."[3] *Yoga* — union or integration with the divine — begins with quieting senses and stilling thoughts, the mind finding rest and refreshment in the Atman.

Letting go and *letting be* are indispensable contemplative habits. These seemingly simple practices have to be learned — they are the fruit of years of spiritual practice through the day-to-day labor of meditation. Attaining inner quiet, seeking stillness of mind and senses, requires enormous discipline. If we can learn to withdraw our attention from its attachment to sensory experience, to stop relying solely on the senses for satisfaction and joy, then we are in a position to become aware of God.

The Maitri Upanishad expresses this with great beauty, accuracy, and paradox: "There is something beyond our mind which abides in silence within our mind. It is the supreme mystery beyond thought. Let one's mind and subtle body rest upon that and not rest on anything else."[4] To rest beyond our mind, and yet to be present in silence within the mind, means that the divine cannot be grasped by the mind's methods: through reason. The divine is ineffable because infinite, and so it transcends the mind's capacities. Yet it "abides in silence within our mind" because it comprehends all things within itself and is immanent in all things, and all things exist within it. To become aware of its subtle presence within subjectivity, one must rest in it through contemplative meditation.

A Clear Perspective

Attachments color our perception of reality, distorting its nature and value. We may think we see reality clearly, but we usually adjust our version of events around whatever is most important to us. For example, compulsive eaters, for whom food is vastly important, will have trouble objectively examining their eating habits. By making hate and fear their attachment, some otherwise religious people spread hate against African Americans and homosexuals, justifying their prejudice by ascribing it to God.

Desires and emotions affect everyone's understanding of reality and life. We all tend to adjust our view of reality to serve our desires. Sensory experience can trap us in bondage to the desires they create. One way to cut the cord of bondage is to unravel its sensory support system. To this end, contemplative meditation is a valuable tool. The Dhammapada, the earliest Buddhist text, wisely observes, "Never surrender to carelessness; never sink into weak pleasures and lust. Those who are watchful, in deep contemplation, reach in the end the joy supreme."[5] The Dhammapada stresses watchfulness and contemplative meditation, both methods of introversion. We withdraw from the world and ourselves in contemplative meditation in order to awaken to reality in an absolute sense, and that is the Atman: the boundless, everlasting spirit within and beyond. Bede Griffiths explained it this way:

> Some people imagine that when one is meditating, one is getting more and more isolated and separated from the world, and that in a sense is true. There is separation on the level of sense and even on a psychological level. But if one reaches the depth of reality then one rediscovers the whole creation in its depth, in its center, in its unity. Then one finds all things in one's Self (the Atman).[6]

The mystic does not turn away from the world, from the senses and reason, in order to escape reality and its demands. Rather, the mystic leaves the world to better understand it. Contemplation allows us to acquire a clearer perspective, free of the distortions created when we see reality through the lens of our desires.

This subtle rationalization is actually self-deception. We break through this self-deception by way of the interior direction of meditation, eventually grounding our perception of reality in the divine self. The mystics of many traditions, not just the Eastern, make the same point. St. John of the Cross, the great sixteenth-century Catholic mystic from Spain, speaking within a similar context, explained at great length the purification of the senses necessary to travel toward union with God.7

Panentheism: Everything Is Within God

Although introversion is the dominant tendency of Hinduism, no overriding philosophy can explain an entire religious tradition. Hinduism also finds the divine in the cosmos, in the created order of the natural world. Many texts in the Hindu tradition express an extroverted orientation in the spiritual life. Many passages describe Brahman as pervading the entire universe, at every level. The cosmos resides in him, in his vast, unlimited consciousness. Again the Maitri Upanishad declares: "In the consciousness of Brahman the universe is, and into him it returns."8 We might call this insight divine *introversion*. It is an example of *panentheism*, not to be confused with *pantheism*. In pantheism, God is exhausted in his immanence in the universe, or is depleted in his inward presence to it. He is not able to sustain transcendence, but is limited to his function of upholding the cosmos through his presence in it.

Panentheism means that everything — the universe, nature, the earth, our life — is within God, in the consciousness of the divine or the divine mind. This very subtle perspective is based on mature mystical experience, not speculation. Many mystics the world over are panentheists. Influential examples include Meister Eckhart, Jan van Ruysbroeck, and the Native American sage Black Elk, whose words at the beginning of this chapter reflect a panentheistic understanding. Even a celebrated New Testament text in the Acts of the Apostles is panentheistic. In this passage, Paul describes our intimate dependence on God to the Greeks: "In him (God) we live, and move, and have our being."9 Thomas Aquinas taught the panentheistic notion that each one of us has always existed in the divine mind as an idea. And an idea in God's mind isn't a mere idea; it actually exists in God.

The Lotus Flower

Metaphors for introversion are found in many traditions. Hinduism, for example, has the cave of the heart, and the heart is also seen in Christian iconography. The heart is also a dominant symbol in the

Jewish, Islamic, Chinese, and Tibetan traditions. The Tibetans, for example, speak of the *good heart* as a primary goal in the spiritual life. The lotus flower is another important metaphor, a beautiful cross-cultural symbol that represents transcendence of the human condition — freedom from bondage and desire.

The lotus flower grows in shallow water surrounded by mud. It seems to be floating alone, maintaining an essential purity, yet its roots connect with many other lotus flowers beneath the water. This is a simple yet powerful image.

Images of Hindu deities, rishis and gurus, bodhisattvas, other Buddhist saints and deities, and the Buddha himself seated serenely on lotus flowers are common throughout Asia. Their seated position communicates both their transcendence of this world and their deep interior wisdom. Through contemplation, they have traveled beyond the constraints of the human condition and have become elevated into realization. They have realized their divine potential, their capacity for greater awareness, deepening compassion, expanded humanity, unlimited love, immense caring, and ultimate concern. Free of hidden agendas, they understand sacrifice and unconditional service to others.

They arrive at this spiritual maturity by shifting their attention away from the senses and all that the senses present as worthy of attention, commitment, effort, and will. By moving beyond a dependence on sensation and reason, they discover the realm of the self, the Atman; they open to the domain of infinite spirit.

In his book *River of Compassion,* Bede Griffiths sheds light on this inner development: "The senses convey a reality to us, but it is as though through a mirror, through the changing phenomena of the universe; only when we get beyond the senses and beyond the *manas,* the mind, which is still determined by the senses, do we see Reality as it is. The intellect, the *buddhi,* sees through beyond the senses to the real."[10]

The Need for Solitude

We have seen how important it is not to indulge the senses if we wish to advance on the spiritual journey, but to seek the awakening of the spiritual or inner senses, as they are called in the Christian tradition. These inner senses are receptivity to the divine presence and a natural ability for subtle perception, intuition, experience, and realization. This is why all spiritual systems stress some form of withdrawal from exclusive reliance on outer sensory experience. Regular periods of solitude can facilitate this experience.

Every tradition has a place for solitude, and the Indian experience is most revealing. Sages dwelling in remote caves in the Himalayas, ascetics living in the forests or by sacred rivers in tiny huts, yogis and wandering sannyasis — all attest to the timeless value of solitude on the spiritual journey. When people willingly withdraw for a time, or for several periods of solitude, they are deeply serious about the inner experience and they will be rewarded with mystical graces. Countless souls have experienced this in India over the millennia. The same is true for Jain and Buddhist monks, Sufis, Jewish and Christian mystics. The laws of the spiritual life are universal: solitude has a central place in every tradition.

Solitude is a great teacher, and has been a guru to all mystics and saints. It provides an environment for the mystical journey to deepen and expand by reducing the influences, stresses, confusion, and noise of the world. Solitude assists the process of interiorization in which the person withdraws attention from the outside, and begins to look within.

Withdrawal from the world soon lends a genuine perspective on life, people, God, nature, and oneself. When we enter a place of solitude, all the things that seemed so important to us recede in significance; what is truly important emerges into clarity. It is difficult to imagine any real breakthroughs without a solitary element in one's spiritual life.

Meditation and contemplation give us daily opportunities for solitary moments. Doubly beneficial are those periods when we journey alone to a place hidden from the world and others, a place where we can just *be* in the presence of boundless realization, a place amidst the restorative beauty of the natural world. In solitude, time seems to stand still. We turn our attention to what is really necessary for us instead of worrying over the endless demands of our desires. Solitude always summons us to the essential, pulling us from the superficial. It is a call to look deeply at ourselves, at our relationship with the divine, and at our spiritual discipline.

Solitude gives us the leisure to examine our deepest intentions, to take account of our actions, attitudes, and priorities. It invites us to abandon our questionable motives for more lofty ones. Solitude, like a compassionate surgeon, cuts away at our defenses to reveal our hidden agendas. Solitude shows us just how necessary it is for us to surrender to the divine, to the logic and demands of the inner journey. And it uncovers our resistance to this need for surrender: all the parts of ourselves we hold back from transformation but which we must inevitably release.

Solitude inspires our intention, and forces us to reexamine it periodically — perhaps even daily, as in the Catholic tradition's practice of examination of conscience. It compels us to renew our intention to follow through on our commitment to the spiritual journey, no matter how difficult and long it may be. Many years ago, while we were conversing about the nature of motivation and intention in monastic life, Thomas Keating told me: "Nothing sifts our motives more than time." His comment recognizes how motives evolve and, we hope, purify with age, wisdom, perspective, and dedication. The motives and intention we begin with on the spiritual journey will probably differ from those when we reach our maturity, or arrive at the end, and cross into the eternal.

Periods spent in solitude — whether in a country hermitage, a house in the suburbs, a monastery cell, a city apartment, or a hotel room — are precious occasions for growth and breakthroughs. They are times to renew our intention to live the spiritual life, to clarify our spiritual commitment, to intensify our inner experience. Such intensifications can explode into other states of awareness, insights, intuitions, and realizations. Our faults have no place to hide, and they surface into our waking consciousness. When we become aware of these faults, we can then leave them behind. Solitude is also a time to intensify our prayer, or spiritual practice. If we are to progress on the inner journey, solitude is essential; we must include it in our lives.

✦ The Outer Path: The Way of Action

The Christian, Jew, and Moslem who point to the sky, the clouds, and the mountaintops in response to the question "Where is God?" are classically suggesting the external or extroverted way to the ultimate. For these traditions, divine reality is external to us. It dwells in a transcendent realm, in heaven — above and beyond this world. This heavenly domain is a place like earth, only different: It is free of age and corruption.

In the Koran, for example, God is so transcendent and ineffable people may not create any images of him. Yet his dwelling place — paradise — is beautifully and concretely physical. Koranic descriptions of heaven are not vague and ethereal, like those of Christians.[11] They depict paradise as lush with vegetation, flowers, abundant fruits, and exotic foods. There is no want in heaven; beauty is everywhere to behold. Koranic images of this paradise are both compelling and inviting.

The way of extroversion is based on a dichotomous understanding of reality, an all-pervading dualism inherited from the Greeks. This dualistic view is primarily characteristic of the West. Applying dualistic thinking to the human relationship with the divine creates both the fundamental objectivity of God *and* a clear distinction between ourselves and God.

The existence of ultimate reality is no less objective in the East. But Eastern thought has many answers to the question of whether a distinction exists between the person and God in the mystical state, some of which are quite subtle. They range from complete identification with God, and hence no separate human identity, to varying levels of unity with God.

This same mystical diversity exists among Western mystics. All of them speak of their union with God, and most retain that essential distinction between the human being and the source. Some, like Eckhart, van Ruysbroeck, John of the Cross, and Louis de Blois, express union in terms that obliterate any possibility of difference. Most of these mystics qualify their unitive experiences by saying that the soul becomes God through *participation*, not through actual union.

Perceiving the Divine in Nature

The outer path also embraces the natural world as a manifestation of the divine glory in, behind, and surrounding it. This commitment is the basis of Native American spirituality. Indeed, in all the indigenous cultures of the world, nature is utterly central to their experience of ultimate reality. But this perception of the divine's presence in nature is not limited to traditional cultures; it is also a perennial experience of Western and Eastern minds.

The way of extroversion, as expressed in nature, is the foundation of natural mysticism. India's long and clear tradition of natural mysticism is expressed through its conception of the *cosmic revelation*. This is the experience of the Brahman not only in the natural world, but in the entire cosmos and in the depths of the heart.

Natural mysticism (which we will explore in chapter 8 in much greater detail) becomes a focus for most mystics at some point in their development. It is a whole living matrix of spiritual insight, an objective presence surrounding us like a great mother. The natural world provides an external medium through which we may seek and encounter the divine, and through it the divine also seeks contact with us. The Native American tradition is a rich source of such instances, instances that are commonplace in their spiritual tradition. The experience of the divine in the natural world is a defining realization for all peoples whose life is surrounded by nature. Nature affects the totality of their understanding. The divine presence isn't a matter of speculation in those societies but of daily awareness based on actual encounters. Nature assumes the role of vehicle for the presence to communicate itself to all of us.

Social Action and Service

The path of extroversion may also pass through social action and service to others, particularly the vulnerable. This dimension of the Western tradition is an enduring hallmark of Christianity, Judaism, and Islam. Again, this presupposes a dualistic understanding, but it also requires a deep appreciation of community. A clear understanding of the distinction between God and us allows these traditions to see the value of this world and the sufferings of the poor, the oppressed, the ill and the elderly, calling forth a healing response from us. Compassionate service and social action present endless opportunities to see God in the poor and oppressed. In our time, Mother Teresa exemplified this expression of spirituality, which she combined with an equally extraordinary contemplative practice. Such active forms of spirituality and witness convey the essence of the Gospel.

✦ The Place of Spiritual Transformation

Where does spiritual transformation occur? Is it exclusively in our understanding and awareness, a function of the inner path, or is it in our will, a function of the outer path? This is a very important question. For millennia, the East has seen transformation as a matter of enlightenment, a new form of awareness that takes hold of the person. For almost as long, the West has seen mystical union as primarily an integration of the divine and the human wills, but in God's terms, not ours. Personally, I feel the change has to be in both in order to be complete. I don't think transformation is total if either the will or consciousness is left out of the equation.

If transformation is only a matter of consciousness, then there is always the risk that the change may never touch the deeply hidden intentions of the heart. If the will is not involved in the radical change the spiritual process initiates, then the resultant "enlightenment" is only partial. It leaves intact the will's autonomous decisions, free of the influence of the knowledge acquired in the enlightenment experience.

This partial transformation is especially apparent in the world of organized religion. A few partially enlightened gurus, roshis, and rinpoches give in to sexually abusing or manipulating their disciples, thus bringing shame on their traditions, their lineages, and themselves. There is also the problem of pedophilia among a small minority of clergy, which brings disgrace to the Church and to the priests and ministers who have engaged in this kind of reprehensible behavior. Clearly, if the mystical process is to be complete, it must include a profound transformation in the will. Achieving an ultimate awareness of the way things are is simply not enough!

How the West Emphasizes the Will

In the West, particularly in the United States, we place great value on the will. The concept of finding new frontiers, being "self-made" men and women, even the individualistic, do-it-yourself philosophy all find their roots in this emphasis on the will. It is the same in religion: We want to know God's will for us, we want to do God's will. From the earliest Hebrew scriptures, and particularly in the Christian tradition since the sixth century, there has been a clear tendency to emphasize the will as being the place where the divine communicates with the soul.

This emphasis has been very influential on the subsequent contemplative tradition of Christianity, which has preferred love, or bridal, mysticism, and in the monastic tradition in general. It has greatly influenced the spirituality of the Trappists, who are a purely contemplative order, the Victorines, and the English mystics, notably the anonymous author of the fourteenth century mystical classic *The Cloud of Unknowing*.[12] It has also had a deep impact on the Rhenish mystics, Eckhart, van Ruysbroeck, Tauler, and Suso, as well as the Spanish mystics, St. Teresa of Avila, and St. John of the Cross. Its influence persists to our time, and shows no sign of abating. There is such a strong sense that we are incapable of truly understanding God that an evolution in this area will inevitably be slow.

Hermetic Understanding

I am convinced we can know more of the divine reality, that the union can encompass our inner awareness as well as our will. Hermeticism can shed some light on this difficulty. The anonymous author of *Meditations on the Tarot: A Journey into Christian Hermeticism* is just as convinced as I am that more than a communication of union to the will is possible. The author is a hermeticist, a person who has the capacity to crystallize mystical experience — that is, to be self-aware in the state of mystical union with the divine.

In his consideration of *Hermeticism,* he analyzes Teresa of Avila's description of her mystical experience. This description spotlights the will's function in relation to God in the unitive experience, while the other faculties — memory, thought, and imagination — simply *accompany* the will into union in a state of suspension. They enjoy the union but cannot operate in their usual way. In Teresa's experience, the will receives the union with God. This characterization is very much the heart of the Christian tradition in its apophatic insistence.

The anonymous writer of *Meditations* reveals a more advanced state of mystical realization in which thought, memory, and imagination may enter the union as equal partners with the will. They may be completely alert in the experience, and bring back a substantial content from the union. He credits this ability as the contribution Hermeticism makes to Christian mysticism by enlarging the capacity of the other faculties through symbolism. Memory, thought, and imagination function on a higher level by means of the twenty-two major symbols, the arcana embedded in Hermeticism. Here is how the author describes mystical union when aided by Hermeticism:

> Practical Hermeticism…applies itself to educating thought and imagination (or memory) to keep in step with the will. This is why it requires constant effort of thought and imagination combined in order to think, meditate and contemplate in *symbols* — symbolism being the sole means of rendering thought and imagination capable of not being suspended when the will submits to revelation from above and enabling them to unite with it in its act of receptive obedience (to God), so that the soul not only has a revelation of faith (through the will's surrender to the divine in union) but also participates in this revelation with its understanding and memory.[13]

Training in practical Hermeticism enlarges a person's capacity to receive the full fruits of divine union so that consciousness — which contains memory (or imagination), thought, and the will — is completely included in the process. Hermeticism provides a way for a Christian type of enlightenment experience to occur in tandem with mystical union, and as part of the unitive experience itself. In this way both the Eastern emphasis on consciousness and the Western emphasis on the will are brought together in the harmony of transcendental experience, or mystical contemplation. This is a more fully awake experience that essentially takes us beyond where the traditions were fixated in the past. It represents an advance into an interspiritual understanding of the ultimate state or condition. Such an insight is part of a larger vision of the spiritual journey itself. It is an example of how interspirituality works in its deeper function of natural, intrinsic synthesis — the function of uncovering convergent experience, where different spiritualities complete one another's understanding and hence becoming more effective and accurate.

✦ The Asramas and Margas: Living the Sacred

When we enlarge our understanding of reality, whether through the paths of introversion or extroversion, we see a brand new world: a sacred world. Our task, then, becomes one of learning to live in this world in a way that honors the divine reality that gives it life.

Interspirituality draws its insights, intuitions, and visions of the future from the collective wisdom of humankind found in all of our religious, philosophical, literary, artistic, social, political, and spiritual traditions. We in the West can draw on the resources of the Hindu view of life, which is informed by the sense of the sacred at every turn. Ritual, sacrifice, prayer and chanting, songs, work, family life, study, eating, bathing, sex, even sleeping — all things of life are sacred because they participate in a cosmos that is bounded on all sides by the transcendent reality of the Brahman and the immanent divine, the Atman. Since life itself participates in a supernatural universe, each stage of life is similarly holy and must be consecrated.

Hinduism identifies four distinct stages in life (the *asramas*) and four spiritual paths (the *margas*) to the final goal of liberation, or moksha. The asramas and the margas are a brilliant contribution to interspirituality. They offer a balanced view of life as profoundly originating from and destined to an eternal Source, who is both the transcendent goal and the inner identity of the person. The margas, or paths, have their resonances in other traditions. As we shall see, they are based on universal personality types and the needs that accompany these types.[14]

The Asramas: The Four Stages of Life

The Hindu view of human existence recognizes four distinct but related stages, the four asramas: student, householder, forest dweller, and renunciate. *Brahmacarya,* or the asrama of studenthood, spans the ages of twelve to twenty-four. The student, who is known as a *brahmacari,* is a beginner, a novice who literally "moves in Brahman." Brahmacaris often live with their teacher, trading service to the guru for learning. They study the scriptures: the Vedas, Upanishads, the Bhagavad Gita, and other texts. During the first stage of life, students concentrate on learning the basic tradition and the ways of the eternal religion. They are involved in the gradual work of character formation, which is greatly influenced by the spiritual and moral values present in Hindu culture and their teacher. Students learn scripture through the memorization of texts, which is assisted by chanting *slokas* or passages. The meaning of the texts may come much later. Students also attend temple to assist or participate in the *pujas,* the temple sacrifices and offerings to local deities. The period of studenthood is devoted to formation in the tradition, in the development of virtuous character, and the cultivation of skills as a Hindu.

Around twenty-four, the individual enters the second stage of life, that of the householder, or *grihastha.* This time of life is devoted to marriage, family, career, and social or civic responsibilities. Most Hindus are expected to marry and raise a family. This expectation is a very serious duty in this ancient civilization in which family is everything. Women especially feel intense social pressure to marry at a very young age. Although it is beginning to change, a terrible stigma is still attached to an unmarried woman. The householder carries on his social, spiritual, and civic duties, and also fulfills religious obligations to attend the temple pujas. Householders are usually — if they are wise — committed to meditation and the guidance of a guru. Normally, they fix and deepen their practice during this active period of their lives. Another responsibility, one which most accept with great seriousness, is to provide for the sannyasis or wandering ascetics. It is a blessing to give any assistance to a sannyasi, and people are eager to help them — their generosity is spontaneous and their concern very real.

When the householder's hair has grown grey or white, and a first grandchild is born, the time has come to retire from the world. This is the third asrama, that of the dweller in the forest, or the stage of *vanaprastha*. The forest hermit may or may not take his or her spouse, although many do. The third stage of life is a time of withdrawal from all the usual obligations of life — religious, social, familial, and economic. It is a period reserved for contemplation, of learning to let go and just be. It is a transitional stage between the extremes of active life and total withdrawal from the world, the purely acosmic (not of this world) life of the sannyasi, the *renunciate*. Some remain in this spiritual station instead of going on to sannyasa, or renunciation.

The fourth and final asrama is that of renunciation, or sannyasa. A sannyasi has absolutely no ties to the world; he or she (the nun is a *sanyasinin*) is free to wander, and normally sannyasis will not stay in one place more than two days. People provide them with food and lodging, and take care of any other needs that may arise. The basic function of the sannyasi is to be a sign to others of the ultimate reality, the Brahman, the Atman, and Saccidananda awareness. They are representatives of the spiritual journey. They convey in their life, example, and presence the depth of human existence. They are constant reminders to everyone why we are here. This asrama is a purely contemplative period of life that allows many hours each day for spiritual practice, in particular, meditation.

The Margas: The Four Paths of Awareness

The Hindu tradition also offers us the margas, four distinct but related paths to cultivate our inner and outer awareness. These four paths are primarily part of the introverted, or inner way, although one of them, karma yoga, has an active, outward direction. The four paths are *jnana yoga, bhakti yoga, karma yoga,* and *raja yoga*. They are called yogas because they are ways to union or integration with the divine reality. The margas are related to four personality types. An individual may have all four dimensions over the course of his or her journey, but normally one predominates.

Jnana yoga is an intellectual approach to the inner life. It is a way of contemplative analysis, reflecting on the identity of the knower in each one of us by stripping away what it is not. The *jnani* yogi realizes that he or she is not the body, the imagination, nor the memory; not the feelings, nor sensations in the body, nor the perceptions of any of the senses; not feeling, and not even thought itself, which is always in flux, but something much deeper, ultimate, and enduring. That is the abiding knower who observes the body, sensations, thoughts, and feelings. Intellectuals and scholars, and all those who cultivate the mind, make good jnanis.

Bhakti yoga is the path of pure devotion to God. *Bhaktins* are usually found performing various rites at temples, or engaged in long devotional practices. These devotional practices may involve chanting or singing *bhajans*, devotional songs, all night long. They may mean making a pilgrimage to the site of an important deity, such as Shiva, Krishna, or Parvati. Bhakti yoga is the way of love and devotion, a path of absolute dedication to God in some form or another. It has many similarities to the devotional piety of the Western faiths, notably Christianity.

Karma yoga is the way of selfless work, or service to God and to others, or even to the community. "Selfless" means that such work never refers back to the individual who performs it, nor does that person claim the good actions for himself or herself. The karma yogi always acknowledges that he or she is not the doer when something good or noble is done for God or others. It is a way of humble, compassionate action, or service. It never counts the cost, nor dwells on the good deed. It never looks for gratification in the good action by focusing attention on it. It simply forgets it, and moves on.

The path of raja yoga is much more specialized than the other three. The *raja yogin* bears some similarity to the jnani, since he or she is also pursuing an intense inner path. Raja yoga is essentially a discipline of intensified meditation practice, and other psychospiritual exercises designed to produce ecstatic experience or profoundly interior states of consciousness or absorption in God. Raja yoga is similar, in some respects, to contemplation in the Christian experience. It also bears some resemblance to *vipassanā* or insight meditation insofar as the raja yogi follows certain inner exercises, and then observes their deep subjective effects on the psyche or consciousness. In many respects it is the most difficult of the margas.

Beyond Ego

In the fully developed mystic, all four ways appear at some point, and then he or she will settle on one path for the remainder of the spiritual journey. All four ways have their equivalents in other spiritual traditions. They are basic paths stemming from people's particular temperaments and capacities.

Each path is a means to transcend the ego level of identity — the spiritually, psychologically, and morally superficial fixation we have on ourselves. There is no doubt we need the ego, in a psychological sense, to develop personal identity in the normal course of becoming an autonomous individual. The ego, however, becomes a serious obstacle to our moral, psychological, and spiritual evolution when it becomes our sole motivational and volitional focus, or when it alone determines our decisions and actions. It is bad enough in ordinary life, but a disaster in the spiritual journey.

The goal is to achieve selfless intention and action, which permits a docility to the higher demands of the spiritual life. Selflessness is the fundamental measure of a person's progress, and it exists as an essential value in every tradition. The path of jnana allows one to reach it and implement it by way of a simple recognition that we are not the ego. Bhakti yoga achieves it through pure love and devotion to God and others. In karma yoga one arrives at selflessness through action that transcends personal gratification. The way of raja yoga moves into selflessness through the practice of intense meditation. All of them are paths to the same goals: self-transcendence and God-realization — and to compassionate, loving service.

The Hindu view of life, with its paths of spiritual development, is a significant vision of the meaning and direction of human existence. We have plenty of religious choices in the West, but each competes with the prevailing preoccupation with cultural materialism. Even people living a devoted spiritual life are affected by this cultural materialism, with its twin pillars of consumerism and entertainment. The Hindu understanding of life, following as it does the four organic stages, presents an alternative for the West and the rest of the world; it saves the world from drowning in the shallows of this fixation on the material, the intoxication with more and more things, by indicating the meaning of life and its direction toward ultimate belonging.

Similar Paths in Other Traditions

The paths identified in the Indian tradition have their analogues in the other traditions. These other systems of faith, with their great diversity of spirituality, all offer a life of either action or contemplation, and sometimes combine them, as Christianity does. Bhakti and karma yoga are very similar to the active life of the Christian, Jewish, and Moslem perspectives. Jnana and raja yoga bear a strong resemblance to the contemplative forms that have evolved in the western reaches of spiritual life, especially in the monastic tradition in the Orthodox and Catholic Churches. In Catholicism, for instance, the Carmelites, Trappists, Carthusians, and Benedictines are devoted to contemplation, while the Franciscans, Dominicans, and Jesuits combine the active with the contemplative. Millions of Moslems cultivate their contemplative lives through Sufism's ancient spiritual practices. In Judaism, the contemplative experience is pursued in the studies of the Kabbalah, and also to some extent by the Hasidism, a later mystical school of Judaism. Islam, Christianity, and Judaism all value the life of action, and we see this in its finest expression in their social concerns. The same is true in Buddhism, where there are active forms of life, and a socially engaged Buddhism inspired by Christianity, and the contemplative life of the monastic structure or *sangha*. Some sort of approach similar to the Hindu is necessary in the unfolding of an interspiritual mysticism for humankind's future.

✦ The Integration of Action and Contemplation

Every form of mystical spirituality makes a distinction between the contemplative or inner experience, and the outer realm of active life, of service to others, of compassionate witness and merciful deeds. Yet the spiritual journey, when it has reached its fullness, unites these two realms of experience. The active and the contemplative are integrated within each person's consciousness; they converge, and are understood to be one.

When we have cultivated a subtle spiritual awareness, no separation between inner and outer exists. The quality of our consciousness permeates everything we do because that awareness is who we really are.

People who have reached this kind of contemplative awareness carry it with them into all life situations. Their mystical perceptions, insights, intuitions — indeed, who they are — saturate their actions. Everything is transfigured by their mystical consciousness. All activity becomes redefined by the power, truth, and depth of what they have become.

When we are learning how things are put together, we often take them apart to see how they are made. When we are beginning the spiritual journey, it is useful to see contemplation and action as separate ideas. As St. Thomas Aquinas says, we distinguish in order to understand their unity. And, in the end, we understand that they are one.

The celebrated Zen Oxherding pictures help us discern this unity of contemplation and action.[15] This charming series of drawings provides a narrative of the evolution of spiritual life from the beginner's stage all the way to enlightenment and back. In one of many sets, the first drawing depicts this little aspirant in search of the ox, a symbol of enlightenment (or, in other traditions, a symbol of the divine reality, the divine lover). Our friend begins by asking someone where the ox can be found; he is told that the ox dwells far away in the countryside, way up in the mountains. So he starts out for the countryside in search of the ox. This whole series of pictures is a wonderful metaphor of the spiritual journey. He meets others on the way, and enquires about where the elusive ox lives; he is told that the ox resides on the far side of a high mountain. He goes on, and asks others on the way; they tell him that he is very near, that the ox is just off in the distance, up the mountainside, grazing. He doesn't become discouraged, and he doesn't give up, even though he encounters many difficulties. He keeps pressing on, never turning back until he reaches his goal. Then he spies the ox in the distance; he calls to it, but the ox ignores him. He calls again and again, and the ox continues to pay no attention. He is being tested.

He moves closer and closer, until he is very near. The ox notices him; it discerns the seriousness of his commitment, and begins to respond. Our friend decides to camp there with the ox. He and the ox hang out together and become friends. In one of the last few pictures, he has mounted the ox, suggesting the unitive experience — integration, or enlightenment. The next image is of an empty circle, which expresses the ineffability of his experience, the incomprehensibility of transcendent nirvanic consciousness, or in other traditions, the mystical union with

God. Then a picture depicts the return to the source, the moving beyond this world to its foundation in the eternal. In the final image, our boddhisattva has returned to the marketplace, but now with bliss-bestowing hands. This last drawing conveys the reality of integration between ordinary action in the world and contemplative experience. He is now enlightened, but he returns to the same ordinary market-place. He perceives everything now through his enlightened aware-ness. With his new perspective, he can bestow great benefits on others; he can assist them on their path to enlightenment and integration. His enlightenment has allowed him to realize that contemplation and action are ultimately one because they happen to the same wise being.

Looking for the ox

Seeing the footprints

A glimpse of the ox

Catching the ox

Taming the ox

Returning home on the ox

Losing the ox

Man and ox disappear

Returning to the source

Returning to town with
bliss-bestowing hands

The Contemplative Process

The natural world and compassionate social service are both means of activating the contemplative in us. Although the Western faiths are essentially extroverted, extroversion is not opposed to contemplation, for contemplation understands the inner and outer from a deep awareness within. When, as mystics, we turn within, we discover this contemplative way, in which we seek God as an objective reality. Contemplation is a way that grasps the common ground between the inner and outer in the depth of mystical consciousness. It is a process of overwhelmingly honest self-knowledge in the light of the divine's presence to us, especially through the various gradations of union. Such metaphors as the *path,* the *road,* the *mountain,* the *stairway,* and the *ladder* all express this progress. They point to a process that takes place in an external world. But contemplation equally involves — and more intensely — the inner life. Although the West has been regarded as extroverted, its contemplative tradition is also highly oriented to interiority. In this interiority, however, it holds to an objective reference point, namely God, who is also, as Augustine says, "more intimate to us than we are to ourselves," or, as the Koran observes, "nearer to us than our jugular vein."[16]

In contemplation we turn within; our introversion keeps the objective of divine reality constant. We also transcend extroversion when we find God in the depths of our own subjectivity — in the heart. We encounter the divine reality that is both the transcendent source and the immanent ground of all beings in the abyss of subjectivity, in the depths of the heart.

Introversion and extroversion come together in interiority, which is really a term for deep consciousness. Consciousness, which is the basis of our human identity, is also the locus of our contemplative mystical encounter with the divine. Meister Eckhart, a Western mystic, articulates this insight with poetic precision: "The eye in which I see God is the same eye in which God sees me. My eye and God's eye are one eye, one seeing, one knowing and one loving."[17]

This "eye" is a metaphor for inner awareness; it stands for consciousness itself, especially in its contemplative mode of interiority. It represents this interior capacity for clarity of awareness. The self-awareness I have of myself as self-aware is the vehicle through which the divine can communicate with me. And I in turn can be aware of the divine, united with it most intimately through this same self-awareness. The extroverted consciousness and introverted consciousness come together in the act of mystical contemplation in which the person is in contact with God. Both the internal and the external paths have the ultimate mystery as "object," but we can only approach the divine through this subtle form of contemplative awareness.

If we were to be thrown into the utter radiance of God's glory without sufficient spiritual preparation, we could not endure it. It would be like coming out of a dark house and being blinded by the light of the noonday sun. We have to adjust our eyes slowly in order to behold the light. That is why so much of the contemplative process is preparatory. We must prepare ourselves to be receptive and sensitive to the divine presence by slowly awakening our spiritual senses. These are our inner means of receiving God's communications to us through the grace of his presence, and the numerous subtle forms he utilizes to give himself to us in love.

God can use any means he wishes to communicate with us. He can use words, even though the divine does not need written or spoken language to make its meanings known. He can achieve direct and clear communication through a simple impulse of the will, a suggestion in the mind, an image in the imagination, a stirring in dreams. And he can communicate through mystical love. This is the experience of countless mystics throughout time, and my own as well.

✦ The Goal of the Spiritual Journey

Whether we take an extroverted or introverted route to the ultimate mystery, the goal is the same: God-realization, nirvanic awareness, boundless consciousness. In most traditions, the goal of the spiritual journey is union with the divine, whether this reality is called God, Allah, Brahman, Atman, Wakan Taku, the Tao, the One. In every form of mysticism in which the divine is experienced in personal terms, the objective is the same: intimacy of relationship, a loving unitive experience that becomes stable between the soul and God.

In the Advaita Vedanta of the Hindu tradition, the goal is to arrive at nondual consciousness, the total integration with the absolute in which the person's identity is absorbed. The individual's being becomes the being of the absolute, and there is no difference, at least in the most radical interpretation of advaitic experience. It is a totally immanent view of the ultimate mystical consciousness. The Buddhist approach emphasizes a similar nondual experience. It regards this experience as absolutely true, whereas all dualistic experience is only relatively so. Buddhist mysticism, or esotericism, is transpersonal and so nonrelational. There is no intimacy because there is no personal absolute to which one may be united. The goal is realization of the ultimate awareness of enlightenment.

Regardless of the tradition, the effects of the spiritual journey on the person are the same. Contemplatives, mystics, and sages, in whatever form of spirituality, undergo a radical refashioning of their being: the theosis, or deification of the person, a transformation that affects their entire life. Their consciousness is greatly enhanced and deepened; they acquire a transcendental, subtle awareness. Their character becomes saintly; their will is fixed on love and compassion, mercy and kindness. They are exquisitely sensitive beings, gentle and patient. They move beyond emotional swings. They are not victims of their feelings, nor ruled by their desires. They are free, and so are capable of giving to others and their communities. Their actions are consistently animated by compassion and love.

Such beings exist in all traditions, and are part of a spiritual fraternity of sages that unite all ages and cultures. They are able to appreciate interspiritual wisdom because they are inwardly free, with no vested interests to defend. Most amazing, perhaps, they are not separate from us. Every human being is on the same journey.

Mysticism is a liberating movement in humankind's experience and history. It is perhaps the most precious treasure with which the human family has been entrusted, and it is our most effective resource for transformation of attitudes, actions, and lives. But we all must be able to participate in this growth — the universal mystical life we can all possess if we allow ourselves to be.

PART II

THE PRACTICAL NATURE OF THE MYSTICAL WAY

Chapter 5

THE MYSTIC CHARACTER

Pluck out your self-love as you would pull off a faded lotus
in autumn. Strive on the path of peace,
the path of nirvana shown by the Buddha.
— The Dhammapada

I once knew a shy, quiet graduate student named Aggie. Aggie was a Catholic, and she was deeply committed to her spiritual life. Her intense prayer experience had greatly opened her heart to others. One day, while walking along the Charles River in Cambridge, Massachusetts, near where she lives, Aggie encountered a homeless woman with two children. The woman and her children were cold and hungry. Aggie took them home and made a meal for them while they bathed. Then she found them a furnished room with cooking privileges, and paid their rent and the food bill until the mother was on her feet again.

I am always inspired by genuine acts of selflessness. To me, Aggie is an example of someone who demonstrates the mystic character. In addition to her desire for prayer, recollection, and quiet, she has a concrete capacity for selfless love. This quality of love is the natural fruit of the mystical life and the contemplative character, and it is the nature and fullness of this character that we will examine in this chapter, as we begin to explore the nine elements of a mature interspirituality: actual moral capacity, solidarity with all living beings, deep nonviolence, humility, spiritual practice, mature self-knowledge, simplicity of life, selfless service and compassionate action, and the prophetic voice.

✦ The Problem of the Ego-Driven Life

Life is a journey from hypocrisy to sincerity, from self-centeredness to other-centeredness and love, from self-deception, ignorance, and illusion to self-honesty, clarity, and truth. We are all immersed in these struggles, whether we realize and accept them or not. Even if we reject them, we have made a choice.

Christian and Buddhist spiritual writers and teachers often use the metaphor of illness as a way of understanding the human situation before transformation. This illness is a lack of genuine wholeness, characterized by self-centeredness, selfishness, and self-deception. We think, decide, and act out of our illness. This is the basic difficulty with the human situation at any time and in any place, regardless of the culture. The work to be done is always the same: transformation.

It is really only through an intense life of spiritual practice that we become aware of our human condition. As long as people are content not to look, not to embrace their ultimate vocation to become deified beings, they will chase after every distraction that comes along as a substitute for a life of depth. In the United States, for example, entertainment has become our collective practice. We live from TV show to TV show, from *The Today Show* to *The Tonight Show*. The personal cost is great: deeper ignorance, confusion, and despair, and less authenticity.

We are all meant to passionately seek not illusion and entertainment but *the real*. Seeking what is real, finally, is the vocation of every human being. All too often, however, we become sidetracked — by our conditioning, our families, our peer group, and all the negative influences of an intoxicating culture that dispenses the narcotics of dissipation and superficiality.

On the spiritual journey, we need to gain perspective on human nature, to glimpse what we are up against in ourselves. What really motivates us, and why? Some may resist this all of their lives; others achieve it finally in old age, when all life's vanity is gone. Whenever you begin this inner looking, you will encounter the shadow of human experience: the *false self*.

✦ The False Self

Thomas Keating's notion of the false self — the tendency to seek our own interests — is a very powerful teaching on the basic obstacle to spiritual progress in human life. Keating says:

> The Self developed in our own likeness rather than in the likeness of God; (it is) the self-image developed to cope with the emotional trauma of early childhood. It seeks happiness in satisfying the instinctual needs of survival/security, affection/esteem, and power/control, and bases its self-worth on cultural or group identification.[1]

We begin building the false self in early infancy, out of fears stemming from our great vulnerability. From the beginning, we have innate needs for security, love, and control. Our need for security is related to our survival. As infants, if our biological needs are not always promptly met, we translate this emotionally as "nobody cares, so I will have to fend for myself."

Our need for love and affection is directly related to our need for esteem. If we are not held, cuddled, kissed, and tenderly spoken to, we don't feel sufficiently loved and esteemed. Emotionally, we translate such neglect as rejection.

Infants also have an instinctual need to control or manipulate their environment. From this they derive their sense of power. If as infants we are frustrated in our attempts at power over our immediate environment — even if it's only the crib — we translate this frustration emotionally as helplessness.

I once heard a story of a newborn baby that wouldn't accept its mother's milk. It kept rejecting her breasts, and a wise, alert nurse noticed how odd this was. She took the infant to another nursing mother and the infant immediately took to her. Later the same nurse asked the baby's mother how she and her husband had felt about their infant before its birth. The woman confessed that during the pregnancy neither of them really wanted the child. The baby, in its profound sensitivity, probably felt their attitude.

The false self begins from these infantile perceptions, and compensates for its sense of lack by creating its own agenda for happiness. If the infant perceives a deficiency in security, the adult compensates by rushing headlong toward material prosperity and security. If the infant felt unloved, the adult makes up for it by constantly seeking the approval of

others. Where the infant felt helpless, the adult compensates by domi-
nating others' lives at work, in the family, everywhere. In all these situations the false self is advancing its programs.

Just realizing the existence of the false self is half the battle to extri-
cating oneself from its power and influence. Many years ago, Bede
Griffiths and I were walking in a park in the Ealing section of London. We
were discussing the nature of sanctity, or holiness. I asked Bede what
sanctity actually is, and he said a very curious but profound thing:
"Sanctity is being aware of how much we are conditioned by the ego."
Father Bede's insight has remained etched in my memory and is a landmark in my own inner geography. I was surprised at the time how psychological and Buddhist his insight was. We don't have to conquer our
false self; we only have to observe it. And through observing it, by being
aware of it, we transcend its grip on us and move toward our own transformation into love and compassion.

It is very difficult, if not impossible, to cultivate genuine love and
compassion for others if we are fixated on ourselves, or if our false self
has distorted our sense of reality. We can find many examples of thoroughly corrupted people. We all know the stock gangster character in
movies and television. Unfortunately, people who prey on the weak, who
have no conscience, who take life as if they were picking strawberries,
exist everywhere. This type of person has a fragmented conscience; it only
works in certain spheres of life. A person for whom a human life is
expendable is deeply disturbed.

Figures like Hitler, Stalin, Mao, and Pol Pot — the systematic mur-
derers of the twentieth century — suffered from a twisted view of reality;
they allowed themselves to be possessed by their delusions. They con-
signed millions to death, and millions more to prison, labor camps, to
misery, poverty, malnutrition, and disease. They, ultimately, lacked all
compassion, all mercy. They were utterly brutal killers, even though they
had others do their dirty work for them. They capitulated totally to their
false selves, their egos. I cannot escape the conviction that there must
have been a lack of love in their lives at a tender age, and this contributed
to the compensations they sought, and the moral monsters they became.
Those responsible for the genocides in Tibet and Rwanda and "ethnic
cleansings" in Bosnia and Kosovo represent the false self taken to its logical conclusion: where it becomes a tin god, bending the will of others to

do its will. I cannot imagine that these misguided souls had any genuine knowledge of their condition, for if they had had any real insight, they might have adopted a different course.

We all have a shadow side, and are certainly capable of evil, but the spiritually and humanly mature person achieves a clear perspective on his or her shadow. Mother Teresa was once asked by a journalist why she does what she does, that is, how she is able to take the dying poor from the streets of Calcutta, nurse and love them. Her response reflected her deep self-knowledge: "I realized a long time ago that I had a Hitler within me."[2] This realization became the basis of her self-transcendence and of her unique holiness.

Clearly, the false self and its hidden agendas — or as Thomas Keating calls it, its "programs for happiness" — needs to be exposed to the light of awareness. As we will discover in the next chapter, it is essentially through contemplation or meditation practice that a salutary self-knowledge dawns in us. Although this sort of insight is always available through our conscience, contemplative practice affords an infallible source of self-understanding. Once we acquire a clear perspective on ourselves, we are in a position to evolve more fully into the ways of love, compassion, mercy, kindness, and wisdom.

✦ Element 1: Actual Moral Capacity

The first element in a global or universal spirituality, and thus part of interspirituality itself, is a fully operative moral capacity. If we were to choose a contemplative or mystic from each spiritual tradition, and our choice was based on the maturity of these individuals in their mystical path, we would quickly discover that each one of them had a fully developed moral understanding and commitment. A person who lies, cheats, steals, and treats others unkindly has a weak and ambiguous moral foundation. A viable spirituality is not possible for such a person. Only when a person is in touch with compassion, love and mercy, is kind and other-centered, is the inner life really possible. The moral dimension makes a healthy inner life an actuality when accepted.

Why We Have Moral Codes

The moral dimension of the spiritual life is universal and unvarying in its essential outlines. It is recognized by all the great world religions as an indispensable part of the spiritual journey. It is simply not possible to live a spiritual or mystical life without this dimension. This is one reason why all religions — not only the major traditions, but all of them, no matter how few people they serve — have a clear moral code that provides norms to guide human behavior.

Hinduism, along with Jainism and Buddhism, emphasizes *ahimsa,* or nonharming, as a guide for our actions. It strongly endorses honesty and an injunction against stealing, and because of this thieves are despised in Hindu society. Ironically, I was once on a bus in Tamil Nadu, in southern India, when someone was caught stealing from a Westerner. The other passengers became very angry, took the law into their own hands, and nearly beat the fellow to death. The whole incident happened so quickly there was hardly time to react; he was spared only because the police intervened.

The Hindu vision, like Judaism and Christianity, places enormous importance on respect and care for one's parents. Indian families tend to be much better at keeping to this teaching than Western families, who have gotten away from their spiritual roots in this regard. The entire moral code of the Hindu tradition is spelled out in exhaustive detail in the Laws of Manu, the legal foundation for Hindu civilization. The Laws of Manu were codified in the Middle Ages, but what they express has been India's view for millennia. On a higher, or mystical plane, there is the tradition of *yama*, restraint, and *niyama*, discipline, meant to guide the yogi, the budding sage. Basically, these traditions are concerned with the self-control that morality imposes on us.

Buddhism's fundamental moral teaching, the Eight-Fold Path, is related to its overall program to disengage the volitional roots of suffering, the cause of the afflictive emotions that are triggered by desire and attachment. Five of the eight steps are directly related to moral life and conduct:

1. Right View (or understanding the nature of human existence);
2. Right Intention (or decision);
3. Right Effort in the determination to be free of desire and achieve enlightenment;
4. Right Speech, which means honesty in speech, and not to gossip, not to use harsh, abusive, and judgmental language; and
5. Right Livelihood, or not to earn a living by doing work that has a

negative impact on others (for example, making poisons or weapons, or living on stolen money).

These moral teachings are augmented in Buddhism by the Five Precepts, which are expanded in the recommendation to refrain from what are called the ten negative actions: (1) killing or otherwise harming others, (2) stealing, (3) sexual misbehavior, (4) lying, (5) gossip, (6) harsh or abusive speech, (7) speech that causes divisiveness, (8) covetousness in mind and behavior, (9) hatred and malice, and (10) twisted or distorted understanding or views.

The whole of Buddhist practice is actually a refinement of these teachings, so that they become expressed in a living attitude and disposition of compassion. We see the fruit of Buddhist moral thought incarnated in the lives of so many sages in their tradition, notably in our time in the Dalai Lama and Thich Nhat Hanh.

The Ten Commandments are the moral foundation of the major Western religions: Judaism, Christianity, and Islam. Most of these commandments have parallels to the above teachings from the Eastern traditions. The commandments to keep the Lord's Day holy, or the duty to rest and pray on the Sabbath, and not to take the Lord's name in vain, are reflected in the Buddhist notion of Right View. The rest of the commandments are in harmony with Hindu, Buddhist, and Jain moral principles — especially not to kill, steal, lie, covet, or commit adultery.

Christianity, through the teachings of Jesus Christ, presents a further refinement of the Law as handed down to Moses in the form of the Ten Commandments. These refinements are germane to the inner experience of the mystic. Jesus exhorts us to follow two new commandments, telling us that they sum up the Law and the Prophets: Love God, and love your neighbor as yourself. Here Jesus is able to distill the quintessence of the biblical tradition's moral understanding. Freeing it from centuries of legalism, he restates it in clear, existentially relevant, and eloquently simple language.

Christ shapes and gives expression to an ethic of love not only in his words but in his life. When Jesus washed the feet of his disciples, when he saved Mary Magdalene from death, and when he cured lepers and others, he was demonstrating love in action. This teaching of Jesus is the supreme achievement of the Gospel, the Church, and the Christian tradition. It is also an accurate expression of the inner consciousness and motivation of the mature contemplative mystic, or mystic in any form.

Towards a Global Ethic: An Initial Declaration, the document of the Parliament of the World's Religions, is itself a reflection of the collective moral wisdom found in the world's religions.3 The Global Ethic, which is intended to guide the human family by providing the basic norms for a common moral vision, a consensus on ethics, is itself the fruit of millennia of inner realization by countless sages, mystics, and saints. Clearly, this was not something foreseen by the framers of the Global Ethic.

"Beyond Morality"

Living the spiritual life has a direct relationship to the formation of moral vision. As we grow in compassion, love, mercy, kindness, gentleness, wisdom, patience, and sensitivity, the meaning of ethics naturally extends beyond simply avoiding certain attitudes and actions. It assumes an interior nature that transforms society's moral code through spiritual wisdom. *It becomes part of the consciousness of the individual mystic, and not something externally imposed by society.* Ultimately, the work of the individual enlarges the entire culture's moral understanding.

It is often said that mystics are "beyond morality." This does not mean they are free to act outside morality. The process of socialization inculcates in each person a moral code, with all its norms and expectations of human behavior, which better informs the individual conscience. But we still need external moral norms and laws. Why? Because the whole aim of ethics and law is only fully achieved by the person who achieves an inner transformation in which they now act from love, compassion, mercy, and kindness. The supremely wise persons in whom this inner change has occurred no longer need an external ethics, a moral code, or even a legal system, but everyone else does.

Jesus and the Buddha didn't need external moral codes; they were already supremely moral in the depths of their being and hence in their actions. The inner life of mystics, grounded in love, compassion, and wisdom, possesses the essence of the highest ethical understanding possible in this life. These sages respect the moral code of their cultures because they understand their importance as stepping-stones to spiritual integrity. They respect morality, and tradition, because they understand their value in people's instruction and transformation.

Thus actualized moral capacity is based in a transformed inner nature. The moral dimension of the spiritual journey has nothing to do with external rules and regulations but with a fundamental, radical reorientation of the person's inner commitment to be established permanently and concretely in love and compassion. Once we are so established, we have acquired all we can from the ethical guidelines of the various religious traditions. We are then good, merciful, loving, wise, gentle, patient, and compassionate simply because that's what we are in our realized nature, not because any system tells us to be this way. We need religious systems to learn these attitudes and dispositions; but once we internalize these values, we no longer need to look to them for the same lessons.

To say that an actualized moral capacity is the basis of the spiritual life is really to suggest that selfless love and compassionate action form the foundation, and that external morality simply provides guidance in the formative stages of development. In my own study and experience, St. Francis of Assisi, St. Teresa of Avila, Thomas Merton, Bede Griffiths, Mother Teresa, the Dalai Lama, and Thomas Keating are a few examples of extraordinary beings who have transcended external morality to become love in awareness and action. They have all arrived at interior freedom. Not victims of the their desires, they are free of afflictive emotions that accompany the activity of grasping, craving, and wanting. They have the gift of pervasive peace that comes as a companion to selfless love and concretely merciful, compassionate, and healing action.

We Take the Spiritual Journey Together

Spiritual maturity is not about pursuing salvation alone; it is about contributing to the salvation or enlightenment of others. This is love's work and goal: extending to members of all species the willingness and generosity to serve their needs for meaning, direction, growth, and belonging. Love and compassion translate existentially into an attitude and practice of availability. All the great founders of the world's religions were genuinely available to their followers. In my experience, this has been profoundly true of many priests and nuns I have known growing up. All these people have the spirit of the bodhisattva, who takes a vow to delay entering nirvana, or final liberation, until all sentient beings are liberated from the cycle of rebirth.

❖ Element 2: Solidarity with All Living Beings

The second element in a universal mysticism is a deep realization of the interconnectedness of everyone and everything. Intense mystical experience confirms the unity of all aspects of reality, cosmic and earthly life and being. Each of these realities are interrelated intrinsically; they form one vast system, which is itself a system of systems.

The perceived interconnectedness between and among all aspects of the cosmos is an essential fact. It is more than simply a question of inter-dependence, which is cultural, economic, and political. The experience of the interconnectedness of everything is part of the perennial tradition, a primordial vision gained from the insight of countless mystics across the millennia. Augustine, Francis of Assisi, Julian of Norwich, Thomas Merton, John of the Cross, Hildegard of Bingen, and Teresa of Avila in the Christian experience; the rishis and Shankara in the Hindu tradition; the Buddha and Nargarjuna of Buddhism; Mohammed, Ibn al-Farabi, Rumi, and Attar in Islam; Moses, the prophets, the mystics of the Kabbalah, and the Hasidim of the Jewish tradition: all were keenly aware of the unity and interrelationship of everything.

This unity undergirding all reality, being, and life creates our sense of solidarity with all living beings, the earth, and the cosmos. The Buddhists establish their entire approach to life on the metaphysical perception of this interconnectedness, which they call pratitya samutpada, or depen-dent origination: Everyone and everything co-arises together. Everything affects everything else; nothing exists in isolation from the whole. Hindus through the Vedanta speak of advaitic consciousness, or the experiential realization that everything subsists in unity, and therefore in an intrinsic state of essential interrelationship. Christians speak of the Mystical Body of Christ, an intuition of a community of being that originates with the early Christians of the Apostolic Age. Muslims have a deep sense of com-mitment to the *Ummah,* the Islamic community or commonwealth of all adherents to the faith of the Prophet. The Ummah names a spiritual com-munion between believers who are united in faith, but also in their dedi-cation to the total welfare of Islamic society. It carries with it the meaning of interconnectedness.

The sense of solidarity with all life, with the natural world, and with the cosmos, is a mystical perception of consciousness. This deep feeling of connection is often triggered by the encounter with the world's suffering. St. Francis, for example, was profoundly aware of his solidarity with all creatures. He related spontaneously to their suffering, and would respond to them. He saw Christ, the divine presence, in all beings. But Francis also had to work at his sense of connection. He had great difficulty with lepers, the social outcasts of his day. Although he recognized that God was present in them and loved them eternally, Francis experienced a visceral reaction of disgust at the sight of lepers. Yet he knew he had to conquer these feelings to truly please God.

One day, while Francis was riding his horse in the countryside, he came upon a leper. Immediately, he felt revulsion, fear, and a desire to flee, but he resisted these feelings. Instead, Francis dismounted, went up to the leper, and looked him gently and lovingly in the eyes. Then he embraced him and kissed him on the lips. Immediately, his fear and revulsion disappeared, never to return. That night, when he fell asleep, the leper appeared to him in a dream with the face of Christ. The leper had been Christ. As Christ himself had said: "Whenever you do it (something kind and merciful) to the least of my brethren, you do it to me."[4]

Mother Teresa had this same ability to perceive the divine in everyone, especially in the unloved, the unwanted, the homeless, and the dying. She never held her love and compassion back, but always responded. She experienced, moment by moment, her human solidarity with everyone. Again and again, on so many occasions in her long life, she confided to public audiences the secret of her rich spirituality, which was very similar to the karma and bhakti yoga: total surrender to the divine presence, to Christ, in the poor. In them she perceived her connection with everyone and everything else.

In ordinary life, of course, this feeling of solidarity comes in fleeting moments — at sports events, parties, family reunions, even political demonstrations — in those rare times of extremity when people come together. The point is to apply this knowledge all the time. As we walk the mystical path, we become more and more aware of our intimate connection with everyone and everything else. And the spiritual life requires that we are ready to respond to the suffering of those we meet along the way because they are connected to us.

It is fascinating to see how science is catching up to mysticism in its understanding of this fundamental unity. As we have seen, quantum physics has contributed to a new understanding of identity. We have also seen how we can ultimately find reality in consciousness itself. As Fritjof Capra puts it in his *Tao of Physics,* quantum physics indicates that the universe is "a complicated web of interdependent relationships."[5] Each relationship is intrinsically connected with every other, and all of them taken together are part of the totality. Capra maintains that quantum physics verifies the account of the contemplative sages of the East — and, we can also say, of the West, South, North, and the eight directions!

British physicist David Bohm, another important voice in quantum theory and mathematics, has developed a new paradigm to advance this understanding of interconnectedness. In his groundbreaking book *Wholeness and the Implicate Order,* Bohm shows that the universe and all reality is both enfolded or part of an implicate order, and that this implicate order unfolds through time. Everything is part of an undivided order of wholeness, which always exists, and is the origin of all we see now in the universe. The implicate and explicate orders are the same reality in different stages of manifestation. The implicate order, before unfolding, is nonmanifested in a state of implicitness. In this state, it is pregnant with all that is contained in its later explicated state.[6]

Bohm conveys his understanding of the total order of wholeness through the hologram. When a hologramic image is fragmented, each fragment contains the whole image. The image is never divided or broken. This suggests that the total order is present in every part. Everything reflects and implies everything else, and each thing is intimately part of everything else. This means that the cosmos and reality are one vast system of order. All parts are bound up in the community of being and consciousness. All are part of the web of existence, and nothing is excluded.

❖ Element 3: Deep Nonviolence

When the spiritual life has put down deep roots, there is a natural, organic evolution into deep nonviolence: the attitude and practice of nonharming. Even individuals who come from aggression naturally progress beyond the need to the resort to violence.

The realization of the interconnectedness of all beings brings with it a sense of the utter preciousness of all life. Every being in every species is precious and irreplaceable. Men and women on the spiritual journey who have made this realization would rather suffer harm themselves than harm another. They extend this attitude of nonharming to all sentient beings and to the planet itself.

A commitment to deep nonviolence is necessary to the emerging global culture, and to interspirituality. Nonviolence adjusts our external actions to our inner attitudes, and makes them consistent with compassion and the demands of love. As we grow in spiritual wisdom, we become more sensitive to the rights of others, including other species. Gentleness, calm, patience, and humility are all aspects of nonharming; they are expressions of this wonderful quality often regarded as an attribute of the divine itself.

The Jains gave this valuable and precious teaching to India, and thence to the world. Here Jainism heavily influenced Hinduism and Buddhism, which have assimilated its truth into their own understanding of human responsibility for nonharming, or ahimsa. Throughout their twenty-five centuries of existence, the Jains have managed to keep their commitment, and avoid conflict: They have never fought a war, an extraordinary accomplishment when you consider that Christians, who boast the Prince of Peace, have fought thousands of wars in their own history. Through the Hindu understanding of ahimsa, Mahatma Gandhi was able to apply this inner resource with great effectiveness in India's struggle for independence. His achievement stands as a permanent monument to the power and depth of nonviolence to change politics and society, to transform conflict into peaceful opportunities to resolve differences.

People who have attained this inner spiritual wisdom have no need to be aggressive. They know that each person, each being, no matter its species, is precious, and so has a right to be and be respected. More than that, they understand that each being should be protected. The spiritually mature have a natural sensitivity toward all other persons and other creatures, and a profound awareness of the dignity and worth of everyone and everything that is.

A striking example that illustrates this awakening to compassion was the experience of a friend of mine, Jeff Genung. Jeff and his family lived in upstate New York for most of his childhood. Many years ago, when Jeff was about nineteen, he went out deer hunting alone. Jeff had hunted from a tender age and was very familiar with guns. On this day, he shot a deer from a distance, but failed to kill it outright. Jeff approached the deer, who was sitting quietly, waiting to die. He stood in front of her, looked into her eyes, and saw an infinite gentleness in her. There was no fear or hostility; there was only forgiveness in her eyes that said, "Don't worry. It's okay. I forgive you and love you."

Jeff was overcome with grief. In all his years of hunting and fishing, he had never been so near to his prey. He had never, through this intimate eye contact, understood the nature of these gentle creatures. Jeff's life was forever changed. He decided he would never hunt or fish again. The deer was a teacher who gave him an indelible lesson in the mystery of life and the interconnectedness of all beings. Since that time, Jeff has formed a deep commitment to nonharming in his life, to which he remains faithful. It has become a significant part of his spiritual discipline. Jeff is bringing up his children in the same wisdom of gentleness and nonviolence.

This insight about nonviolence is not something that most societies understand. Even India betrayed ahimsa before Mahatma Gandhi's body was cold. The West doesn't grasp the importance and necessity of nonviolence, and the United States in particular has built a culture of violence. Movies create the appetite for all sorts of gratuitous aggression, and so reinforce violence as a value in the culture. Our children grow up with the conviction that violence is a fundamental part of life. Through constant exposure to violent entertainment, they don't learn anything else. Hollywood forces violence on us as a way of life. Moviemakers bear a huge responsibility for the effects violence has on society.

Hollywood gives the impression that somehow violence is innate to the human species, that we are stuck with it. Nothing could be farther from the truth. In the 1980s the United Nations, through UNESCO, commissioned an international group of behavioral scientists to study the problem of violence in human life. Their mandate included the question of whether or not violent behavior is innate. After five years of exhaustive research on this issue all around the planet, this group formulated its findings in a document called *The Seville Statement on Violence*.7

These scientists unanimously concluded that not only is violence not innate to human beings, but it can be overcome through education. They found that aggressive behavior is something learned over time. They emphasized the hope implicit in these findings that humankind can evolve beyond the need for violence. The Seville Statement has been quite influential in certain educational circles, and eventually it will find its way into the mass consciousness. This document is significant because it disproves the cynical contention about the nature of violence in human life, and it especially discredits Hollywood's irresponsible manipulation of the global psyche. The Seville Statement also confirms the universal experience of mystics throughout the ages in setting aside violence as their consciousness evolves.

The Universal Declaration on Nonviolence, which also emerged during the late 1980s and early 1990s, addresses the primacy of the spiritual insight of nonviolence.[8] This document was inspired by a collaboration between the Dalai Lama and Christian monastics. They wanted to do something together for peace, something to aid the future human community. This document, very much like a manifesto, is a declaration of independence between the religions and war-making. Although the declaration has been signed by thousands of individuals and groups, it is still little known outside Catholic monastic communities. It applies the spiritual resource of nonviolence to teaching the religions themselves to be responsible for a more peaceful future. It holds them responsible for rejecting not only individual acts of violence and aggression but the systematic violence of war itself, especially as sponsored by organized religion. It was the insight gained from spiritual practice that produced the awareness that this kind of declaration was necessary. Although it is barely known now, it will some day surface and help guide humankind.

All the heroes of nonviolence have been either mystics or men and women of prayer. It is true of the Jains, the Hindus, and the Buddhists. It was true of Jesus and the early Christians, of Tolstoy, of Gandhiji, and Martin Luther King Jr. It is equally true of the Dalai Lama and all those countless Tibetans who are solidly committed to a nonviolent means of resolving their issues with the People's Republic of China. It is true of Desmond Tutu in South Africa, and Cory Aquino in the Philippines. All these religious traditions, cultures, and individuals recognize the value that comes from an attitude and practice of nonharming. Intense spiritual practice generated this insight, and it represents a permanent acquisition in the moral resources of humanity.

✦ The Mystic or Contemplative Character

Each of us is called to be a mystic. To be a human being means that we are invited into the possibility of transcendental life and experience. We are not here simply to pursue a profane existence spent plotting the course of our human happiness. That is what seems to happen to so many of us, but it needn't be that way. We are meant for greater things.

The call into life is a call into being, a summons into a deific possibility for us, an opportunity to actualize our potentiality to realize higher levels of consciousness. Such a possibility, however, takes perspective, work, and discipline; it doesn't come easily, nor in most cases does it just happen. Understanding the mystical dimension of life takes great effort, but it is not impossible. It is open to all of us as our birthright.

To embark on the inner experience, we have to understand that life is a spiritual journey, a process toward fulfillment. We are not meant to remain here, but to move on to better things. We can begin to have a substantial taste of that in this world. Our life here is under a cloud of illusion and delusion; we are pulled now in this direction, now in that. It is important for us to be self-directed: We must decide where our life is going, what direction it will take and why. That kind of decisiveness requires courage and perspective; it means that we must cut ourselves free from our cultural conditioning.

We live in a culture that is blind to the spiritual life. It is spiritually illiterate, morally confused, psychologically dysfunctional, and heavily addicted to violence, entertainment, and consumerism. It is "religious" to a point — that is, as long as it doesn't cost too much. Most Americans, we are told, believe in God, but too few realize that life is a spiritual process, a journey in which certain skills of self-mastery have to be learned. We cannot depend on our culture either to guide or support us in our quest. We must do the hard work of clarification ourselves.

Some of us are fortunate enough to meet exceptional individuals in our lives who can guide us in the ways of the spiritual journey, and challenge us out of our spiritual lassitude. Such people are a great gift and a real advantage. They are our best hope to gain perspective and direction; they are also a source of knowledge of methods of prayer and spiritual practice, of light on the stages to be traversed. It is true that when the student is ready, the teacher *will* appear. The student hears the inner call to be, and decides to heed it. The heeding of the call summons the teacher from within, and so the spiritual master arrives.

Who are these spiritual teachers? What characteristics do they have?

What do we look for in them? What is the mystic or contemplative character they and indeed we possess? First, these spiritual teachers were once like us; they started out earnestly seeking the realization of the inner life; they persevered and so progressed. They are really no different from us, just further along on the journey.

Wisdom

The contemplative or mystic character that has shaped them is animated by wisdom. They understand life, its pitfalls, its heights, and its great potential. They are usually extremely gentle, always patient and kind. They are never in a hurry, but move with deliberateness. They are profoundly merciful, and willing to respond in mercy to any being who suffers, always aware when encountering others. They have become channels of love and compassion; indeed they are compassion and love itself. They are capable of spontaneous responses to people in need. Their compassion and love, their mercy and kindness, know no bounds. All their actions flow out of who they are, and there is a perfect consistency between those actions and their enlightened state of consciousness.

Sensitivity

The mystic character expresses an almost infinite sensitivity to all beings, human and otherwise. They are individuals of grace who incarnate an exquisite sensitivity — a state of being completely awake to all the important opportunities that present themselves to us every day. Sensitivity is also an attribute of presence to others. It is the ability to be fully there for others, without any agendas. This sensitive presence is able to respond through deep listening — really listening with the heart to both what is said and left unspoken.

This capacity for sensitivity is rare. It is a generosity and magnanimity of heart, a willingness to sacrifice for those in need, who suffer, who need us in some essential way. Sensitivity puts others first; it never considers self, but setting self aside, reaches out in a healing, appropriate way to all those who need us. Sensitivity is never rude or unkind; it always seeks the good of others. It never imposes on them, but patiently waits until an opening occurs. Sensitivity, which is definitely a divine quality, is a form of selfless affection that is free of sentimentality. It is love transformed by divine union or enlightenment.

Shifting from Self to Others

Mature contemplatives, no matter what tradition they come from, are not fixated on self but are profoundly other-centered. This other-centeredness is an infallible sign of grace and holiness. Part of compassion and love is this shift from self to others, and it is definitely present in one who has submitted to the demands of the spiritual journey. The mystic knows that the system of the false self is the way of illusion. It is based on ignorance of the true self, which is essentially a relationship to others. Other-centeredness has its roots in the realization that what matters is the interconnected whole, not just the happiness of one individual. Other-centeredness is facing reality.

A wonderful story from Theophane Boyd's *Tales of the Magic Monastery* illustrates this shift. Theophane Boyd is a Trappist monk, and this fascinating little book is a gem of spiritual wisdom. One Christmas, as a boy, he visited the magic monastery. Near the entrance to the monastery, at the outer gate, sat a blind beggar. As the child went to pass through the gate he placed a dollar in his bowl. The old man cried out: "Who will lead me into the heart of God?" The boy was bewildered for a brief moment. Then he went and sat in front of the old gentleman, took his two hands in his own, and said tenderly: "Together we will go into the heart of God!"9 This utterance, in its eloquence of simplicity, sums up the other-centeredness of the Christian saint, what Christ himself exemplified in his life and witness. This quality of other-centeredness is a reality all mystics, when their love and compassion are fully formed, have in common.

Accepting Others as They Are

The mystic character accepts others as they are, and does not attempt to change them against their will. This is a critical point, because most people lack fundamental tolerance. This attitude doesn't come easily; it only happens as wisdom dawns in the midst of the inner life's unfolding. People tend to be very judgmental, a ruthless practice to which many are habituated as a matter of course. I have been amazed at the amount and intensity of judgment among monks and nuns in the Catholic Church. This is curious, since Jesus himself has counseled against passing judgement on others. We can only judge others if we can fulfill two conditions:

that we know the other's heart totally, and that we love them uncondi-
tionally. Only God can possibly meet these two conditions, therefore *only*
God can judge. Despite this truth, people continue to play God, and pass
harsh and unfair judgments on others.

In the Christian experience, especially in the early monastic life of the
desert tradition of Sinai, Palestine, and Syria, great emphasis was placed
on the practice of nonjudgment. To reject judging a brother or sister was
regarded as a sign of spiritual wisdom. I call the tendency to judge others
an act of *projection*. I don't use this term in the psychological sense, but
in a purely spiritual context. Instead of attending to their own inner work,
judgmental people are actually doing another's "work"; they are project-
ing outside themselves, imputing motives or intentions on others, as if
they know the others' hearts. The spiritual journey only begins in earnest
when we no longer experience the need to judge others, when we begin
to take responsibility for our own inner development.

The mature contemplative is beyond this practice of projection. He or
she is too busy accepting and loving others to judge them. Mother Teresa
made this point succinctly. Once, when she came to the United States to
open a hospice for AIDS sufferers, a reporter asked her what she thought
of these people. He was looking for a pious putdown of these poor souls,
but Mother Teresa simply replied: "I never judge them. I only love them."
That is the wisdom of the mystic character, the wise, mature individual
who, having ceased to project, is now free to accept and to love. That is the
challenge and the call of the spiritual life: to transcend self in order to love
beyond self-interest and our own opinions about ourselves and others.

For some ten years, from 1982 to 1992, I was a member of a small
experimental lay monastic community in New Boston, New Hampshire,
called Hundred Acres Monastery. The name Hundred Acres was the
ancient designation of the land on which the monastery was located. The
founder of the community was Father Paul Fitzgerald, a Trappist monk.
I used to marvel at Father Paul's acceptance of everyone. He was a person of very few words. In all the years I knew him and attended his
masses, he only gave one sermon or homily. Father Paul simply had no
need to speak.

I learned a lot from Father Paul about acceptance. He never dismissed anyone. Father Paul took the long view of human development.
He had a very deep faith that God was in charge, and so was unwilling to

take the prerogative away from the divine. In his acceptance of others as they were — even when they were obviously wrong — he was sort of a Taoist Catholic: someone who lets nature take its course. A master of detachment, Father Paul had relinquished the need to control much earlier in his life; he replaced the desire to control with the desire to accept and to serve. He never deviated from this approach in the many years I knew him, right up until his death. Very little in life was a big deal to him, and we used to joke that Father Paul could sleep through a nuclear war. This was his most impressive virtue, a form of wisdom that originated in his years of contemplative practice, particularly the commitment to silence that characterizes the Trappist life. He was a mystic in a very quiet, humble way.

✦ Who Is a Saint?

The preeminent form of mystic or contemplative character is the saint: one who, although limited, has achieved some perfection in his or her capacity to love and to care for others. We all know the names of various saints throughout history. What all these people have in common is their surrender to something beyond themselves.

This is the secret of their effectiveness: a freedom from themselves that allows them to avoid acting out of the false self. Their capacity for self-transcendence is nurtured through their intense spiritual discipline, one of the subjects of the next chapter. The mystic character is the potential of the human to become God-like, and it is in these extraordinary figures that we glean just how possible it is to achieve it.

There is really nothing else in life more worth doing. And to assent to the spiritual journey is to say "yes" to our own ultimate growth as well as that of others. There is no greater gift we can give to others than to assist them on their way, to be there for them in their questions, their darkness, and their triumphs. The mystic character is thus also a midwife in the spiritual life of others — a cause of enormous joy.

Chapter 6

SPIRITUAL PRACTICE: THE CRUX OF INNER CHANGE

Spiritual life is like living water that springs up from the very depths of our own spiritual experience. In spiritual life everyone has to drink from his or her own well.
— St. Bernard of Clairvaux

All over the world, every day, men and women are actively living intense spiritual practice. In tens of thousands of places in India and elsewhere in Asia, mystics are living the spiritual life in secret, hidden from the world. By sacred rivers (India's seven include the Ganges, the Krishna, the Ravi, the Jammu, and the Kavery) or off in caves in the Himalayas, in Rishikesh, Hardwar, or Gangotri, in tiny huts throughout the forests of the subcontinent, sadhus, sannyasis, yogis, and other ascetics are immersed in the contemplative life of intense meditation and self-denial.

Prayer or spiritual practice assumes many forms. Trappist monks and nuns rise at 3 A.M. every morning to begin their day. Their order is completely dedicated to the inner experience, pursued through community prayer in the chapel, and private contemplation in their monastic cells. Jewish contemplatives keep aware of God on the Sabbath and daily engage in remembrance of and conversation with him. The Dalai Lama wakes every day between 3:30 and 4 A.M. to meditate and perform his prostrations. Writer Ken Wilber, a Western Buddhist, also wakes at 3 A.M.

to meditate for two hours, exercise, eat breakfast, and then write for the next ten to twelve hours.

In the many religious orders of the Catholic Church, and in the monasteries of Mount Athos, as well as in the various monastic centers of the Orthodox tradition, a similarly rigorous observance is followed with great perseverance and regularity. Their devotion and sacrifice never lessens.

The same is true of the Sufi dervishes in Turkey, who are transfigured by their ecstatic whirling dances. It is true of all those who sit in meditation, no matter their tradition — be it Zen, Vipassanā, Tibetan, or Christian forms of contemplation. All are given over to the inner work that is slowly changing them from within. Each has embarked on the journey to that "place" of ultimate realization, bliss, and peace. All are exploring who they really are beyond mere social identities and roles assigned by society, family, or even their faith. The vast majority of them will not give up the struggle but will press on until they are freed from within and set loose from this world of illusion, or impermanent reality.

This is the task for each one of us. We are all invited to plunge into being and seek the ultimate roots of our identity in the great mystery.

The heart of the spiritual life, the enduring substance of the journey, is the refinement of our own inner landscape — humility, egolessness, selflessness — that occurs through spiritual practice. Spiritual practice is how the mystic approaches the inner self and relates to others, the world, nature, and the cosmos. Spiritual practice is the cutting edge of radical interior change and the basis (along with grace, in the theistic schools of spirituality) for profound self-knowledge to emerge in our lives. The last part of this chapter will examine the nature of this radical inner change. First, however, we will consider the elements of humility, spiritual practice, mature self-knowledge, as well as the nature of transformation.

✦ Element 4: Humility

The spiritual life is impossible without the virtue of humility. Humility of heart is a great treasure because it keeps us honest, cutting away self-deception, falsehood, and inauthenticity. It forces us to be real, even when it is uncomfortable. It rescues us from superficiality, and compels us to always be true to ourselves and to others. Humility of heart forces us to stand in the light of truth. Humility is a difficult virtue, but it is indispensable to progress in the interior life.

For many Americans, humility is not only undesirable, it is virtually incomprehensible. Those who don't know its true nature view humility as weakness. But humility of heart is not about bowing and scraping before others; it is about honesty and self-truth. It includes modesty about oneself but is essentially a virtue related to what *is*, rather than what seems to be.

Humility of heart is an egoless understanding — as opposed to the false self's projections — of one's own limitations, of where one stands in relation to others on the way. This is the foundation of the spiritual journey, which must be grounded in the truth of ourselves. Thomas Keating has said that "The greatest accomplishment in life is to be who you are, and that means to be who God wanted you to be when he created you." No other accomplishment in life compares to this attainment. The humble man or woman has chosen to be fully who they are; in the God-centered forms of mysticism, they are regarded as dear to the divine. St. John of the Cross, the great sixteenth-century Spanish Carmelite, wrote: "To be taken with love for a soul, God does not look upon its greatness, but upon the greatness of its humility."[1]

My favorite example of humility of heart in my life is my uncle, John Cosgrove, who raised me. Although ordinary in most ways, Uncle John was a rare spiritual being. A professor of early childhood education at Rutgers University and later at St. Joseph College, he was not an intellectual, but was well-read and had been virtually everywhere, for he loved and believed in travel. His humility expressed itself in a lack of boasting, vanity, and self-assertiveness. He was free of ego and the false self; he was always other-centered. As my uncle, he was always concerned about me and my development. He was never preoccupied with his own problems, even when these problems were extreme.

Twenty-five years before his death in 1985, my uncle was operated on for prostate cancer. The surgeon performing the operation had been drinking and was in a hurry to leave for a skiing vacation in Colorado. He rushed through the ninety-minute procedure in forty-five minutes, and accidentally cut a vital nerve that controls urine flow. The doctor never acknowledged his mistake, but because Uncle John had been awake for the operation, he saw the horrified reaction of an assisting nurse. From that day on, Uncle John was incontinent and had to wear diapers. He bore it with heroic patience. He never sued the physician, who was dismissed years later for incompetency. Uncle John let the matter go, and kept the man in his prayers. Some people would describe his behavior as wimpishness, not humility. Yet Uncle John was absolutely fearless.

Uncle John was my first spiritual teacher, and I look back with enduring gratitude to his presence in and influence on my life. There is not a day that goes by that I don't think of him and say a prayer for him.

Humility of heart is closely related to egolessness. Egolessness is to live out of the depths of the heart in a spirit of kindness, mercy, love and compassion. Along with humility, it represents good-heartedness, the pure heart open to grace, or the truth. It is really love animating the person's motives, actions and ways of regarding others. Selflessness is a fundamental element in the spiritual journey, and which, like humility, is required for the spiritual life to awaken and prosper. This form of wisdom is summed up by the *Tao Te Ching:* "The sage has no mind of his (or her) own. He is aware of the needs of others."[2]

✦ Element 5: Spiritual Practice

Spiritual practice, the work of our transformation, is the means of inner growth and change toward human maturity glimpsed in the best of religious experience. It is critically important in authentic spirituality, and thus in a multifaith approach to spirituality or interspirituality. Through this disciplined habit of relating to the divine, the living, transformative power of inner reality takes hold. Without a spiritual practice of some kind, spirituality is a hollow affair; it has no substance and is reduced to the formalism of external religiosity.

Daily spiritual practice is the "technology" of inner change. Without it, such change is inconceivable. Devotions alone are insufficient; the practice must be contemplative. Only such intense forms of inner discipline lead to the interior breakthroughs that provide real progress in the spiritual life. This insight is found in all the spiritual traditions, and marks the difference between a genuine mystical process and popular religion, or a purely devotional type of spirituality. All spiritual practices are transformative, be they contemplative forms of prayer, meditation, and sacred reading; a restful, active participation and presence in liturgy and ritual; music and chanting; yoga and certain martial arts; hiking and even walking. They change us within and make this inner change consistent with our actions in the world in our daily lives. Seekers and saints of every tradition have cultivated a spiritual practice and have thus cultivated a profound self-knowledge.

Spiritual practice shapes our understanding, character, will, personality, attitudes, and actions by enlarging their scope through the light of compassion and love. Thomas Merton became a great teacher to millions because he embraced the daily observance of a contemplative discipline. He didn't just talk and write about contemplation, he *was* a contemplative. He didn't simply dream about being a mystic, he *was* a mystic. His path was contemplative prayer and he lived in a monastic setting, with long periods of solitude. Contemplative prayer, beyond words and thoughts in the inner silence of the heart, led him into the fullness of the divine mystery. Contemplative prayer was his spiritual practice, and he was always trying to communicate its secret to others.

Lectio Divina: An Effective Contemplative Practice

For some 1,500 years in the Benedictine tradition of the Catholic Church, a contemplative practice called *lectio divina,* which means literally "divine reading" or spiritual reading, has existed.3 Lectio divina organically grew out of the choral prayer and reading of scripture by monastics, and has been perfected over the course of centuries. It remains an important practice among Catholics in our time, and has now spread to the laity through the church's contemplative movement. It has become quite popular in parishes to perform lectio along with some sort of contemplative prayer (usually Centering Prayer, discussed below).

Lectio divina may take anywhere from forty-five minutes to an hour and a half, depending on the person doing the prayer. It has four distinct but related stages: *lectio, meditatio, oratio,* and *contemplatio.*

The lectio stage is divine or spiritual reading — usually a passage from the bible or the New Testament, or from the early Christian literature known as the Fathers of the Church (for instance, the writings of Augustine, Origen, Cyprian, Evagrius, John Cassian, Gregory of Nyssa, Basil the Great, among others). One reads not for information, but for *inspiration,* that is, as input to inspire one's prayer. Lectio is never an intellectual exercise. It doesn't really matter how much we read, simply that we read with complete attention, a kind of devout listening with the heart. It may be a page, a paragraph, a sentence, or a word, but finally, it sparks an interior movement. We are inspired, and so we stop reading and enter the second stage of lectio: meditatio.

Meditatio has nothing to do with what meditation means today — a contemplative kind of sitting, an absorption in an inner process of simplification or observation of interior states. The old term connotes a discursive, thoughtful kind of prayer. To avoid confusion between these two meanings of meditation, the traditional Latin term meditatio has been dropped in favor of the word *reflection,* for that is precisely what it is: an inner musing on the content, or at least spirit, of the reading. Again, the reflective moment in lectio divina has nothing to do with analysis. This type of reflection is more a deep musing — a slow, digestive process of intuitively pondering the hidden meaning of the sacred text. Its significance is captured in Luke's observation of Mary as "pondering these things in her heart" when she didn't understand the words or actions of her son, Jesus.4 A spontaneous movement in the depths of our being suddenly inspires us to express our commitment to and love for God. At this point, we enter the third stage of lectio: oratio.

Oratio simply means prayer, but a very profound sort of prayer. A better term for our age is *affective prayer,* a prayer of the heart that engages the emotions and feelings. In affective prayer, we simply give free rein to our intentions in relation to the divine. We express an aspiration of the will awakened by reflection and informed by reading. We impose no limit; we express whatever spontaneously arises from the inner depths of our being, unimpeded by social expectations. Affective prayer is often exultant, joyous — almost ecstatic — as it lifts a person to the heights of feeling and intuition. It is a complete receptivity to the presence of God, and a loving response to him. When affective prayer reaches the end of its term — as it quite naturally will — we enter the fourth stage of lectio: contemplatio.

Again, in our time the term *contemplatio* suggests contemplation. The preferred word in lectio, however, is *rest:* resting in God, luxuriating in the divine presence. The fourth stage of lectio is meant to facilitate the awakening and cultivation of contemplation through rest. One simply *rests* in the presence without any thought or analysis, without entertaining the imagination, or calling up the memory; it is not a time of doing but a time only to *be.* Contemplative resting is the process of creating a psychological space within ourselves for the divine to do whatever it wills to accomplish in us. In this effortless *letting go,* we allow God to take us wherever he desires. Unhampered, this fourth stage of lectio quite spontaneously and organically leads us into contemplation.

Active and Passive Contemplation

Contemplation can be of two kinds: receptive or passive, and concentrative or active. Receptive prayer is a form of contemplative prayer that allows us to get out of the way and let divine grace work freely in us. Concentrative prayer is a much more active form that requires our constant effort. Mantric meditation, the Jesus Prayer, devotions like the rosary, and prayerful veneration of icons are examples of a concentrative approach to the awakening and development of contemplation.[5]

It is useful to understand the distinction between *active* and *passive contemplation*. Active contemplation pertains to our own effort at the contemplative practice, and all that we do in our spiritual lives to bring about the radical change within. It is also known as *acquired contemplation*. Passive contemplation, in contrast, is all that is achieved by God in us. It is also called *infused contemplation* because it is the divine's action flowing within the depths of our being that is doing all the work. All we have to do is to assent and show up for the times of prayer, and be loving, kind, merciful and compassionate.[6]

The distinction between active and passive contemplation is the relationship between what the Christian mystical tradition calls human effort and divine grace. Indian mysticism also has two metaphors to communicate this distinction: the mother monkey and the mother cat. God is the mother in each instance. The mother monkey, which represents active contemplation, carries her baby around her stomach, but the baby has to make the effort to hold on. There is thus a delicate balance and interplay between the effort of the baby holding on, which represents the individual person, and God, represented by the mother monkey who lends her body to carry the baby.

The mother cat, in contrast, carries her babies in her mouth. The kittens need only assent to be carried. This metaphor expresses the state of pure contemplation. The mother cat is like God passively infusing spiritual graces, especially union, to her children, while the kittens, or us, need only agree to receive the divine presence through these graces. Our effort is minimal in passive or infused contemplation, but it is there nonetheless, since we have to will the union to happen; we cannot be indifferent to divine grace and its fruitful activity in us.

Centering Prayer

Centering Prayer is a practice of the Contemplative Outreach organization founded by Thomas Keating. It provides a very useful method of cultivating contemplation among Christians and others. Centering Prayer is a reliable guide to the development of the interior journey in our age.

Thomas Keating has elaborated a complete teaching of the spiritual evolution of the person in our time. People from all walks of life, and from various traditions, have embraced this way with great and enduring benefit. Keating understands the entire extent of the inner process, the spiritual journey, from his own rich experience as a Trappist monk.7

The practice of Centering Prayer involves remembering four basic guidelines. The first guideline concerns the choosing of a sacred word, which is sacred only because it symbolizes or represents our consent to the presence and action of God within us. Our intention is what makes the word sacred.

Choose a sacred word — any word of one to four syllables (for example, father, mother, sister, brother, joy, love, mercy). You are not choosing it for the meaning, but simply to carry your intention to surrender to the divine presence within your being. You may want to select this sacred word during a time of prayer in your home, asking the Holy Spirit to guide you in this selection.

The second guideline follows from the first. Sit quietly, either in a comfortable chair or on a meditation cushion. Remain still throughout the period of centering. Close your eyes, and gently introduce your sacred word, expressing your consent to God's presence and action within you. Don't hold on to the sacred word. Let it come and go as it will. This is the receptive way.

The third guideline concerns what to do and what not to do when thoughts become a problem during Centering Prayer. Thoughts are a normal function of the human being; they are an occupational hazard of having a mind. We cannot avoid them. They are like monkeys chattering away in trees, to use a metaphor from the Indian tradition. They arise quite naturally, and are impossible to eliminate. When you find that you have become preoccupied with thoughts, that they have taken center stage and are a problem for the quality and integrity of your meditation, just turn ever so gently back to the sacred word, thus renewing your intention to assent to the divine's presence and action within your being. Whatever you do, don't fight the thoughts; if you do, you will only drive them deeper into your mind. They will dig in like a tick and ruin the peace of your experience of Centering Prayer.

The fourth guideline concerns the transition from Centering Prayer back to normal awareness. When you come to the end of your Centering Prayer period, don't jump back up into your daily life. Remain where you are for another two minutes, and take your time coming out of the experience. When we meditate, we reach a deep level of rest and awareness, and it can be unpleasant to jerk yourself from it too abruptly. In fact, doing so can cause a headache, an upset stomach, or dizziness. So allow yourself a couple of minutes to come out of it.

Remember, Centering Prayer is about spiritual attentiveness to God. After a while, you will find the divine doing most of the work, particularly as you are more and more pulled into passive states of contemplation. Your work is simply to make yourself more and more receptive to God, to effortlessly let go of all your hindering baggage. In the end, the mystical journey is more about what we release than what we acquire on the way.

Our lives are so cluttered in our consumer civilization. Our busy schedules and the external clutter in our homes reflect the psychological clutter within ourselves. Contemplation, Centering Prayer, meditation — these practices are about inner simplification, a process the divine initiates in us and brings to completion in time.[8]

In each sitting of Centering Prayer, we pass through what Thomas Keating calls "moments," four distinct but related stages: (1) the Sacred Word, (2) Rest, (3) Unloading, and (4) Evacuation. The Sacred Word is at the beginning of the prayer. We have introduced the sacred word, and with its introduction the circular process of the four moments begins. We are aware of thoughts, but they are remote and not a particular problem. We are lovingly waiting for God, gently knocking at the door.

After a few minutes, we enter the second moment of Centering Prayer, Rest. Now we experience a deep sense of peace, quiet, stillness, and refreshment. It is a period of interior silence and a tangible sense of the divine presence. Centering Prayer is a process of becoming more and more aware as we become more sensitive. Our inner, spiritual senses awaken; these are essentially capacities to know and relate to the divine reality. But this stage only lasts a short time, perhaps ten minutes or so, and we are plunged into the third moment, Unloading.

Our deep relaxation and rest also relaxes our defense mechanisms. As a consequence, the unincorporated, raw emotional contents of our early life and infancy surface from the unconscious; these can assume the form of a flood of primitive, intense emotions, or thoughts. Then, after a few more minutes, the fourth moment of Centering Prayer commences.

Evacuation is the discharge of these undigested thoughts and primitive feelings, which are then dissipated, freeing us from their hidden influence. Following this process, we begin again with the sacred word the next time around in our next sitting, and on and on it goes.9 I have experienced much of what Abbot Thomas describes in this schema, although in my experience of this form of meditation I am primarily aware of the divine presence and the pervasive peace that emanates from it.

It is the Holy Spirit, the divine itself, that is accomplishing a process of healing in us. This is what Thomas Keating calls the *Divine Therapy*.

The human condition, as we have seen, is basically one of illness. We feel isolated or separated from God. The mystical life is a way in which God can gradually heal our illness by slowly restoring us to a unitive relationship with him. We are *ill* precisely because we mistakenly think we are separate from God. This Divine Therapy also includes our contribution of practicing the virtues, and communicating love, compassion, kindness, and mercy in all our relationships.

Here is how Keating describes it: "The healing process is primarily the work of contemplative prayer, which along with the homework of daily life constitutes the Divine Therapy."10 Contemplation, especially through its infused or passive forms, is the way in which God works his will in our lives. We must be prepared to collaborate with him in the labor of our inner transformation from isolated individuals to mystics — the inherent dignity of each one of us. In this process of the four moments of Centering Prayer, the spirit excavates ever deeper into our unconscious experience, and frees us from all our undigested emotional material, all the raw energy that has held us back for so long.

Christian Meditation

Like Centering Prayer, *Christian Meditation* is a form oriented to cultivating contemplation in the fullest sense of the term; but unlike

Centering Prayer, it is a *concentrative* way of prayer. John Main learned this method of contemplative meditation from a Hindu guru in the 1950s, when he was stationed in Malaysia as a British diplomat. Later, returning to England, Main entered a Benedictine monastery and began teaching Christian Meditation in the 1970s. He died in December 1982, but his movement has spread all around the world, due to the untiring efforts of his disciple and successor, Laurence Freeman, another Benedictine.[11]

Christian Meditation is a mantric form of meditation that counsels the perpetual, conscious repetition of the mantra from the beginning to the end of the meditation period. Like a hammer pounding away at our thoughts, the mantra wears away the support system for our false selves by replacing each thought with the mantra itself. The mantra eventually becomes a vehicle that takes us to deeper and deeper states of inner quiet, peace, and stillness, where we can transcend our thoughts and the false self, and know the joys of divine union with God.

Christian Meditation lets us set the false self aside. Although its emphasis is different from Centering Prayer, the goal is the same: union with God and transformation of the person, and the latter through the former. Such divine union can also occur following Sufi, Hindu, Taoist, and Sikh forms of meditation. Unfortunately space doesn't permit us to explore all of these types here.

Christian Zen

Another form of contemplative experience, which can be called *Christian Zen*, is becoming more common in our time. Figures like German Benedictine Willigis Jaeger, German Jesuit Hugo Enomiya-LaSalle, American Jesuit Robert E. Kennedy, American layman and professor Ruben Habito, and Trappist monk Kevin Hunt are all Christian Zen masters, or roshis. They are dramatic examples of interspirituality, of intermystical wisdom and practice.

Without abandoning their Christian faith, they have adopted Zen meditation, or *zazen*, as their means of contemplation. They have become quite adept at combining these two venerable and ancient traditions. The rich experience of the monks of St. Joseph's Abbey with Zen over a period of fifteen years, for example, has borne fruit in the lives of many Christians. Christian Zen constitutes a genuine hybrid, a natural and organic interspiritual phenomenon.

Zen

Of course, Zen Buddhism itself has a long tradition of the inner life. *Zen* is a mahayanan form of Buddhism, the later school of the Great Vehicle, like the Tibetan tradition of Vajrayana, the Diamond School. Zen is specifically a Japanese form of Buddhism that has been greatly influenced by the natural mysticism of Taoism and Chinese Ch'an Buddhism. This form of Buddhism is based almost exclusively on spiritual practice. It strips away externals to focus only on what is absolutely necessary: zazen, or sitting meditation, which is a regular and highly disciplined practice.

Zazen emphasizes a straight posture, rhythmic breathing, and a peaceful, nondiscursive state of mind. This is augmented with *koan* practice, the zazen intensive retreat, and interviews with the *roshi* or teacher. The koan is a nondiscursive riddle meant to trip up the logical or rational mind and position the practitioner to experience *satori,* or kensho, the mystical breakthroughs in consciousness in which a person experiences nondual awareness, a unitive mind in which no separation is experienced in relation to reality and others. Satori and kensho are forms of enlightenment experience. Zen is a no-nonsense form of contemplative practice, a long, difficult, but infinitely rewarding path.

Vipassanā: Insight Meditation

Vipassanā or Insight Meditation is another Buddhist form. It derives from the Hinayana tradition, or that of the Lesser Vehicle, the original form of Buddhism. This southern form of the Dharma is also called Theravada Buddhism, the Path of the Elders.[12]

Vipassanā is based on interior observation of states of mind, perceptions, and sensations. This profoundly contemplative form of meditation usually goes on for several hours each day. During six- to eight-month retreats, the practitioner may sit for ten hours and then perform walking meditation for another eight. Like Zen, it is a long and difficult path, but similarly rewarding. Jon Kabat-Zinn and Jack Kornfield are some of the better-known teachers of Vipassanā in our time, and the Insight Meditation Center in Barre, Massachusetts, is one of the more important retreat facilities in this tradition.

Tibetan Buddhist Meditation

Tibetan Buddhist meditation, or *Vajrayana* practice, is a multifaceted approach that employs a number of techniques. We can only discuss them here in very general terms because the forms are not revealed to those who are not serious initiates.

In Vajrayana, a number of meditation practices, usually involving visualization, are meant to activate certain capacities in us. For example, one type of meditation practice is meant to stimulate the growth of forgiveness and compassion. One way to do that is to visualize a deity or a bodhisattva that embodies those qualities, thus awakening those qualities in oneself. They already exist in us; we just need help to access them, and visualization is one way to accomplish that actualization.

Another Tibetan meditation practice cultivates lucid dreaming, the act of remaining conscious in the dream-state so that we can make spiritually useful or beneficial decisions.

A further method of meditation trains the individual to be fully conscious and with a peaceful mind during the death process. *The Tibetan Book of the Dead* is an important guide to what to do and not do at death. It contains detailed descriptions of after-death states. Of course we can only scratch the surface of Tibetan Buddhism's immensely wise traditions.

The crown jewel of Tibetan Buddhist practice is sky meditation to awaken and develop *Dzogchen,* or the perfected state of the mind, the original and eternal state of awareness, which is nondual, alert, and vast.[13] In sky meditation, we simply sit in a relaxed manner, gaze into the sky, and realize that our consciousness is vast like the sky, and that this immensity is the nature of the nondual, original awareness. It is what we are! It is the nature of the mind itself. It is the Buddha-nature, our original nature, the abiding reality of who we truly are when freed of our limitations and ignorance. Our own ultimate awareness is unlimited.

Transcendental Meditation

Transcendental Meditation, coming from the Hindu tradition, is what is called an open or receptive method because there is nothing to do but simply be, to let go of control, and open up within. Transcendental Meditation, or TM, as it is named, utilizes a mantra, or word form. It allows the person to become more and more receptive to the divine presence within the heart, or depths of consciousness. The mantra draws us into a state of complete relaxation, and this permits us to access more subtle states of awareness.

Through a kind of rolling repetition, the mantra becomes self-moving. It only needs us to start the process by introducing the mantra each time we sit. The mantra allows people to relax and achieve inner calm through an almost effortless activity. Perfect for busy people, TM is a good method to learn the surrender of control so necessary to the spiritual journey. The mantra is always working in its own way, in its own time, and at its own pace. TM will lead us into greater integration of body, mind, spirit — the unconscious with the conscious and the superconscious.

TM is most effective in connecting us with our interior landscapes. But it requires that we let the mantra do the work. Through the agency of this mantra, TM draws us into interiority and the experience of the immanent divine. TM has undoubtedly guided millions on their pilgrimage to awaken to the inner life.

Yoga and the Martial Arts

Yoga, and martial arts such as t'ai chi, Aikido, capoeira, and others, can also be effective forms of spiritual practice. These are more active means, but they each have a contemplative, or meditative dimension. In each, through the integration of body and mind through movement, it is possible to reach mystical levels of perception and realization, even the very highest.

O Sensei, the founder of Aikido, was certainly a great mystic, and Aikido was a mystical practice for him. He constantly hinted at this insight, but he wanted people to discover this mystical dimension on their own. Properly understood, one can reach the same kind of consciousness through these forms of practice as one can through meditation. We will discuss these forms in more detail in chapter 8.

Mass, Liturgy, and Conventional Prayer

Depending on the needs and temperament of the person, mass, liturgy, and more conventional kinds of prayer are also useful means of spiritual practice. Mass can trigger deep states of awareness of the divine reality, and can even lead to a unitive experience with God. The mass is a powerful symbolic activity that can propel us into eternal time and sacred space. Indeed, all liturgical ritual can have this kind of power over us. Many people choose the mass, or Eucharist, and other forms of ritual as a means to transform awareness, partially because it is all they have ever known, but also because it works for them. Liturgy has properties that can act on very deep levels of perception.[14] The symbolism of liturgy can be very contemplative, but it takes a very disciplined person to reach that level of awareness, something that often only happens in monasticism.

The more conventional forms of prayer can also be a viable form of spiritual practice; it has worked for countless saints of all traditions throughout the ages. Prayer is a means of self-transcendence as well as a point of contact with the divine. Many mystics make the point that it leads us into self-transcendence precisely because of this contact, or unitive relationship with God. Prayer can be pure, clear, profound, and intensely single-minded. Prayer had a radically powerful effect on St. Francis of Assisi, for example: Francis would pray all night on his knees, weeping for his sins and the sins of the world. In the last two years of his life he became blind from his tears, and spending the entire night on his knees in communion with the divine.

Bede Griffiths's spiritual practice centered on two hour-long periods of meditation a day, the Eucharist, or mass, and three periods of common prayer in the temple of his ashram, which was really a chapel. He also engaged in hours of spiritual reading every day. But Bede was also accustomed to pray in the traditional sense, and it was this kind of prayer that proved to be a turning point in his early life. Before his conversion to Catholicism in 1931, and his subsequent entrance into a Benedictine monastery, Bede did social service work in a poor section of London. He decided at one point to spend an entire night in prayer on his knees, much like Francis of Assisi. It was difficult at first, particularly fighting off sleep, but eventually, as he continued into the night, he was taken out of himself, beyond time and space. Before he knew what had happened, it was morning; some eight hours or so had elapsed since kneeling down to pray. When he rose, he felt as if his body had no weight, as if he were floating. He experienced a deep stirring of sorrow for his sins and failings in his life, and he wept for the first time.

Although Thomas Keating is now focused on more contemplative forms of spiritual practice, earlier in his monastic life the core of his spiritual practice was to pray on his knees before the Blessed Sacrament, or the Holy Eucharist, every morning from 4 to 7 A.M. Clearly, this kind of prayer experience was transformative and contributed to the extraordinary being he has become. Those years of kneeling in the chapel made a deep impact on his spiritual life. The combination of asceticism (the kneeling) with a recollected form of prayer that became contemplation for him made him the mystic he is today.

Devotional Spirituality

Devotions, like the rosary and the Stations of the Cross, can also be an effective means of spiritual practice; they also allow us to transcend ourselves, to reach beyond our limited sphere to all those who suffer and need us in some special way. Devotional spirituality can be incandescent in the energy and power it generates in us, in our awareness.

I remember watching my uncle, during the last three years of his life, as he said the rosary several times a day. The rosary became his spiritual practice, his vehicle to contemplation. I believe he became a mystic saint through the rosary; it assumed a meditative practice for him, doing the same work in him as the more traditional forms of meditation practice discussed above.

Chanting, Singing, Dance

Chanting and singing can also lead to ecstatic states of consciousness. I have seen this in Gregorian chant — the way it pulls you into your center as a recollective practice, into the divine. In India, people are fond of *bhajans,* popular hymns or songs sung in a sacred context. These songs are simple, but they are hypnotic, even ecstatic. Sometimes, people in temples and ashrams will stay up all night singing only one bhajan! They completely lose themselves in their singing, becoming absorbed in the spiritual impulse of the song and transfixed by its rhythmic power. It is extremely seductive and effective in altering consciousness, and can be a compelling form of contemplative experience.

Bhajans, chanting, and music in general are very useful aids in the spiritual journey. Another story about St. Francis illustrates their power: One day, an angel appeared to St. Francis, holding a violin. The angel looked at Francis, then gently stroked the strings of the violin with his bow. The music was so heavenly in its ethereal beauty and sweetness that it sent the saint instantly into ecstasy. Such is the mystical power of music — when it is the right music.

Ecstatic forms of dance can also be radically transformative. Dance is an ancient form of spiritual practice that has mystical and ritual properties, even liturgical qualities. In its mystical properties, dance is unitive, integrative, contemplative, joyful, and bliss-bestowing.

In Sufism, whirling dervishes dance into union with God through their ecstatic turning; many tribes in Africa and other areas where indigenous forms of spirituality exist have ecstatic, rhythmic dances. There is no doubt that certain types of dance are designed to alter consciousness, particularly in a ritualistic context. Watching the whirling dervishes in Turkey, or the ecstatic dances of the Masai in Kenya and Tanzania, one is carried away by the potency of these sacred forms of dance to propel their practitioners into other states of awareness.

The Goal of All Spiritual Practices Is the Same

Spiritual practice is to the mystical life what food and water is to the body. Just as we cannot survive very long without food and water, we cannot survive on the spiritual journey without a contemplative practice of some sort. It is the inner source of nourishment and growth, and it unites with the efforts of the divine, or the ultimate nature of the mind itself.

There are as many forms of spiritual practice as there are individuals. Forms may differ, but the goal is the same: integration and transformation. To achieve authentic spirituality, genuine mysticism, we must adopt some form of spiritual practice.

◆ Element 6: Mature Self-Knowledge

Some twenty-five centuries ago, Socrates counseled, "Know thyself." In the same way, mystics have genuine, mature, honest self-knowledge. They are radically open to acknowledging faults and limitations, and do not shy away from coming to terms with them.

Spiritual progress depends on a maturity in our self-understanding. We must know ourselves fully. Humility is the basis of an honest, mature self-awareness that accepts ourselves as we are, without covering up, making excuses, or blaming others. We live in a culture in which the average person tells a lie thirteen or fourteen times a day, and many of these lies are to ourselves! Humility will not allow us to lie to others or to ourselves, and certainly not to God. A mature self-knowledge depends on truth and honesty.

Profound inner change takes root gradually within us as we gain this precious self-knowledge and uncover all the hidden motives that lie buried deep within us. This self-knowledge can also be seen as a gift of divine grace, and contains the wisdom to guide us in our mystical or contemplative development. In some traditions, such as Hinduism and Buddhism, this grace can be mediated through a spiritual master or guru, but it represents a significant factor in our growth to spiritual maturity and wholeness in most — if not all — traditions.

Self-knowledge, when it reaches its full potential, becomes the basis for very radical inner change. Mature self-knowledge happens when we move beyond denial — denial of our faults and limitations, our buried motives or hidden agendas — and beyond judgment of others, beyond projection on others our own need for inner work. The more we see ourselves as we really are, rather than as our ideal self-image dictates, the more we are on the road to the fullness of the spiritual life, and the ultimate actualization and realization of our potential for divine love and compassion.

Joy

In a number of theistic forms of mysticism, self-knowledge is an illuminative state of consciousness initiated by the divine itself. The closer we come to God, the more we know the intimacy of divine union, the more we are aware of how imperfect we are in relation to divine perfection. We cannot long endure this perfection if we are not growing toward it ourselves.

Sufi master Shaykh Fadhlalla Haeri, in his practical work *The Journey of the Self*, remarks about how contentment and joy — bliss — dawns in the life of the person who has achieved real self-knowledge. He observes, "Once self-knowledge is mastered, one attains a joy and happiness which cannot be measured by any of the normal senses. This joy is of a higher value, and gives greater solace and comfort, than anything else we can seek or find in this world."[15]

Coming into the clarity and truth of self-awareness, self-understanding, free of illusions and delusions, we know a continual joy, a fullness of bliss that will never pass away. It is the bliss of wisdom, that wise understanding that embraces us as we realize our inner poverty but our potential for mystical wealth — psychological and moral treasures beyond the grasp of the greedy of this world, where inequity and injustice are so widespread. Self-knowledge, like all mystical knowing, gives us an invincible certitude about ourselves and divine matters. This certitude, and the clarity of our understanding, partially accounts for our joy and contentment.

All the great souls I know and have known, from the various spiritualities of the world's religions, have all been people of great joy, humor, and contentment. From time to time they would allow it to gush forth in laughter, humor, or just sheer joy itself.

Indeed, the joy of the mystic is a property that accompanies the process of inner change. Abbot Columba Mormion, a Belgian Benedictine and spiritual writer, was fond of a saying, "Joy is the echo of God's life in us." Joy is also an infallible indication of spiritual maturity and integrity.

Humor

In my opinion, the sense of humor is the seventh "sense." We have the usual five senses, and then many see a pyschic or sixth sense, but then there is the sense of humor. Life is incomplete without it.

A sense of humor not only expresses our natural and supernatural happiness, our contentment, it is also a very useful check against self-deception. It is very easy to take ourselves much too seriously. Humor allows us to transcend our seriousness and become lighter, inwardly more free.

Whenever I would get too serious and pious about my own inner process, my uncle would unfailingly come to the rescue with an appropriate outburst of his inimitable wit. He would gently poke fun at my seriousness by making hilariously silly faces. This simple act would immediately bring me to my senses, and I would laugh along with him. He had a natural genius for finding humor in any situation.

At the risk of revealing all my uncle's physical failings, I remember when it became necessary, as an old man, for him to have all his remaining teeth extracted. The dentist took out seventeen teeth! A few days later, before he got his dentures, I noticed as he was getting ready for bed that he had a toothbrush and toothpaste in his hands. Naturally, I exclaimed, "Uncle John, what are you doing?" He grinned a toothless grin and said,

"I'm just bringing back happy memories!" Humor, like self-knowledge, is filled with truth. It is essential for our human and spiritual evolvement.

✦ Transformation As the Reality of Inner Change

The spiritual journey changes us to the core of our being. If it didn't, it wouldn't be real. This quality of inner change is what I understand by the term *transformation:* a radical reordering and alteration of our character, and all our old habits of thought, feeling, and action.

Spirituality is always meant to make us better by unlocking our potential for divinity, to be *like* God in some participatory way. This is what the Christian theologians of the early Orthodox church called theosis, or deification, becoming like God. It is what Eastern traditions mean when they speak of awakening the Buddha-nature within us, or the Atman. If spirituality does not offer access to actualizing our potential for this higher form of life, which is what we are made for, then what ultimate value can it possibly have for us?

Seven Levels of Transformation

The transformation to which mystical life summons us has seven basic levels: (1) consciousness, (2) the will, (3) the emotions, (4) the character, (5) the imagination, (6) memory, and (7) action or behavior.

Consciousness affects our understanding of life and reality. Through the practice of the spiritual life, our awareness grows and expands; it takes in more. The more it expands, the greater becomes its capacity to understand, to change, to actualize what we are potentially: images and likenesses of the divine reality. As our understanding increases, ignorance dissipates and we can then modify or alter our motives, outgrowing the selfish ones.

Our *will* then knows an inner change, a purification that effects a far-reaching transformation in our character and behavior. The will becomes stable in desiring the good, in transcending self-concern and preoccupation, so that we can respond to others with love and compassion. The will seeks less the goods that are mutable, desiring the ones that are unchanging: wisdom, spiritual knowledge, the virtues, mystical awareness, unitive vision, and attaining higher spiritual life.

The *emotions* achieve a greater stability and order. They no longer operate on their own, but are brought into harmony with the integral person. The emotions now serve the spiritual journey; they are no longer a source of distraction.

The change in consciousness, will, and the emotions gradually habituates the *character* to be reshaped in and by the virtues, values, and spiritual treasures of the inner journey. The character then makes the shift from self-preoccupation to love, from hypocrisy to sincerity, from sin to holiness, from ignorance to wisdom, from human limitation to the liberating power of grace. The character takes on the form and substance of virtue, slowly being deified in the process. It becomes a beautiful manifestation of holiness, radiant with virtue and a loving presence. The person's character is then an icon of truth, virtue, wisdom, compassion, mercy, kindness, and love. A natural beauty emanates from such beings, attracting others to the inner life that they themselves incarnate and witness.

The *imagination,* like the emotions and feelings, is united to our understanding, will, character, memory, and actions to form an integral and effective center of willing, knowing, acting, and being. The imagination is not operating in its own field irrespective of what is happening in the inner life of the person. It is in harmony with the will and intention of the person, not dragging it away with images of another life or commitment. The same is true of the memory and its operations.

The *memory* is healed by our inner transformation, by the mystical power of deifying grace. Memory is at the service of the person's inner growth; it no longer sits in isolation, wallowing in its hurts, injuries, and traumas of earlier life, but becomes completely present to the eternal now.

A living, mature, integrated spiritual life transforms our *action* or behavior, conforming them to the requirements of love. It compels our behavior to be in harmony with compassion and practical wisdom, which knows the sufferings of others and the appropriate responses to those sufferings. Our actions become consistent with our virtue. We can no longer act inconsistently or in isolation from what we have realized. We must act from our inner life and from wisdom itself.

All the great examples of heroic holiness, expressed in love and compassion throughout history, in all the traditions of humankind, attest to the relationship between inner transformation and outer action. If they are not in harmony, if they are not consistent, then the relationship and the transformation are either inauthentic or incomplete.

All Spiritual Practice Is About Inner Transformation

The existence of spiritual masters in each tradition is palpable evidence of the perennial, universal validity and effectiveness of spiritual practice as an aid to genuine self-knowledge and radical, total inner change.

All spiritual practice is ultimately about this inner development that reaches fruition in selfless love, compassion, mercy, and kindness. All the spiritual practices — chanting the names of God, the numerous forms of meditation, spiritual reading, reflection, affective prayer, music, art, dance, walking, drumming, yoga, the martial arts, contemplation — are directly related to self-knowledge and inner transformation. We cannot ignore the overwhelming empirical evidence they offer for the profundity of inner change; they stand as a permanent witness to their value and efficacy to lead us to a complete reversal of the old self, addicted to selfishness and the false-self system. Following this path isn't easy, but no better way to lasting happiness and tranquillity of heart and mind exists. All ways lead finally to this place that transcends all we thought we knew before.

Chapter 7

OUT IN THE WORLD:
THE SPIRITUALITY
OF ACTION

At the evening of life, you will be examined in Love.
— St. John of the Cross

The sage does not accumulate (for himself). The more he expends for others, the more does he possess of his own; the more he gives to others, the more does he have himself.
— Tao Te Ching

In a clever cartoon you may have seen, a man who looks like a biblical prophet is walking around in front of a hotel in New York City. He is carrying a sign printed in bold letters, proclaiming "Jesus Is Coming." Across the street, a little Buddhist monk in saffron robes holds up another sign with equally prominent letters, proclaiming "Buddha Here Now." This cartoon is not only humorous, it raises the serious issue of the here and now vs. the unknown future of another reality. Genuine spirituality doesn't turn its back on the world; it always remains open to its call. Interspirituality requires engagement.

Dietrich Bonhoeffer, a German Lutheran theologian during the time of the Nazis, gave up his comfortable and secure situation at Union Theological Seminary in New York City to return to Germany and oppose Hitler. He knew it might cost him his life, and it did; but he had to risk everything for the sake of justice. His sacrifice was a prophetic act that originated in his deep faith and a spirituality of engagement. Genuine spirituality always expresses itself in action for others.

A viable spirituality today is socially engaged; it does not turn its back on the sufferings of the world, but squarely faces them and contributes to their mitigation and alleviation. We turn now to an examination of the more outward expressions of the inner journey, the social dimension that is found in all traditions of spirituality. This social dimension has three important elements: simplicity of life, selfless service, and the prophetic or moral voice. These elements of a universal spirituality apply the fruits of the mystical life to the sphere of social concerns, and the demands of compassion and love in active society. These elements are more important than ever today, when our planet is so threatened. We must turn to the spiritual and moral resources of humankind's mystical traditions to guide our individual and collective action.

✦ Element 7: Simplicity of Life

Simplicity of life concerns our relationship with the planet, the natural world, other species, and other human beings. What we do here —how we live our lives, how we use and abuse the earth's resources — is an important moral issue. Simplicity of life is an inner focus on what is necessary. As we grow in mystical consciousness and become inwardly integrated, our life naturally becomes simplified, uncluttered by property and money.

Examples of Simplicity

Simplicity, or poverty — the term more commonly employed in the Roman Catholic tradition — is an attribute of spirituality that has been present as long as people have walked the inner path. Mystics naturally gravitate to simplicity of life, which then is incarnated in their actions by a lifestyle that sets aside wealth and power.

Jesus counseled this kind of simple life; he was not interested in power and wealth. St. Francis of Assisi and his early followers lived a life of simple poverty, although this simplicity was abandoned by his later followers. Countless mystic saints of India from the dawn of her tradition have embraced voluntary lives of poverty and simplicity. The sannyasi has only two pieces of cloth (a *dhoti* and a shawl, for his clothing), a walking stick, and begging bowl. Mahatma Gandhi himself lived in this manner. He was completely committed to simplicity of life and lifestyle; he lived dispossessed of the goods of this earth. He knew how distracting they could be, how they become sources of division and conflict, as Karl Marx also observed with his distinction between the haves and the have-nots.

Mother Teresa truly understood and embraced the value of simplicity and poverty. In all her communities throughout the world, her sisters live as the poorest of the poor *among* the poorest of the poor. This commitment has disconcerted many of her supporters, especially in the wealthy countries of the West. Again and again, when she opened a house in a large North American or European city, well-meaning friends would furnish these houses with the best appointments, only to have Mother Teresa order their prompt removal. She understood the power of voluntary poverty and simplicity. She realized how these qualities contribute to our sense of vulnerability in the face of temporal existence. How can we be truly spiritual beings when we have had everything handed to us, without effort or labor?

Another important figure in the Catholic tradition is a French priest by the name of Charles de Foucauld, who lived from 1858 to 1916. A nobleman, he had lived a dissipated life before his conversion to the Catholic Church changed his life drastically. He founded a small, semi-monastic community in an oasis of the Sahara Desert, where he was eventually martyred by Muslim fanatics. Charles de Foucauld was passionately committed to the Gospel, and he took Christ's evangelical counsel of poverty to heart. He lived a very austere life of self-denial, fasting, constant prayer, recollection, and poverty. During his life, no one who came to join him ever stayed; he never lived to see his community develop and flourish. Today, however, it has. He and Mother Teresa are among the brave few who have been faithful witnesses to holy simplicity and poverty.

Why Simplicity Is an Urgent Issue

Simplicity of life is one of the inner resources that advances our common responsibility. It can have a major impact on altering how we relate to the earth, other species, and the poor. This element of global spirituality is necessary because we must simplify our lives if the Ecological Age is really to take root. When we voluntarily embrace a simpler lifestyle that does not require squandering our precious resources, degrading the environment, oppressing other species, and depriving the poor, simplicity of life reveals itself concretely as a great generosity of spirit.

In our social realm, the adage "live simply so others may simply live" wisely demonstrates the practical efficacy of true spirituality. This dictum is a way to concentrate our minds and our efforts on changing how we live. It is not enough merely to talk about the need to change. We *must* in fact change! This change has to begin with each of us, or else our words are meaningless.

Simplicity of life and poverty have largely disappeared in the Roman Catholic Church and in most other Christian communions. Priests have become very attached to their material comforts, with no spirit of sacrifice in how they use resources. An example of gross failure in this regard occurred in July 1995, when more than 550 people died in Chicago during a heat wave, while less than twenty-five miles away in a suburban monastery, an air-conditioning system operates twenty-four hours a day from early June to September. Where is the simplicity, compassion, and social concern in this failure to act?

Simplicity of heart and life require an appreciation of insecurity, vulnerability, marginality, and detachment, which a certain experience of material poverty facilitates. There is no "upper-class," "middle-class," or "lower-class" spirituality. There is only the summons to transformation as part of human experience, and its requirements are universal.

Simplicity and Humility

Simplicity has a way of focusing our attention on what is absolutely essential; it goes to the core of our being and strips away all the distractions that compete for our attention. It directs us to the utter seriousness of the spiritual journey, and relieves us of any crutches we may have relied on.

Simplicity, as a virtue, knows only what is real. It will not tolerate useless complexity in how we live; it always challenges us to reduce everything to the essentials. It is not impressed with many things, but with few things used well, especially in service to others. Simplicity of life sees reality as it is; like humility, it is only comfortable with the truth. Simplicity is truth in how we live, unadorned and free, available and inviting to all, open to the world, and welcoming of its demands on us.

In terms of the inner process of the mystical life, simplicity makes us more and more attentive to what is happening within us; it doesn't allow us to neglect the fires of our spiritual life, but ever calls us back to give an accounting. The person who understands simplicity, and has the virtue of a simple heart, is like the man mentioned by the Chinese sage Chuang

Tzu, who desires to be obscure and withdrawn into solitude. Chuang Tzu says of him, "The man of Tao remains unknown. Perfect virtue produces nothing. 'No-Self' is 'True-Self.' And the greatest man is Nobody."[1]

Simplicity of heart is always related to humility and meekness. As St. John Climacus, a father of the Desert tradition of early Christian wisdom, observed: "A meek (or humble) soul is a throne of simplicity...."[2] Humility allows us to keep our natural purity, or simplicity, and simplicity of heart is itself this purity of soul that allows us to retain our innocence. Climacus declares: "Innocent is he [or she] whose soul is in its natural purity as it was created...."[3]

We are born with this kind of simplicity, and it is the inherent property of children. Climacus tells us that this natural simplicity, or purity, makes us blessed; but that purity of heart — the simplicity that comes after much inner struggle with our weaknesses — is of far greater value for us. This kind of simplicity brings infinite rewards.[4]

When we have humility and simplicity we are free of hypocrisy. Climacus mentions how God is himself simple, and how he desires that the souls who "come to Him..."be simple and innocent."[5] St. Teresa of Avila speaks of humility as having an infinite value, and she regards it as more important than merely intellectual knowledge. She declares: "Believe me...one act of humility is worth more than all the knowledge of the world."[6]

Simplicity Enriches the Spiritual Journey

Simplicity clears away all the inessentials of existence and makes a life of genuine depth and meaning possible. When we remove the clutter from our lives, we become inwardly free to give ourselves to the mystical journey, to seek union and communion with the ultimate mystery.

Simplicity of life allows us to become single-minded about the inner experience, and not to waste our precious time and energy on useless efforts that only distract us. All the great founders of the religions, and countless mystics and saints in these faiths, freely chose simplicity because they understood its value.

Gandhi was very clear on this point. He eloquently applied the truth of simplicity of lifestyle even to the economic sphere: "The earth has enough for mankind's needs, but not for its greeds!" Simplicity is at once an inner law of the spiritual life, and a basic demand of justice and wise economics. It has perhaps taken the ecological crisis to prove the Mahatma right, and to vindicate the teachings of Christ on this point expressed in the living words of the Gospel. A person who does not understand and practice the virtue of simplicity is only playing around on the spiritual journey.

When one embraces simplicity of life, one then begins the spiritual journey in earnest. To take this step goes a long way in accepting the seriousness of the mystical challenge. Only when we can plunge into a commitment to live simply can we enter more authentically into the realm of the interior journey.

The spiritual journey is not a game; it is the most ultimate and most real human adventure. It is not subject to the vagaries of this impermanent existence, but is rooted in the eternal. Simplicity of heart can make all the difference in terms of living the interior experience *while* relating it to others, to the natural world, to other species and to the community at large. It sets an example that has great value for others.

✦ Element 8: Selfless Service and Compassionate Action

Selfless service and compassionate action together constitute another universal element of interspirituality. Any truly viable spirituality for the third millennium will need to include our commitment to the social dimension. Given the enormous suffering among the poor and oppressed, the ecological degradation of the earth, and threats to world peace and stability, men and women of spiritual wisdom must make a positive contribution.

The Western faiths have always taught that we have a moral responsibility to all our vulnerable brothers and sisters, especially those who are pushed by events and circumstances to the extreme margins. The need is very great in our time. As the rich get richer, the problem of homelessness worldwide has grown to alarming proportions. The United States alone has more than five million homeless; they have become nonpersons who haunt our cities and our consciences. Christianity, Judaism, and Islam have much to teach the world and the other religions about selfless service and concrete compassionate action, and Buddhism is becoming more inclined to social engagement as inspired by the example of these faiths.

Learning to Serve

Genuine spirituality is always open to service. It never attempts to evade it, especially as need arises — and the need is great.

The spiritual life summons us to selfless service in particular. This is a form of action that, as the Bhagavad Gita so powerfully emphasizes, does not seek a result; it is not attached to the possible fruits of any action, so it is not performed with any purpose in mind other than to respond to the perceived need in the moment. Selfless service doesn't come easily. It is something one must learn through education and practical experience. Two examples elucidate this difficulty:

Three Christian monks, each wearing a religious habit, were walking together from the Parliament of the World's Religions toward their car a block or two away. They were deeply engrossed in a discussion about the importance of reaching out to the homeless in some concrete, effective way. As they walked, they passed a homeless man who was prostrate on the street. He cried out to them plaintively, but they ignored him and kept walking. As he continued to call after them, the youngest of the three monks wanted to respond. He turned and looked at the man, but did not quite know what to say or do. He looked to his seniors for a cue. They continued to walk, engrossed in their conversation, ignoring this homeless gentleman as if he didn't exist. Reality had presented them with a golden opportunity for service, a challenge to do something about homelessness that went beyond their rhetoric. While it is no doubt true that each of these monks is essentially a good person, none of them had received any formation in service.

The second example comes from Dharamsala, India, the capital of the Tibetan Government-in-Exile. His Holiness the Dalai Lama has said and written on a number of occasions that Buddhists can learn from Christians something about the necessity of an active, compassionate service to others in need. He has this attitude and disposition himself; his compassion is clearly discernable and it shines out through his inspiring example. In Dharamsala, the "Little Tibet" or "Lhasa" of North India, live some two thousand monks and nuns. Twenty or so lepers roam the streets of upper Dharamsala at McLeod Ganj, finding strategic locations on the roadside in order to beg from foreigners. The Tibetan monks and nuns have no real contact with the lepers, who are mostly Hindus and a few Christians. This phenomenon shouldn't exist where there are so many monastics who could quite easily reach out to them and affirm them as persons. It is actually this affirmation they are seeking more than the money. Like the homeless in America, lepers are nonpersons in India, and yet every one of them has a name, a history, and a family. The Dalai Lama is very much aware of this situation, and there may be some center eventually established for these lepers, where Tibetans, Indians, and Westerners could together care for them. There is already considerable discussion going on among Tibetan Buddhists about social service to the poor, and some breakthroughs may come before long.

This problem of inaction exists in every part of the world, and the failure to respond plagues every religious tradition. Each tradition could no doubt offer many similar examples. Elderly "bag ladies" can be found on the doorstep of the Vatican! Whether they are homeless, AIDS sufferers, or lepers, the appropriate response is always to extend compassionate attention and loving action. The ability to respond and follow through tests the mettle of all spirituality.

Life gives us so many opportunities to help those less fortunate than ourselves, but often we miss these challenges because we are not sufficiently alert to what is being offered us when we meet someone who asks us for some of our time and a little portion of our resources. Actually, such people help us more than we help them. Even though they are not aware of fulfilling this role for us, and may have no intention of assisting us in any way, the homeless, poor, and disadvantaged are teachers who silently open the door to us to stretch beyond our normal indifference.

To be selflessly available to others, to respond to them in a loving, compassionate way — not a sentimental love, but an unconditional, self-sacrificing presence — is a sign of great spiritual and human maturity. It is a witness to the seriousness of our commitment to the inner process of growth and its outward fruits. It is a sign of a deep-seated, aware sensitivity at work in us. It allows us to come forward and respond to our economically and socially deprived brothers and sisters. We cannot afford to miss these opportunities, nor to fail to accept them when they present themselves. To do so is to basically retard our moral, human, and spiritual development. To do so is an admission of our spiritual immaturity.

Contemporary Examples of Selfless Love

Life provides us with many extraordinary models of selfless love and compassion, of sacrifice for the sake of others. We can find such examples in our families, among our friends and associates at work, and among more celebrated figures. One such shining figure is Dorothy Day, who founded the Catholic Worker movement in the earlier part of the twentieth century.7 I was fortunate enough to meet her a few times in New York as a graduate student at Fordham University. She was a powerful example of someone capable of completely transcending herself to be a brilliant light of selflessness and compassion to the homeless poor in our cities.

Like Mother Teresa, Dorothy Day was totally available to the poor. She was also a severe critic of the Vietnam War, which she and many others saw as unjust, immoral, a terrible waste of life and precious resources. In her Catholic Worker houses, which exist today in every major North American city, she took in the homeless, giving them a place to live in the midst of her communities of like-minded people, whose highly developed social awareness was often augmented by contemplative practice.

What was so persuasive about her vision of life with the poor was that she allowed them to live *with* her. She became vulnerable to them and with them; she didn't isolate herself from them, but kept a simple room like many of her friends from the streets. In the Mary and Joseph Houses in Manhattan's Lower East Side, she integrated the street people into the daily life of her very active Catholic Worker community. They shared all aspects of life with her: meals, prayer, work, recreation, joys, sorrows, hopes, dreams, and struggles. Dorothy Day was a tireless champion of the rights of the unloved, rejected, and socially marginalized of America. She often said, quite rightly, that if each family took in one street person, homelessness would disappear. Hers was a spiritual vision that rolled up its sleeves and plunged into the raw, exposed humanity that economic desperation creates.

A mutual friend, Jeannette Noel, told me a story that illustrates Dorothy Day's selflessness and dedication to radical simplicity and poverty. A few years before her death in 1980, during a very hot New York summer, her community wanted to install an air conditioner in her room because she was having some difficulty breathing. They brought the air conditioner to her room, but she refused to permit its installation. She wanted them to give it to one of the permanent guests of the community. For hours, various members of the community tried to persuade her, but she was inflexible. Finally, Jeannette said to her, "Look here, Dorothy, you've got poverty down; let's work on humility now!" After Jeannette's intervention, she surrendered her resistance, and agreed to the air conditioner. This humorous incident indicates the depth of her commitment to simplicity and her essential selflessness.

I have also been moved by the selflessness of Thomas Keating. Watching him over the years, I have noticed his constant availability to those in need of him. A mutual friend of ours, Michael, an Italian American from Brooklyn, had been an A student until his mother suffered a nervous breakdown. Without his mother's supervision, Michael took to hanging out in the streets with his friends. His father, a hardworking man with little education, was not much of a disciplinarian, and had little understanding of his son's complexity and intelligence. Michael soon turned to heroin, and then to petty crime to support his habit. When he wasn't with his friends, he worked in a cemetery as a landscaper, keeping the grounds in order.

Michael went from bad to worse. Then he met Thomas Keating through some Franciscan brothers. When Michael walked in, Thomas discerned a diamond in the rough and decided to try and help him as much as he could. Michael kept trying; he had a brilliant mind and was an avid reader of literature and spiritual books. Thomas directed him in his spiritual life, and a wonderful friendship developed between them. Michael would do well for six months, but then he would run back to his former life — even mugging people to support his return to drugs.

Michael hurt a number of people in this way, however unintentionally. He was like a cow who gives milk and then knocks the bucket over, spilling the contents. For many years he went back and forth between a life on the streets and attempts at inner change. Finally, he contracted AIDS through his indiscriminate use of needles. He struggled for about five years, and succumbed to the disease at age forty-five.

Thomas Keating never gave up on Michael, even though most of his friends had. He was always there for him, and never failed to respond to his endless requests and needs. Thomas gave of himself, never counting the cost, never keeping score. He saw the deeper goodness of Michael's nature, something Michael himself didn't recognize, except in moments of grace. After Michael died, Thomas told me, "He never gave up; he kept trying. There was something of great value in him, working in his nature, and the point is not that he may have failed, but that he persevered in his efforts at transformation." Thomas's great charity, his selfless love, and his boundless compassion are guided by his rare depth of wisdom.

When I was in graduate school, before attending Fordham University, I studied at the McAuley Institute of St. Joseph College in West Hartford, Connecticut. There I met Sister Mary Sarah, a saintly member of the Mercy Sisters who was my professor of Latin for three years. I took five or six courses in this challenging language and her kind patience was always an inspiration to me. She was never in a hurry; she relied on humor to encourage me. All our courses were independent studies, and she pushed me as far as she thought I could go. In this way, I translated a number of fragments from ancient and medieval texts, and sometimes, whole treatises, acquiring a love of Latin in the process. I owe her much, and I found her to be one of the most loving and selfless people I have ever known. She was always there for me, and for everyone else who sought her assistance.

Although they are all professionally religious, these contemporary examples make clear that holiness is within everyone's potential. There are tens of thousands other examples of saints, of selfless people of profound simplicity and humility of heart, in all the religions of the world, all throughout recorded and prerecorded history. Most readers could easily recite a long list of such saintly souls. The capacity for largeness of heart is the inner nature of all of us when we are liberated from the false self and its hold on our motives. The mystical journey makes this shift an actuality in us, and this shift from ego-centricity, from the false self to love, is a permanent acquisition once it takes root.

✦ Element 9: The Prophetic Voice

A further vital component in a universal spirituality, and so in an interspirituality, is the awakened and utterly necessary function of leadership in the area of justice. I call this the operation of the prophetic or moral voice in situations that require witness and response.

The prophetic voice vigorously acknowledges the unjust events and policies that cause enormous tension, misery, and dislocation in the lives of countless numbers of people. Wars; the plight of refugees (most of whom are women and children); unjust economic, social, and political conditions that enrich a small class of rulers while oppressing the masses; threats to the environment — all are matters that should evoke the moral voice and our willingness to respond. We no longer have the luxury of ignoring the many challenges to justice in all its forms. We have a universal responsibility to apply the moral or prophetic function wherever we see justice disregarded, threats to world peace, oppression by states against its people or a neighboring nation, or some other danger as yet unforeseen.

The History of Prophecy

The witness to justice all over the world — prophecy — has a long history. There are the many celebrated examples of prophecy in ancient Israel, where the patriarchs Abraham, Isaac, Jacob, Moses, the prophets Isaiah, Jeremiah, Elijah, Ezekiel, Hosea, Daniel, and the rest raised their voices against tyranny and injustice to the poor and oppressed. They admonished kings on two points: (1) faithfulness to God and his covenant with Israel; and (2) strict observance of justice, of compassion to the poor, the orphan, the widow, and the foreigner. Whenever the kings and the people neglected these, catastrophe befell the Jewish people. The prophets championed the cause of the poor, the oppressed, the economically, socially, and politically vulnerable. Their impact on civilization through Judaism, Christianity, and Islam has been and is great, and it continues to be influential.

One can discern the spirit of their influence on people like Martin Luther King, Mahatma Gandhi, Dietrich Bonhoeffer, Edith Stein (the Jewish Carmelite nun who gave her life at Auschwitz and who was canonized by the Catholic cChurch), Russian prophet and writer Alexander Solzhenitzyn, and Archbishop Oscar Romero, the spiritual leader of El Salvador who opposed the vicious policies of the right-wing government and paid the price of his prophetic witness when he was assassinated. Bede Griffiths, Thomas Merton, Mother Teresa, and Thomas Berry are other contemporary prophetic figures who have given compelling witness to justice in their own ways, drawing attention to the need for change. Tom Berry, for example, continues to speak and write about *ecojustice*. There is no more eloquent a voice for the sanctity of the earth than this modest priest from North Carolina. All of these individuals and countless others have exercised the function of the moral voice and prophetic action.

Speaking Out: Tibet and the Catholic Church

We have a universal responsibility to speak out when we see injustice, oppression, and the abuse of human rights, the rights of the earth, and other species. This is a critical operation of all spirituality, particularly through the collective voice of religious and spiritual leaders; it is a function desperately needed now, in the Interspiritual Age, because most spiritual and religious leaders are curiously silent before these kinds of challenges.

Although much has been said in recent years, for example, about Bosnia and Rwanda, where the cost of speaking out prophetically is rather low, virtually nothing has been uttered by any religious or spiritual leader about the systematic violation of the human rights of Tibetans by the Chinese colonial government in Tibet. Personally, I find this silence disturbing and morally indefensible; it indicates a lack of courage and moral strength that hides behind considerations of prudence and discretion. It appears as collusion, through a conspiracy of silence, with the People's Republic of China.

China invaded Tibet in 1950, and thus began the tragedy of the Tibetan nation. For nearly a decade, the Dalai Lama and his people tried to co-exist with the oppressive Chinese. Finally, in 1959 the people revolted against the Chinese invaders and were harshly put down by the People's Liberation Army. As the oppression steadily grew until intolerable, the Dalai Lama, his government, and a hundred thousand of his people fled into exile. Later, the Chinese killed 1.5 million Tibetans; imprisoned and tortured tens of thousands; and destroyed six thousand monasteries. They imported millions of Chinese nationals; deforested Tibet; and stationed hundreds of nuclear warheads on the roof of the world.

There is a pressing need for the spiritual leaders of the world to address this tragedy. Tibet is really a test case in measuring the mettle of the planet's spiritual leadership. It is a significant opportunity for the religions, in their evolution toward a community of religions, to contribute substantially to the emerging global culture of peace. There will never be a truly viable community of religions, a culture of genuine peace, or a universal society, unless the religions can muster the courage and wisdom to speak out and act collectively, to apply the prophetic voice when confronted by such a blatant challenge as China's arrogant violence in Tibet.

This action has a direct relationship to the intensity of the inner life in the mystical journey. The depth and quality of spiritual life grants the courage, wisdom, perspective, and moral clarity to confront, nonviolently, evil with the truth. Gandhi, Martin Luther King Jr., Thich Nhat Hanh, and Archbishop Desmond Tutu are models to whom the world can always look. From them we can derive the inspiration to stretch beyond the often myopic focus of the religions, a myopia dictated by political considerations — not a reflection of the deeper commitments of the various traditions.

Authentic spirituality compels us to engage in moral and political struggle, to sustained action, when justice is at stake. This is doubly true of those who commit to a multifaith spiritual journey, who should be more aware of threats to justice and committed to a universal understanding that emphasizes our essential interdependence. If men and women who are leading rich inner lives cannot or will not respond to events and situations that require them to do so — such as cases of injustice, oppression, and environmental degradation — then that scenario negates religion's potentially prophetic and incisive contribution of encouraging an enlightened global community. An attitude of "business as usual" simply reveals a bankrupt moral and spiritual authority in the face of grave moral evil, such as exists with Tibet. This is the problem with many of the Christian churches in their relationship with the People's Republic of China.

Perhaps most grave is the failure of the Catholic Church and the Vatican to fulfill their prophetic responsibility. Under the leadership of Pope Pius XII, who reigned from 1939 to 1958, the Church adopted a policy of complete silence regarding the Nazis and the Holocaust. It absented itself from the moral struggle with Hitler's regime when others who accepted the challenge paid the price with their lives. Rome's lack of leadership in this area represents the worst, most inexcusable moral failure in the history of Christianity.[8] Had the Vatican given a vigorous witness against the evils of anti-Semitism and the policies of the Nazis, Hitler's war plans may have been derailed and the Holocaust may never have happened! Weakness at the center of Christendom — extreme papal reti-cence and inaction — only emboldened an already out-of-control Hitler.

Christianity had actually nurtured anti-Semitic sentiments in her bosom since the first century and the break with the Jewish community at the time of the Church of Jerusalem — an especially bitter rupture. Anti-Semitic feelings and occasional attacks on the Jews in the following centuries were the soil in which Hitler's obscene brutalization of the Jews developed. It is critically necessary to understand that the Holocaust did-n't occur in a vacuum. It was conceived in the Church through nearly twenty centuries of hatred for the Jewish people, and in particular by blaming them for the death of Jesus Christ. While the popes since the col-lapse of the Nazi regime, and especially since the Second Vatican Council have systematically and thoroughly dismantled the cultural supports within Christianity for anti-Semitism, the Catholic Church needs to apol-ogize wholeheartedly to the Jewish community, both for its centuries of anti-Semitism and its gross failure to speak out against Hitler and the Holocaust.

Unfortunately, the Vatican is repeating this same mistake with Tibet and her much-oppressed people. It has done the same with East Timor, Haiti, and a number of countries in Latin America, where it has embraced ruthless dictatorships. The same pontiff who presided over Catholicism's conspiracy of silence on the plight of the Jews, Pius XII, was reigning when the Chinese army overran Tibet in 1950. The Vatican's policy on the Tibetan situation has been the same as their policy on the Jews: absolutely no words or action on the oppression. No Vatican official has ever addressed the sufferings of the Tibetan people or what the Chinese have done in Tibet.

Despite the Vatican's silence, various forums of the Catholic Church have made many symbolic gestures of sympathy toward the Tibetans, and have recognized Tibetan Buddhism as a faith tradition. The Dalai Lama and Pope John Paul II have met four times during this pope's long pon-tificate. On his first visit to the Vatican, before the time of John Paul II, the Dalai Lama did have a wonderful exchange with Pope Paul VI, who reigned from 1963 to 1978. The Dalai Lama has told me that he and Pope John Paul II are friends, and that the two of them have a lot in common, particularly the experience of Communist oppression of their people. While he has found the pope personally empathetic, this welcome commiseration has never translated into public expressions of papal support.

I have no doubt the pope is indeed deeply anguished over what the Tibetan people have endured, but I suspect political considerations regarding China have influenced Rome's policy of silence. If this is indeed the case, then it is a cause for profound concern. These political aims, even though they may involve spiritual motives — such as securing the rights for the Church in China, and serving what may be as many as eighty million Chinese Catholics — cannot take priority over the demands of justice the Gospel clearly requires.

In its behavior toward Tibet, the Vatican is following a norm of expedience. It is placing its own interests above those of humankind. To confront the Chinese regime morally, prophetically, and nonviolently would be a powerful service to and example for the nations, religions, and cultures of the world. It would be an impressive instance of applying the moral voice in a desperately needed ongoing situation of horrendous oppression.[9] The failure to respond to this challenge will inevitably affect the credibility of the Vatican's claim to moral leadership of the planet.

History will not ignore Rome's lack of leadership on the Tibetan tragedy, just as it hasn't with the Holocaust. If Rome were truly visionary, it would reevaluate its inaction over such oppression. Not to do so will result in the continuing cycle of simply repeating its mistakes in the future, while paying the cost of reduced relevance to an agonized world. Its credibility is at stake: In these instances, when humanity looks to Rome for courageous leadership, it finds only cautious bureaucrats.

Tibet is a test to measure whether or not the human species has the ability to evolve in its moral consciousness — whether or not it can stretch beyond its present ways of approaching situations of injustice, tyranny, and threats to the ecosphere. If we cannot grow morally, then it becomes difficult to justify our long-term future on this planet. Judging from the timid role the Vatican and other religious institutions have played on the issue of Tibet and other problems, it's not easy to be confident. Institutions are just as much creatures of habit as individuals are, and so, it's risky to predict that the Catholic Church, or any other center of spiritual leadership, will suddenly discover the courage to act differently in the world.

If Rome, or any tradition, were genuinely open and receptive to the transforming power of mystical spirituality, like many Tibetan teachers,

Hindu sages, Christian contemplatives, Sufis, Jewish mystics, and shamans, the impact on humankind would be substantial, far-reaching, and permanent. Spiritual leadership, guided by a deeply alive, universal spirituality is always ready to take a stand when required by the demands of justice. To focus and make concrete this insight and element of a global spirituality, of interspirituality, again Tibet is a test for us all.

Religions, interfaith organizations, nongovernmental organizations, all contemplatively aware persons, and all decent people must stand unambiguously with Tibet in its consistently nonviolent moral struggle with China. We should avail ourselves of the lessons to be learned in endorsing the Dalai Lama's (and so the Tibetan people's) approach, thus identifying with their higher moral ground. Supporting Tibet in this way would educate us in nonviolence, habituating us to this path of peaceful action, while allowing us slowly to emerge with an enhanced identity as the community of religions *because* we have learned and exercised the prophetic function together. We will have learned the importance of the moral voice precisely because we will have exercised it! This is the kind of action required of those who are working toward a universal civilization; such a society can never be based on a silent acquiescence to injustice of any form. An effective and mature spirituality always produces the fortitude necessary to rise to the challenge of the prophetic function in relation to the actions of governments, nations, cultures, religions, and individuals.

The Role of Interfaith Organizations

Interfaith organizations are increasingly becoming forums for the traditions to meet through some of their more enlightened members. Unfortunately, the leadership of these groups have shown the same extreme reticence as the Vatican to speak out on Tibet, East Timor, and many other issues of human rights. The Temple of Understanding in New York City has been a refreshing exception, but both the World Conference on Religion and Peace and the United Religions Organization have fallen short of their potential. No matter how they may try to justify their lack of moral leadership, or prophetic action, no matter how reasonable their objections to such a role, they are diminished by their silence.

One of the most important steps the interfaith organizations can take together is to convoke an international consultation of religious and spiritual leaders with experts on Tibet. With the active participation of the Dalai Lama and his advisors, this group could examine the problem thoroughly in the light of the current situation in China and Tibet, explore options for a resolution of the lingering tragedy, and make recommendations for a unified course of action. The venue for the consultation might be the Vatican itself, and perhaps with the assistance of the Parliament of the World's Religions, or even the Peace Council. Such an event would be a positive development.

An organization inspired by the interfaith vision is currently attempting to raise the profile of Tibet around the world, and particularly among the membership of the various religions. Founded by Ma Jaya Sati Bhagavati and Brahmadas, this group is called the Council for World Tibet Day. World Tibet Day itself happens each year on or around July 6, the Dalai Lama's birthday. This event has the potential to galvanize support for the Tibetans and gradually raise the consciousness of the world toward efforts to finally resolve the Tibetan issue.[10] The Council for World Tibet Day also sponsors the Interfaith Call for Freedom of Worship in Tibet, and their website offers numerous prayers from various traditions and figures that convey the desire that Tibet and its people will be restored to their land, culture, and freedom.

The Interspiritual Age will focus this prophetic function for us as a collective responsibility of the religions, interfaith organizations, nongovernmental organizations, and various other organizations concerned with the planet in its totality. This function will transcend the manipulating influence of political forces and special interest groups, whether these be governments, organizations, religions, or private citizens. It will be uncompromising in its applications and operations. It will always be guided by considerations of spirituality.

The spiritual life in its depth and maturity grants us the gift of prophecy by giving us the wisdom, or perspective we need, and the courage to act. If we cannot speak out and act in the face of challenges then we have no real moral credibility. Others will then step in to fill the void in leadership.

✦ The Fruits or Capacities of the Spiritual Journey

Mature spirituality, in its contemplative or mystical forms, awakens and develops a number of significant gifts. They are universal, and so must be seen as part of interspiritual wisdom. These capacities include: openness, presence, listening, being, seeing, spontaneity, and joy — all elements that help us take compassionate action in the world.

They are regarded as capacities because they make possible our sensitive, compassionate, loving relationship with human beings, other species, the earth as a whole, and the divine itself. These capacities benefit interreligious dialogue and collaboration. And they are essential in the great task of building a new, truly universal global civilization. They are indispensable skills for the work of dialogue, cooperation, peacemaking, and the exercise of the moral voice in prophetic witness and action.

Openness

Openness is a receptivity to everything and everybody. When we are open we become naturally willing to serve those who need us. An English nun, Sister Madeleine Simon, once made this observation to me about openness and its necessity in the spiritual journey: "We are really only ready for Heaven when we are completely open!"

It can be said that the divine itself is openness. The Christian understanding of the Trinity emphasizes the very mystery and archetype of total openness. We must also be open and receptive to God, to boundless awareness, reality, others, nature, the non-human species, the earth, and the cosmos. In this wonderful ability to be open, we can learn a lesson from the flowers, which always incarnate this principle for us. A flower simply opens to the light and warmth of the sun and receives the moisture from the earth and the rain. Nature is full of such lessons, as we shall see in the next chapter.

Presence

The inner journey also grants us the ability to be genuinely *present* to others in all senses. When we are present, we meet them in the eternal now, where everything is continually arising. Through this incomparable gift of presence, we fashion and shape ourselves as a home for the divine within us, a place for ultimate realization of creation and all others. The present moment is thus sacramental because it is filled with the reality of the ultimate, with God, as the Jesuit spiritual writer Jean-Pierre de Caussade reminds us in *Abandonment to Divine Providence*.[11] Presence is also the path of mindfulness that Buddhism (especially

Zen), Hinduism, and all the other spiritual traditions recommend in some form or another.

One sign of enlightenment and spiritual maturity is this ability to be present to others, and to do so without expectation. It is not an easy capacity to acquire. Ordinarily, we follow a policy of personal convenience in our relationships with others. We aren't really present or available to others without some incentive. To surrender to the present moment with an open and trusting heart is a sign of great spiritual progress.

Listening

Deep spirituality also gives us the capacity to listen. The nature of this deep listening is much more subtle and comprehensive than the ordinary mode practiced by most people. It is a complete inner attention, a devout listening with one's whole heart. It does not matter whether we are listening to the divine, to the natural earth, to other people, to members of other species, or to ourselves. Everything is an avenue to the divine. Ultimate reality expresses itself and speaks through all things in each moment. All we have to do is listen.

We all love people who really listen to us. When we find a good listener, we cherish that person. This rare gift tells us something substantial about the inner depth of such a person.

Being

Individuals who are mystically awake also have the ability to just *be*. Indeed they are vitally conscious of the importance of this capacity for simply *being*. We are part of a technological society that stresses doing, and so most of us are always rushing around, involved in numerous activities and tasks. I will always remember Bede Griffiths's reaction to the fast pace of life in the West, particularly in America. He disliked the endless racing around in cars, and ceaseless chatter on phones. He grew to dislike phones intensely, and he's not alone in that sentiment!

Contemplative spirituality is a call to being: to just be who we are in the deepest sense of our nature, our contemplative, mystical being. We all have this dimension of being by virtue of our humanity; everything else we do only adds to what we already are. The ability simply to be is actually the method of contemplation, mysticism, or spirituality itself.

In this, the flower is again our teacher. The flower doesn't do anything; it just is. The flower doesn't read books, answer letters, give speeches, or attend school. It just is. Native Americans and other indigenous peoples, when they are authentically living their unique culture, exemplify this capacity, skill, or talent to just be.

Seeing

Closely associated with the ability to be is the capacity to see: to see reality as it is, to see ourselves as we are without pretense. This *seeing* arises from the depths of spiritual discipline; it is a knowing from the heart.

Mystical seeing, which also depends on self-knowledge, is really the gift of perspective, of being able to see everything in its proper place. It means being able to rise above the pettiness of life and see the larger picture. Perspective, as a fruit of the inner life, allows us to attain real balance in our awareness of everything with which we come in contact.

Many years ago I learned one of the great practical teachings about this attribute from a Carmelite nun, Sister Mary Roman. A Jewish convert to Catholicism, she was a professor of German at Wellesley College when she entered the Catholic Church. Until its closing in 1997, her monastery was in Barre, Vermont. I was in a small monastery in New Boston, New Hampshire, and when I first entered the monastery, I visited Sister Mary. She and I and her community of twelve nuns had become friends over the years, and from time to time I would drop in on them. I asked her if she had any advice for me, as I was embarking on monastic life. I have never forgotten her incredibly wise words: "There is only one thing I would suggest, and it is this. Keep a sense of proportion. Don't overreact. See things in perspective. You will come to realize that very few things in life are worth getting disturbed over. If you maintain a sense of perspective, you will grow in wisdom, depth, and holiness of life."

In this observation, Sister Mary Roman was following the counsel of her guide, St. Teresa of Avila who possessed profound perspective. In virtually every convent, monastery, and parish of the Catholic tradition — something all nuns, brothers, bishops, and priests have on holy cards — is this bit of compelling and useful advice: "Let nothing disturb you. Let nothing worry you. Everything is passing away. Only God is changeless. God alone suffices."

This insight isn't only true of life in the cloister; it is just as true in our busy lives. Sister Mary Roman's advice to me, reinforced by the counsel of St. Teresa, has proven to be a powerful and enduring teaching both in my spiritual life and my day-to-day life, from dealing with misunderstandings or slights to remaining calm in socially tense situations to maintaining patience in traffic. Her words have guided me through serious as well as trivial matters. It is the small things that often cause the most trouble because of our tendency to overreact instead of letting things go in silence.

Spontaneity

As it matures, the inner mystical life also awakens in us the possibility for real *spontaneity* in our actions and responses to others. This spontaneity inspires us to acts of kindness, mercy, compassion, love, charity, patience, and gentleness. Spontaneity again highlights an other-centered focus, often to a heroic degree of selflessness; it is a very significant part of the social dimension of spirituality. Spontaneity allows one to smile generously and effortlessly when meeting perfect strangers, to buy a meal for the homeless, to express simple joy when it's unexpected.

Joy

The crown of all these capacities is a unitive *joy*. Joy is an unmistakable sign of the deeper life. It comes as an abiding gift when an individual has reached union with the divine. Joy is the presence of God in us or the completion of our goal in the earthly pilgrimage. This inner bliss that saturates our being, life, thoughts, actions and relationships, is an expression of spiritual plenitude, the fullness of the inner journey. It nearly always manifests itself in a contagious sense of humor (which, as I said earlier, I am convinced is the *seventh* sense!). The celebrated image of the laughing Buddha expresses this quality of joy, and I have experienced it hundreds of times in so many people whose inner capacity of depth expressed itself in an extraordinary external capacity for happiness.

Profound Peace

This joy, and all the other fruits of the inner experience, culminate in a mystical, supernatural, or nontemporal peace. It is the peace that is the possession of the divine, the peace that rests in the absolute.

The Fruits of Spirituality Work Together

One of the most striking truths of a mature, more complete spirituality, as it is incarnated in lives from all the traditions, is that such persons not only have all these elements in common, but these spiritual factors all work together in the inner life in each of these individuals. If they have humility of heart, they will also express selflessness with others and themselves; they will be naturally committed to deep nonviolence, and will have a profound inner sense of their interconnectedness with the cosmos. All their qualities, virtues, and capacities are directly related to their spiritual practice and always involve intense self-knowledge, which is grounded in humility and simplicity of heart.

Those who are selfless, humble, simple, nonviolent, and other-centered in attitude, motivation, and action are also open, present, listening, rooted in being, real in the view of others, and are spontaneous, joyful, and profoundly peaceful. These inner attributes all work together in the transformation of the person. Ultimately, they are more important than our mystical knowledge because they concern what we are, and who we have become, in the light of our potential to be.

PART III

THE MYSTICISM
OF THE
NATURAL WORLD

Chapter 8

NATURAL MYSTICISM: READING THE BOOK OF CREATION

*To sit with the eagles and their flute-like songs, listening to the longer
flute of wind sweep through lush grasslands, is to begin to know the
natural laws that exist apart from our own written ones.*
— Linda Hogan

Nature is herself a divine revelation with its own...mode of prayer....
— Seyyed Hossein Nasr

I trace my awareness of the universe, its existence for me, to an experience I had on a starry night in the early 1950s, when I was five years
old. We were living in Windsor, Connecticut, a small town just north of
Hartford. This was a quiet, semi-rural, pastoral setting with beautiful
farms dotting the landscape. One evening after dinner, as twilight was
approaching, I wandered out into the back yard. It was a lovely spring
evening, with the scent of flowers floating in the night air, the silence
pierced by a solitary owl and a few other nocturnal denizens. Lying back
on the earth, I looked up and beheld the starry heavens for the first time.
As I looked in rapt attention, I was overcome by a feeling of total awe and
utter amazement. I lay there for several minutes, completely absorbed in
a kind of natural contemplation, wondering, "Where did all this come
from? What is it?" Almost immediately, an answer arose from within me
— not as an audible voice, but as an inner, intuitive conviction, what mystics refer to as an *audition* that emanates from God or angelic beings. It
said to me: "Some day you will know!"

My first encounter with the cosmos was mysterious, magical, numinous
— a sacred experience. Shortly after that youthful "cosmic awakening," I

knew that I wanted to be a priest. Priesthood was my only understanding of the spiritual life at that tender age, an image I latched on to in order to express my desire to live a holy life.

We don't all need to become priests in order to cultivate our mystical heart! Most of us can probably point to such moments in the inner geography of our development, moments in which the universe, the earth, or the natural world have communicated to us something of their numinous quality. Such experiences are common; everyone has them sooner or later, whether they realize it or not. They are essentially perceptions of natural mysticism, or nature mysticism.

Natural mysticism is the way of primordial revelation. It unfolds and makes clear the whole realm of the natural world, the mystery of life in all its attributes, and the universe in its entirety. This revelation is ongoing, perennial, and always available to each one of us, in every culture, in every time, in any moment of our lives. It is thus the first and permanent source of revelation.

The Interspiritual Age is witnessing a new flowering of natural mysticism and natural contemplation. It welcomes natural mysticism's role in a universal understanding of mysticism itself. It realizes that natural mysticism is an important part of spirituality, and that spirituality — indeed, interspirituality — would be incomplete without the inclusion of the mystical wisdom that comes to us through the natural world and the cosmos. Natural mysticism thus has to be a part of every person's formation in spiritual consciousness. It cannot be ignored or left out.

✦ What Is Natural Mysticism?

The term *natural mysticism* expresses the perception and awareness of the numinous reality of the source in, surrounding, and emanating from nature and the cosmos. Everything in this domain is an occasion for the revelation of the divine. This immanent presence pervades the whole of reality in what we can see, feel, touch, smell, and hear, what we can intuit and inhale. Cosmic mysticism is the experience of the divine immanence, the *isness* of the omnipresent, eternal spirit in all things, and all things in it.

Natural mysticism is also the realization and tangible experience of unity. We perceive that we are one with everything on the earth, in the universe, and, with ultimate reality. We are not separate.

Natural mysticism can also be expressed through an encounter with mystery in the natural world that reveals our capacity for mutual understanding between ourselves and other species. For example, an owl brushes up beside you as you sit on a hill in the wilderness, and you are introduced into a mystic knowing. You see the wind stirring the trees like hands playing a harp, and you perceive something of the divine presence. When we are caught up in the breathless immensity of a sunrise or sunset, are we not given a glimpse of a hidden revelation? Each of these instances can occasion awe, wonder, joy — an intense delight in our connection with something infinitely greater than ourselves.

Natural mysticism, like all other forms of mysticism, involves the whole person. It grants us these perceptions and experiences with an overpowering certitude, an unshakable knowledge that is the fruit of the direct experience itself. Such deep encounters absorb us in the vividness, intensity, and numinous character of natural mysticism. Such moments clearly reveal our inherent connection to and relationship with nature, earth, the cosmos, and the divine.

Natural mysticism uncovers this family identity among all these levels of reality. We see the intimate spiritual resemblance among these areas of experience and consciousness, an inner connection and bond between and among all things: the true nature of reality as *interconnectedness*.

The apprehension of belonging that is implicit in such an intense experience of unity, the awareness of the presence saturating ourselves and everything else, and our perception of ourselves and all things in this presence — this is an important step in understanding our relationship with divine reality. This perennial rung on the ladder of the mystical journey is indispensable to a more complete understanding of this inner process.

Nature Mysticism Is Continual Cosmic Revelation

Natural mysticism is a cosmic revelation of the true face of the natural world. The universe, the earth, and the natural world, as well as all the other species with us, are the chief actors in the spiritual journey. The natural world is the platform on which we make the spiritual journey, and is basically a sacramental system, one in which natural contemplation, an ability that is inborn in us — perhaps in all beings —

awakens and nourishes us in our inner lives as we travel ever toward total relationship with or realization of the source.

Natural mysticism has always made the cosmic revelation known to the human sphere from the dawn of our consciousness. Long before any of the historical religions existed, long before writing and tradition, the divine reality communicated its light to us through all that is. Every ancient and medieval culture has known this truth in some form; it is part of the primordial tradition, the perennial philosophy, the universal wisdom that underpins the old cultures with their different religions.[1]

The recognition of the divine presence encompassing everything, present in all beings, all things that are, is the cosmic revelation.[2] It is the perception of the hidden power of the divine in all aspects of creation. It is, as Bede Griffiths observes, "the revelation of ultimate Truth, given to all mankind through the Cosmos, that is, through the creation."[3] It is similar to the all-pervading Tao in the Chinese tradition, God in the Western religions, the Great Spirit of the Native Americans, and to the eternal Brahman in Hinduism.

The Brahman and the Atman

One of the most compelling and fascinating examples of cosmic mysticism is found in the eternal religion of India. India discovered — or her sages were discovered by — the divine presence everywhere and in everything. This divine presence in which the cosmos, the earth, nature, the human, other species exist, which holds everything and is also the ground of own awareness, is the eternal Brahman. The inner spark of this existing mind in consciousness is the Atman, the eternal self. The cosmic revelation came full circle in the Vedic tradition because it realized experientially that the Brahman was also present more intimately in the Atman.

The Brahman and the Atman are the transcendent and the immanent, the outer and the inner. The mystery of the outer and the inner is that they have the same ground of identity: they are the same. It is this recognition that is the genius of India's discovery and formulation of the cosmic revelation.

The Cave of the Heart

Ancient humankind experienced the hidden divine power in everything: in the depths of interiority as well as in the cosmos, in the earth, and in nature. It discerned the presence behind all natural phenomena and consciousness. It understood that the human, the universe, and all beings were part of a cosmic unity that subsisted in the divine consciousness.

It is important to grasp this further subtlety of the cosmic revelation in its upanishadic form, the revelation of the divine in the depths of the heart, the guha. The same divine reality that holds the universe within itself also dwells in our hearts, in the deepest part of our subjectivity, in the very act of our arising to awareness within us. The divine presence immanent in the whole universe, in the natural world, in life and being, also inhabits the depths of our inner life.

Bede Griffiths conveys this insight through the image of Shiva Nataraja, the Dancing Shiva, the god who is the Lord of creation and destruction:

> He is represented with four arms dancing in a circle of fire, dancing at the heart of creation. It is a cosmic dance; it represents the power which permeates the whole universe. The idea is that God is dancing in the heart of creation and in every human heart. We must find the Lord who is dancing in our hearts; then we will see the Lord dancing in all of creation.[4]

The Dancing Shiva is a compelling symbol of the twofold direction of the cosmic revelation: *without,* in the vastness of the universe and nature, and within, in the infinite spaces of the heart. This is another example of India's gift to the world, to interspirituality. This is the core vision of the ancient Hindu world, and the external vision of the source present throughout the cosmos on all levels is the collective experience of humankind before the rise of modern civilization.[5]

Rta: Divine Order

The Vedic understanding of the cosmic revelation, its mystical apprehension of the divine reality in the universe, emphasizes the existence of an all-embracing divine order, harmony, and activity. The name for this universal order, harmony and activity is *rta.*[6]

Rta is the source of the purpose, design, and beauty evident in everything. It accounts for why things work as they do. It is the intrinsic natural law of all creation. In the sphere of human life, rta is the moral law that is in continuity with and expressive of cosmic order and harmony, the universal law. Rta is a profoundly rich and nuanced concept that derives from an experiential wisdom in the domain of cosmic revelation, or natural mysticism.

The Three Worlds

The Vedic revelation, which is also the cosmic revelation, viewed reality as having three distinct but interrelated levels. All reality was characterized by this threefold understanding, the so-called doctrine of the three worlds, an understanding of the nature of being and reality found in all the ancient cultures. This tripartite view represents the original metaphysics of the old civilizations, and lives on in the perennial tradition. Bede Griffiths comments on the Vedic understanding of the three worlds:

> The Vedic seers had reached an understanding of the threefold nature of the world, at once physical, psychological, and spiritual. These three worlds were seen to be interdependent, every physical reality having a psychological aspect, and both aspects, physical and psychological, being integrated in a spiritual vision. The cows and horses of the Vedas were not merely cows and horses, they were also cows and horses of the mind, that is, psychological forces, and beyond that they were symbols of the cosmic powers, manifestations of the Supreme Spirit.7

The Cosmic Revelation in the West

The cosmic revelation, the first one in our history or prehistory, is even mentioned in the biblical tradition as preceding the whole experience of Israel and the Western notion of revelation as a historical process of God disclosing himself to the human community through various encounters with patriarchs, prophets, and saints.

The Book of Wisdom gives a strong indication of this primordial cosmic revelation: "From the greatness and beauty of created things comes a corresponding perception of their Creator."8 The divine reality is perceived as the source of creation, its power, grandeur, and glory.

Similarly, in St. Paul's Letter to the Romans, we hear an echo of this earlier teaching. Paul no doubt drew inspiration from it when he declared: "Ever since the creation of the world his [God's] invisible nature, namely, his eternal power and deity, has been clearly perceived in the things that have been made."9 These two passages suggest a knowledge of the first or cosmic revelation, but it is obscure, lost in the mists of pre-history before the emergence of biblical revelation.

✦ Readers of the Book of Nature

Many mystical writers and saints throughout human experience have been nature mystics as well as fully formed contemplatives. I call these men and women "readers of the book of nature," because of their capacity to understand and benefit from the whole symbolic order of the cosmos.

Francis of Assisi

St. Francis of Assisi, the thirteenth-century friar, was a celebrated nature mystic. He exhibited total openness to and solidarity with the natural world and all the creatures who inhabit it. In this, his spirituality was similar to that of the Native Americans. He accepted all beings as brothers and sisters, and treated them with love and respect.

Francis was famous for his ability to communicate with birds and animals, and even with fish. He reached out to them on all occasions, and felt a deep connection with them in God. All creatures were instantly attracted to him because his ego never obstructed the flow of relating. Birds would allow the saint to hold them, and he would counsel them in the ways of the divine. Wolves (like the holy wolf of Gubio, whom he tamed) and other wild animals would listen to his admonishments.

Francis's cosmic mysticism was based on his relationship with God, his immense joy, and his deep perception of the unity and interconnection of all living beings, including flowers, trees, mountains, winds, water, air, and sun. He sang of his cosmic mystical intuitions in his lyrical prayer, "The Canticle of Brother Sun."

In loving the creation and all beings in it, Francis was also loving God, and he was loving all these beings in God. He experienced the divine in everything, and everything in the divine. Francis' mysticism was panentheistic because his was a vision of the totality in God.

At the same time, he was such a completely God-centered mystic that he held a strict distinction between the infinite reality, love, and mercy of God, and the imperfections and limitations of the human. He was perhaps the greatest saint in the history of the world, and he was certainly one of the most profound mystic sages. For all ages to come he will inspire others to the heights of divine life, and the ever-flowing current of God's love circulating in the creation and in all things.

Bede Griffiths

All nature mystics seem to have this Franciscan quality of sensitivity to the cosmos. Bede Griffiths is a good example. His own spiritual journey really began in nature mysticism.

Bede Griffiths was a youthful agnostic, a brilliant intellectual who lived much in his mind in the earlier part of his life. As a youth he attended Christ's Hospital, a public school established for children of the British working class. In his autobiography, *The Golden String*, Bede relates how he went for a walk on the last day of school before his departure. As the dusk was quickly approaching, he heard the birds singing differently than usual — or rather, he heard them for the first time. This simple experience granted him a sense of the divine's presence in the natural world and radically altered the course of his life. He tells us:

> Now I was suddenly made aware of another world of beauty and mystery such as I had never imagined to exist, except in poetry...I experienced an overwhelming emotion in the presence of nature, especially at evening. It began to wear a kind of sacramental character for me. I approached it with a sense of almost religious awe, and in the hush which comes before sunset, I felt again the presence of an unfathomable mystery. The song of the birds, the shapes of the trees, the colors of the sunset, were so many signs of this presence, which seemed to be drawing me to itself.[10]

From then on, everywhere he went or looked in the country he discovered the presence:

> I liked the silence of the woods and the hills. I felt there the sense of a Presence, something undefined and mysterious, which was reflected in the faces of the flowers and the movements of the birds and animals, in the sunlight falling through the leaves and in the sound of running water, in the wind blowing on the hills and the wide expanse of earth and sky."[11]

His natural mysticism positioned him spiritually and intellectually to understand the cosmic revelation in the Indian and other traditions. This whole spiritual dimension affected the direction and quality of his search

as he set out for India to seek the "other half " of his soul. Bede's mystical perceptions have made an important contribution to our understanding of mysticism in general, and nature mysticism in particular.

William Wordsworth

Bede turned to the Romantic poets to understand, interpret, and
express his natural mysticism, particularly to William Wordsworth, one
of the greatest. Wordsworth, who lived from 1770 to 1850, was preemi-
nently a nature mystic. He followed the religion of nature, and had little
use for organized, institutional religious life. He was in touch with something more primary, more immediate as the source of an inner faith:
nature itself. The natural world, in his daily encounters with it, evoked
intense religious awe. It inspired his deep and broad insight about life
and the divine reality that lives in his verse.

One of the most fascinating insights of this remarkable poet is the
natural revelation of the divine that surrounds us in childhood, which
every child breathes in and is surrounded by all the time, and *knows* without knowing. Natural mysticism is the environment of childhood; it is
what nurtures us. The child is exposed to the cosmic revelation from
birth and infancy. This is the child's world, a world that has a fresh, magical, numinous quality. For Wordsworth, children are born as nature mystics. They approach the divine, and are approached and enveloped by the
divine reality, through the natural world. It is the medium through which
they experience and process their religious experiences; it is their teacher,
friend, and constant companion, the source of wisdom, value, and enthusiasm. They see all of life through this timeless mother before everything
is *interpreted* for them in the categories of others.

In his ecstatic ode "Intimations of Immortality from Recollections of
Early Childhood," Wordsworth gives form to his natural mysticism and
his theology of childhood as the time when God reveals himself to the
child in and through the natural world.[12] In this poem he unfolds the natural spirituality of childhood. God is the "object" of this mystical experience, and childhood is the process of a natural contemplation that is
nourished and formed by the divine. The poet exalts in the knowledge
that we have come from God "trailing clouds of glory" and we will return
to him. He alludes to how we have been here before, and so, to the soul's
pre-existence, to how our "birth is but a sleep and a forgetting." Each

child is "Nature's priest," celebrating the cosmic liturgy. He describes how the whole of nature and all the creatures are involved and respond. He remarks on the incredible joys of children in their natural state united as they are with God without comprehending. Their task is to luxuriate in the light of the divine presence. The immediacy of nature is their consciousness and atmosphere, the school in which their inner formation occurs. The spirituality of this ode is summed up eloquently in the first and last stanzas:

> There was a time when meadow, grove, and stream,
> The earth, and every common sight,
> To me did seem
> Apparelled in celestial light,
> The glory and the freshness of a dream. . . .
> To me the meanest flower that blows can give
> Thoughts that do often lie too deep for tears.[13]

The American Transcendentalists

The American Transcendentalists Ralph Waldo Emerson, Henry David Thoreau, Margaret Fuller, Bronson Alcott, Theodore Parker, Emily Dickinson, and to some extent, Walt Whitman, are examples of nature mystics in American culture. They possessed a penetrating understanding of the relationship between God and human identity in the context of the natural world. Like Wordsworth before them, they were extraordinary visionaries on the fringe of society, although prominent and influential in their day.

The transcendentalists were deeply interested in Hindu mysticism, or the Vedanta, and were greatly influenced by its views of the absolute, especially as developed in the Brahman-Atman identity. Their mysticism was very close to the type formulated in the cosmic revelation, for they experienced the divine reality both as encompassing nature, the cosmos, and all beings, but also as present in the soul, or self. In knowing the divine, intuition provides the methodology of discovery, and it is more reliable than any merely external authority. It is through the intuitive capacity of each one of us that God is directly and immediately accessible to us.

The transcendentalists felt the presence of God in their intuition, but they advised that intuition should be guided by reason, and not follow its own course unaided. They discerned that God speaks directly to the self within us. They stressed the value and importance of personal mystical experience over beliefs, doctrines, rituals, and institutions. All their insights derived from their inner life. Their movement was a reaffirmation of the inner way of introversion or interiority.

Emerson experienced the presence of the divine in all things. He perceived the presence in his own being, and with God, in his own way: in the divine's own awakening to itself eternally, and in the entire universe as well. He knew himself to be one with all creation. Emerson describes his awareness when his ego was suspended.

> Standing on the bare ground, my head bathed by the blithe air, and uplifted into infinite space — all mean egotism vanishes. I become a transparent eyeball. I am nothing. I see all. The currents of the Universal Being circulate through me. I am part or [(a)] particle of God.[14]

Emerson's experience is panentheistic and formless, formless because he is taken out of himself in utter illuminative consciousness beyond this world and its limitations. He becomes a "transparent eyeball" because the eye of wisdom and intuition is open.

Forrest Reid

Natural mysticism is more than the perception of the divine in the natural world. It is more than the revelation of the numinous mystery in the cosmos. It is greater than the sense of unity with creation and all beings. It is more than the simple knowledge of the interconnectedness of everything in the web of existence. Although it includes all of these, and many more factors besides, it takes the mystic to the depths and foundation of reality. Natural mysticism has an inner dimension of consciousness itself. Some nature mystics acquire this realization through intense inner experience. A good example of this inner awareness is found in a novel by Forrest Reid, a British writer at the beginning of the twentieth century. In his novel *Following Darkness,* Reid records what is presumably his own experience:

> It was as if I had never realized how lovely the world was. I lay down on my back in the warm, dry moss and listened to the skylark singing as it mounted up from the fields near the sea into the dark clear sky. No other music gave me the same pleasure as that passionate joyous

singing. It was a kind of leaping, exultant ecstasy, a bright, flame-like sound, rejoicing in itself. And then a curious experience befell me. It was as if everything that had seemed to be external and around me were suddenly within me. The whole world seemed to be within me. It was within me that the trees waved their green branches; it was within me that the skylark was singing; it was within me that the hot sun shone, and that the shade was cool. A cloud rose in the sky, and passed in a light shower that pattered on the leaves, and I felt its freshness dropping into my soul, and I felt in all my being the delicious fragrance of the earth and the grass and the plants and the rich brown soil. I could have sobbed for joy.[15]

These experiences, and the states of consciousness they access, are not as rare as might be expected; they are far more common, and are part of the normal development of nondual mystical consciousness. Forrest Reid's description is a unitive experience in the midst of nature, an advaitic container with surrounding nature as the content. It emphasizes the unity of the person with the natural world but the locus of this unitive perception — its direction, if you will — is *within*. This *within* the self, or person, means that it is happening in consciousness, that all reality is mind-dependent. This form of a natural mystical state, its dominant characteristic, points to the primacy of the *within*, or of consciousness itself. The dualism of the inner and outer breaks down under this intense immediacy of perception. An identity with consciousness itself surfaces and one simply knows everything in the range of perception as *within*.

Indigenous Wisdom

All indigenous cultures are based on natural mysticism. This is true of Aborigines in Australia, the Maori of New Zealand, the Chewong of Malaysia, the Desana of the Northwestern Amazon, the San Bushmen of Africa, and all the Native American nations. Nature is the mothering matrix of their life and well-being. They are self-consciously part of the natural world, and not separated like the so-called historical civilizations.

Indigenous wisdom is based on the experiential understanding of an inherent integrity to creation, and the human is part of that natural unity. This realization is awakened in indigenous people from birth. They grow up with a deep sense of their connection with the natural world, all other creatures, and the cosmos. All of nature is friend and relative. To be a friend and a relative connotes a universal family of nature that is tied together by internal relations expressing an intimacy of identity and source. These societies experience and view the world as part of themselves, and they a part of it. They do not regard themselves as superior, or in any way opposed, to nature, but see themselves as in essential harmony with all that is. Nature as family, friend, teacher, sustainer, and lawgiver is always present as their constant support.

The relationship of indigenous peoples to the earth is mystical — the basis of their culture, life, and spirituality. They hold special places sacred because divine-human encounters occurred in them. They don't limit the sacred to a church, synagogue, mosque, or temple because they know that the divine spirit cannot be contained in any building, no matter how sublime the edifice may seem to us. The earth itself is their church; the vast, open sky is its ceiling. For example, native Australians often prefer to sleep outdoors. They use their houses simply to store their possessions. Similarly, through countless millennia of natural mystical experience, they and other indigenous peoples have understood that they cannot own the land. They can dwell on it, but no one can actually own it.

Native people exhibit a strong bond with the ancestors, with the great spirit, and the other spirits who are like angelic beings. Native peoples have a subtle relationship with these beings, and their connection with them is important. They seek contact with them at certain junctures in life, particularly the transition from adolescence to manhood, when in some cultures the vision quest becomes a vehicle for this rite of passage. The Dakota Indians have a beautiful prayer that is recited before a boy departs on his vision quest. This prayer concerns the inner realization of our oneness with all things, and is a powerful expression of Native American nature mysticism. It is meant to guide him on his vision quest:

> O Wakan Tanka, grant that this young man may have relatives; that he may be one with the four winds, the four Powers of the world, and with the light of the dawn. May he understand his relationship with all the winged peoples of the air.... O Grandmother and Mother (earth)... this young man wishes to become one with all things.... For the good of all your peoples, help him![16]

The prayer, addressed to *Wakan Tanka,* the *Great Mystery,* the *Sacred Presence,* asks that he "may have relatives," that he may see his inner connectedness with animals and birds, and so be accepted by them as a close relative, and also that he will be given spirit guides from among these animals and birds. The word *Wakan* implies power, holiness, and spiritual reality, and yet it evokes primarily the quality of the sacred itself. Petaga Yuha Mani, a Sioux medicine man, whose name means "He Who Walks with Coals of Fire," reflects on the nature of *Wakan Tanka* and his relationship with creation, the natural world, and us:

> Life is like a huge design. Each part of the design is made up of the happenings, acts, and interactions of people with each other and the world. You must know that this design is completed by the intervention of Wakan Tanka. People and this world and all that is in it are only a part of Wakan Tanka....Wakan Tanka is all that is wondrous, awesome, powerful, and infinite, and yet he is also personal, compassionate, loving and tender. Perhaps this is why we call him Great Mystery.[17]

Native Americans and other indigenous persons who have not been completely absorbed into the surrounding technological society and corrupted by it, have a special relationship with other species. This fact is well attested to by both specialists and casual observers. Birds and animals often don't seem to fear these individuals as they do people of modern urban culture. Our relationship with the other species, with the exception of our pets, is strained. These other beings have learned from much experience that they have a lot to fear from us. Similar to Francis of Assisi, Native people often have a wonderful capacity to relate to animals and birds. They feel the pull of a mutual attraction, a mutual respect and curiosity.

Animal Spirit Guides

Animal and spirit guides — and some animals are spirit guides — present wise direction in moments of decision. Native Americans know that all beings are part of the web of life, and we have responsibilities to this great web of interconnection. Native cultures are keenly aware that nature, the earth, the Great Spirit, and the spirit guides have taught them everything they know. It is all a gift from the divine realm through the mediation of these more familiar spirit guides who inhabit all worlds.

The mysterious, numinous reality of nature can break in suddenly upon us when we least expect it. We are always surrounded by the natural world even when we are unaware of it, and so shouldn't be surprised when something extraordinary happens. Let me share an example from my own experience:

On a particularly windy autumn day in Chicago, I was waiting for a bus on my way to a class in comparative religion I was teaching at Columbia College. As I stood at the bus stop on the corner of Hyde Park Blvd. and 53rd Street, engrossed in thought, a falcon suddenly literally fell from the sky and landed in the middle of the street about ten feet from where I was standing. Startled and amazed, I was drawn into a state of wonder and bewilderment.

The falcon seemed to be hurt. It lay completely still and appeared to be in a state of shock (and perhaps a little embarrassment — this sort of thing isn't supposed to happen to such a regal bird). There are a lot of falcons in Chicago, and they prey on the city's ubiquitous pigeons. This falcon had probably been sitting on a ledge above the street, and a gust of the wind blew it to the ground before it had a chance to react. I was concerned for the poor creature because it was lying right under the traffic light in the middle of a busy thoroughfare.

Without thinking, I immediately walked over to the bird; knelt down, and examined its condition. The first thing I noticed was how incredibly beautiful the falcon was, and how utterly clean. It was large, cocoa-brown and white. It was dazed but very alert. The bird wasn't especially apprehensive, but it watched me with complete attention. Realizing how sharp a falcon's beak and talons must be, I was cautious.

Time stood still. I knelt there over this noble being for what seemed an eternity. Without uttering a word, I communicated to it not to be afraid, and it wasn't. The creature clearly knew that there was nothing to fear from me. At least ten minutes passed, and I was wondering if any serious damage had occurred from the fall. During this entire time the bird never moved; it's eyes were riveted to mine. Gradually, the falcon became more relaxed. And then, just as suddenly as it came, it flew off. Curiously, no cars came our way during this mysterious meeting.

Most Americans would say that a falcon had fallen off a ledge, recovered, and flown off. Native Americans would say that this mysterious encounter was actually a meeting with my spirit guide in the form of the falcon, that this bird is my spirit guide. Such encounters are common in the experience of Indians and other indigenous peoples, and their sacred literatures are filled with such examples.

Indigenous peoples, at least those who still live at least somewhat traditionally, seem to be master contemplatives in the sphere of the natural world. They understand its laws, its values, and its mysteries, and they respect these with earnest commitment. They are able to perceive things that most Westerners cannot, and they are capable of genuine communication with other species.

The basis of their natural contemplation and their ability to communicate with the animals, birds, and fish, is their immense openness to the earth and all other beings. Birds and animals are their companions. In the Native American vision there is no rupture in the relationship with our brothers and sisters among other species. The original unity and relationship is intact, and it is a daily experience for these remarkable people. Their understanding of the natural world and the other species stretches back perhaps fifty thousand years.

Natural mysticism is really the Native American religion, but it is not religion in the usual sense. It is a living, day-to-day spiritual reality they have led for countless millennia. Indigenous peoples living out their natural mysticism perceive the world differently from the wider culture that surrounds them. They have a direct awareness of the divine in the immanence of nature, in other beings, and in their own community existence. Theirs is an incarnational spirituality, an inner life bound up with the external reality of manifested being and the created order. Native Americans, whether they realize it or not, have a sacramental vision of the natural world around them, and they are intimate participants in this sacramental system of cosmic mysticism. It is this awareness of the sacred permeating everything that has saved them and their precious culture from the barbaric onslaught of European civilization. The world must incorporate their natural spirituality as an important dimension of a universal, interspiritual mysticism.

Natural Mysticism in the Art of Nicholas Roerich

Nicholas Roerich, who lived from 1873 to 1947, is one of those rare artistic visionaries who comes along once a millennium to awaken humanity to a new level of consciousness through art, writing, and inspiring example.[18] Roerich was a wide-ranging genius, and his art is intentionally meant to communicate a sense of the divine presence through the human encounter with ultimate beauty in the cosmos.

Roerich felt this presence in everything. He understood the sacral character of the natural environment, and also saw nature as always expressing the reality of the divine. In more than seven thousand paintings, he portrayed his inner assimilation of the spirituality of nature and related it to the mystical journey in the world's religions. He lived in several cultures around the planet, including Russia, Europe, America, Tibet, and India, and his art evolved into a universal expression of the spiritual life, especially as it is enhanced in and through the natural world. Like the Chinese painters of the classical period, inspired by Taoist nature mysticism, the Japanese artists influenced by their fellow craftsmen in China, and the English and American landscape painters of the nineteenth century, Roerich was impassioned by the cosmic revelation present in the natural world.

This fascinating Russian artist of Swedish descent had a mystical relationship with the land, particularly with mountains. He painted a whole series of landscapes depicting the Himalayas in various times of the year, and at different points of his life. For Roerich, as for so many mystics, mountains are associated with ascent to the ultimate mystery. They are identified with the solitary quest of the sage in prolonged meditation, a theme found in a number of Roerich's paintings, notably, "Krishna — Spring in Kulu" and in "Milarepa." This ascent passes through the extraordinary beauty of these peaks. They naturally pull the viewer into intense and prolonged contemplation of their immensity, mystery, structure, light, and colors.

"Krishna — Spring in Kulu" by Nicholas Roerich (Courtesy of The Roerich Museum, New York)

"Milarepa" by Nicholas Roerich (Courtesy of The Roerich Museum, New York)

"Pink Mountains" reveals a vast space in the Himalayan sphere above the clouds. The scene is depicted from the vantage point of one mountain height looking to higher ranges separated by a valley below the clouds. The clouds themselves suggest a misty sea. Off in the distance at a greater height, radiant hues light up the distant peaks, casting them in shades of lavender, purple, and pink. In "The Great Spirit of the Himalayas," Roerich renders the silhouette of a face carved in the stone of a mountain pass. It is a face in deep contemplation, blissful but resting in transcendent peace. This is the Spirit of the Himalayas, the mystical, meditative culture of Tibet.

In "Treasure of the World — Chinta Mani," Roerich depicts the Tibetan legend of the horse Chinta Mani descending from the mountains, amidst the lower rocks, carrying the treasure of sacred fire on his back as he humbly and cautiously negotiates each step. The sacred fire is a symbol of illumination; it is in the same line of tradition as Agni Yoga, the yoga of divine fire, inner realization. Chinta Mani, the legend has it, appears in an age of darkness, when humankind is in great extremity, and evil is rampant. The sagely Chinta Mani brings his incomparable treasure to light the way for the world, to enlighten all those who are receptive to the grace he brings. The transcendent quality of the fire is suggested by a bluish aura. The rocks have strange faces, perhaps conveying a sense of urgency or the forces that are oppressing the world. "Treasure of the World" has a diaphanous feeling to it, and nature is part of this atmosphere.

"Treasure of the World — Chinta Mani" by Nicholas Roerich (Courtesy of The Roerich Museum, New York)

Roerich's paintings are mysterious, almost ethereal. All the scenes he paints are clearly of the real world, yet it is a world transfigured by the mystical. Words or language often constrain consciousness, while great music and art awaken consciousness to new levels of experience and understanding. Roerich's art looks through this world to its source in the eternal. Viewing his works, one enters this reality. It leads one beyond the image to what does not change, to the divine itself. Roerich is always trying to bring us to this realm that transcends this impermanent existence. His art is an attempt to invoke this reality for us, to stir it within the depths of our inner life.

For Roerich, the natural world isn't simply the backdrop for revelation; it is a revelation itself. He is keenly aware of its intrinsic power to move us from within. As Thomas Berry put it in a talk at the Parliament of the World's Religions in Chicago on August 29, 1993: "The outer world (of nature) is needed to activate the inner world, the world of poetry, imagination, and spirituality."[19] It is needed to evoke a sense of the divine. It is, actually, our first encounter with it. The extraordinary beauty and glories of the natural world reveal the utter truth of the spiritual dimension. Nature is revelation, sacrament, and we are just passing through; it has important lessons to teach us on our way.

Each of Roerich's canvases summons us to look more deeply and discover this hidden realm that is just below the surface. Each calls us beyond what we know to the great unknown of the ultimate mystery. Many of his paintings are themselves theophanies; they reveal the sacred, the holy, the divine in its living truth. Roerich saw clearly art's potential as a vehicle in awakening people to the mystical process and the interior transformation of contemplation; in this process of discovery and transformation, the natural world is a great and enduring teacher.

✦ Natural Contemplation As the Capacity to Read the Books of Creation and Life

Although modern science has given us extraordinary understanding, the medieval and ancient cultures often had a more profound relationship with the natural world than modern technological societies. They saw deep meanings, patterns, and connections in nature that elude most contemporary people. C. S. Lewis once observed that the difference between these cultures and the modern world is that while these old civilizations saw meaning in everything, ours has no idea of meaning in nature at all.

Natural contemplation is the ability to perceive or intuit the inherent meaning in all things. It is an intuitive faculty that is activated by nature. It is a sensitivity to the presence of the divine reality and all things in it. This is what Thomas Merton calls natural contemplation, from its Greek roots *theoria physike*. Merton writes: *"Theoria physike* is contemplation of the divine *in nature,* not contemplation of the divine by our natural powers. And in fact 'natural contemplation' in this sense is mystical, that is to say, it is a gift of God, a divine enlightenment."[20]

Nature, being, and human life are pregnant with intrinsic meanings, or natural symbols that, like vehicles, take us to higher realms of meaning.[21] The natural world is honeycombed with these meanings in the form of hidden symbols. The natural contemplative, or the nature mystic is able to make contact with this symbolic dimension in nature, being, and life. All of reality is revelational and partakes in this order of innate symbols that trigger higher states of awareness.

The natural world, the cosmos, and life are often spoken of as the Books of Creation, or Nature, and Life. The Franciscans of the Middle Ages had a wonderful understanding of these levels of perception. St. Bonaventure said that the Book of Creation and the Book of Life are augmented by the Book of Scripture.[22] He elaborates the metaphor of the book in order to express the theophanic, or revelatory dimension of existence.

The three books mutually shed light on one another's meaning. It is clear in the Book of Creation that each being or creature reflects the reality of the divine either as a vestige, as in corporeal nature, or as an image of God.[23] For Bonaventure, as for the Christian tradition generally, an intellectual creature or being is an angelic or human being. To compensate for the limitations and deficiencies of the Book of Creation, the divine has also given us the Book of Scripture. It provides the principles that allow for a fuller understanding of nature's book. But not everyone is able to read the Book of Creation, nor follow the Book of Scripture, so God gives us another book, the Book of Life.[24]

Bonaventure's Book of Life includes the beatific vision, mystical illumination, and the special activity of grace in various spiritual experiences that are granted to certain souls. According to Bonaventure, the Book of Life perfects our knowledge of the mystery revealed in the natural world and in scripture.

The Book of Creation instructs us in a number of metaphysical principles and truths, for instance, that there is a God, that he is the source of the universe and life, that he is wise, all-powerful, and good. Bonaventure also regards the cosmos itself as a stepping-stone to the divine wisdom of contemplation: "For we are so created that the material universe itself is a ladder by which we may ascend to God."[25] The universe is a vast system of symbols, a treatise of spiritual knowledge. Bonaventure recognizes that this symbolic theology allows us to understand the place of sensible things in the scheme of one's spiritual journey. Consonant with the notion of creation as a great book, he also uses the metaphor of the mirror. He sees the entire world of perception as a mirror through which we may pass over to God.[26] Everything is thus a vehicle in our journey to the divine source.

Bonaventure was a follower of St. Francis, and Francis himself once said: "If your heart were pure then all of nature would be to you a Book of Divine Wisdom." The subject of Nicholas Roerich's 1924 painting "The Book of Wisdom" is a Himalayan vastness contemplated by a sagely figure seated before a panorama of mountains. St. Bernard of Clairvaux once said that he learned all the mysteries of the Incarnation (the doctrine of Christ as the Son of God) by watching the trees while working in a garden. The sacred literatures of the world are filled with such examples of this intuitive, contemplative ability to read the Book of Nature and Life.

Seyyed Hossein Nasr has a deep appreciation of natural contemplation and the Books of Creation and Life. In these books, he says, we encounter a revelation of the divine mystery. Referring to the Book of Creation, Nasr says, "The cosmos is a book containing a primordial revelation of utmost significance and man a being whose essential, constitutive elements are reflected upon the cosmic mirror and who possesses a profound inner nexus with the cosmic ambiance around him...."[27] The universe is a theophany, a revelation of God. Nasr maintains: "To see the cosmos as theophany is to see the reflection of one-Self in the cosmos and its forms."[28] This "one-Self" is God. Nasr is aware that the whole cosmos is an elaborate symbol of the divine, an insight he expresses through the metaphor of the book, just like Bonaventure and so many other writers before him. Nasr says: "In traditions based upon a sacred scripture the cosmos also reveals its meaning as a vast book whose pages are replete with the words of the Author..."[29] Here he refers to the cosmic revelation, what every nature mystic knows directly.

Nasr, a Sufi, is one of the few writers of our time who is aware of the cosmic revelation coming through the universe and the natural world. His nature mysticism and natural contemplation are integrated with his fully formed God mysticism and soul mysticism. In natural contemplation's integrity, it is related to all other forms of the mystical life. Nasr comments: "It is only by actually experiencing the perilous journey through the cosmic labyrinth that man is able to gain a vision of that cathedral of celestial beauty which is the divine Presence in its metacosmic splendor."[30] We must pass through the realm of nature and the universe to acquire the awareness of God's presence in its transcendent reality.

✦ A Spirituality of Creation

A creation-centered spirituality, or an ecospirituality, is a contemporary form of natural mysticism that combines the moral issue of the environment with the traditional emphasis of the nature mystic. Thomas Berry in our time is an eloquent spokesperson for the aesthetic and spiritual values of the natural world.

Thomas Berry

Tom Berry calls the aesthetic and spiritual values of the natural world "modes of divine presence" and also the "numinous," a term he borrowed from Rudolf Otto, especially as found in his *The Idea of the Holy*.[31] By the word numinous, Otto is referring to a pre-ethical understanding of the nature of the sacred, a view that emphasizes the divine's ineffability, mystery, awesomeness, and mystical qualities. The numinous expresses the divine or sacred reality as it affects the human realm, but with none of the moral connotations that have been added by organized religion. The numinous is the divine in its utter wildness, free of any human attributions.

The notion of the numinous is an essential category of Berry's thought, and it expresses his brand of natural mysticism. His ecospirituality is really more of a *geo-logy* than a *theo-logy*, and his appropriation of Otto's term gives form to his *geo-logy* as an articulation of the pure immanence of the divine reality. Berry's use of Otto's term lacks the dimension of transcendence, of the great beyond. Each natural being, every wonder in creation reflects in some way the divine reality, making it present. Addressing the dire threats to other species, threats emanating from the human sphere, Berry refers to the immanent presence of the divine in the natural world: "We should be clear about what happens when we destroy modes of divine presence. If we have a wonderful sense of the divine, it is because we live amid such awesome magnificence."[32]

Our sense of the absolute is derived from our experience of creation's splendor, although many schools of mysticism demonstrate the direct intervention of the divine in giving itself in love to the individual. Berry regards natural or cosmic revelation not simply as primordial and perennial but as always primary. He observes how much our understanding of God is based on our experience of the natural world. He feels this mode of experience is being obscured, that we are in danger of losing awareness of this primary source of revelation:

> Because our sense of the divine is so extensively derived from verbal sources, mostly through the biblical scriptures, we seldom notice how extensively we have lost contact with the revelation of the divine in nature. Yet our exalted sense of the divine itself comes from the grandeur of the universe, especially from the earth, in all the splendid modes of its expression. Without such experience we would be terribly

impoverished in our religious and spiritual development, even in our emotional, imaginative, and intellectual development.33

Berry's ecospirituality is firmly underscored by the value of the earth and what he calls the "earth process" — the reality of the planet in all its biodiversity, natural cycles, and environmental situations. His spiritual vision is of the divinity of the earth itself, which he regards as a living organism (as proposed, for instance, in the Gaia hypothesis).34 Berry wants to draw attention to the concrete, existential, theological significance of the planet, not to the earth as a reflection of or springboard to the ultimate mystery. He feels that emphasis on transcendence, the Christian doctrine of the Redemption and even on divine immanence distracts us from the earth's supreme value:

> Even our sense of divine immanence tends to draw us away from the sacred dimension of the earth itself. This is not exactly the divine presence. We go too quickly from the merely physical order of things to the divine presence in things. While this is important, it is also important that we develop a sense of the reality and nobility of the natural world in itself.... The natural world is not simply a usable thing, not an inert mode of being awaiting its destiny to be manipulated by the divine or exploited by the human.35

Berry defends a more subtle understanding and appreciation of the natural world. The earth is the matrix of our life and health, as well as being the medium of all our higher values, aspirations, and dreams. The earth is defended for practical reasons: It is the mother of our higher existence just as much as it is our sustainer in biological terms:

> The natural world is subject as well as object. The natural world is the material source of our being as earthlings and the life-giving nourishment of our physical, emotional, aesthetic, moral, and religious existence. The natural world is the larger sacred community to which we belong. To be alienated from this community is to become destitute in all that makes us human. To damage this community is to diminish our own existence.36

This last statement, which is an ethical appeal identified with our own ultimate self-interest as a species, really brings us to the heart of Berry's project: to save the earth by changing our relationship with it, a change that also affects how we understand ourselves. Part of this change requires that we see ourselves as fundamentally involved with the natural world, as essentially connected to it, as we are emergent, reflective beings who have arisen out of the earth process itself. We are not separate from the cosmos, but in the "eye" of it, for we are its self-consciousness. Berry's anthropic principle asserts that the universe is arranged for the human reality to emerge, to be protected and sustained in being by the universe itself. Berry maintains:

> Creation...must now be experienced as the emergence of the universe as a psychic-spiritual as well as a material-physical-reality from the beginning. We need to see ourselves as integral with this emergent process, as that being in whom the universe reflects on and celebrates itself. 37

The anthropic principle places the human reality at the heart of creation, as the goal of the universe itself. The cosmos aims at human self-consciousness. In Berry's formulation of this view, human self-awareness is the means through which the universe perceives itself, its beauty, splendor, and the endless creativity expressed in its teeming diversity of forms. Berry, however, doesn't consider the human reality to be the final goal of the universe, but simply a noetic function within it. Human self-consciousness in knowing the universe provides a knowledge through self-awareness to the cosmos itself.

Personally, I feel the universe is itself aware, and doesn't need the human or any other intelligence to fulfill this role. Rather, the cosmos shares its intelligence and awareness with *us*. Berry says that we are not the apex of creation, as the Christian doctrine of the Redemption or its understanding of the anthropic principle holds, but a *means* of the universe's contemplation of itself. His is an alternative version of the anthropic principle, unique to him and his emphasis on a spirituality based on ecological necessity, justice, and sensitivity.

Berry feels that humankind must become the servant of the earth's protection, the guardian of a viable earth process. We must redirect the negative trends we have set in motion, for the ecological crisis, out of which Berry's thought has developed, is human-made. It must then be resolved by humanity, as it assumes its new role of protector of the natural world, rather than its persecutor, oppressor, and destroyer.

Berry advocates an eco-based spirituality grounded in the numinous or inner reality of the cosmos. He bases his spirituality, really his brand of nature mysticism, on the monumental fact of the universe-event (the expansion and evolution of the entire cosmos from its primordial origin some eighteen billion years ago), through its development, and the eventual appearance of life. This is what he calls the "new story."[38] The new story is science's new cosmology, with its numinous character exposed. It is a functional cosmology, the new myth meant to give humankind a universal focus, uniting humanity's efforts in saving the earth. This cosmology also includes the human story, but the human venture is subsumed under the great cosmic dance. He sums up the notion of the new story, the universal cosmology, in the graphic terms of cosmic history:

> The story of the universe is the story of the emergence of a galactic system in which each new level of expression emerges through the urgency of self-transcendence. Hydrogen in the presence of some millions of degrees of heat emerges into helium. After the stars take shape as oceans of fire in the heavens, they go through a sequence of transformations. Some eventually explode into the stardust out of which the solar system and the earth take shape. Earth gives unique expression of itself in its rock and crystalline structures and in the variety and splendor of living forms, until humans appear as the moment in which the unfolding universe becomes conscious of itself.... We bear the universe in our being as the universe bears us in its being. The two have a total presence to each other and to that deeper mystery out of which both the universe and ourselves have emerged.[39]

Thomas Berry's natural mysticism, his ecospirituality, is refreshing and eloquent in the panorama of the cosmic drama it encompasses. His work is to place the human sphere in a right relationship with the earth and the natural world. It is vitally important in doing so that the traditional ways of the spiritual journey, as means to inner transformation, be preserved. They are the very tools we require to bring about a radical change in human perspective so that we become genuinely sensitive to, and in harmony with, nature and the cosmos.

Panentheism

Related to Berry's vision of ecospirituality is the principle of panentheism, as promoted by writer and theologian Matthew Fox. Panentheism is an essential principle of creation or ecospirituality, an understanding that stresses the sacramental character of the natural world.

Panentheism, as a sacramental vision of nature, being, and human life, becomes the ultimate ground upon which a naturalistic mysticism is erected. The truth of panentheism — that all is in God — implies not simply nature mysticism, but the cosmic revelation as well, with its reliance on intrinsic symbolism in nature, the cosmos, and life. It becomes the inner truth of both.

This panentheistic approach, the whole experience and notion that all is within the divine, means that it is all happening right *now* in the source's consciousness; it is about the primacy of this consciousness. Panentheism is actually theophanic awareness. All things reveal the divine because all things are in God, in the divine consciousness; they exist in him, and he is likewise in them. Panentheism is the good fortune of knowing the secret of creation, the correct formulation of the relation of creatures to God. All things become open to us in relation to him. Panentheism is simply a capacity to perceive the divine in everything.

✦ The Mystical Experience of Totality

One mystical state of consciousness allows us to see the totality of all that is and all that can be in one instant of time. I deliberately say see rather than know because it is not possible to know everything, but it is possible at least to perceive, in a unifying vision, the sum of all reality, all worlds in all universes. Many mystics have reported this exalted state of consciousness.

The English poet William Blake alludes to this experience when he says we can know "infinity in a grain of sand and eternity in an hour." St. Gregory the Great, in his *Dialogues,* a work on the life of St. Benedict, the father of Western monasticism, reports an experience Benedict had in which he saw "all things gathered up into a ray of light." St. Francis of Assisi had an overpowering experience in which he saw the height, depth, and breadth of the Godhead, another version of the mystical totality. The Buddha is said to have realized the fullness of all knowing. Each of these is an instance of seeing the totality. I mention it here in this section only because it is a special state of awareness that involves creation.

The experience of totality came dramatically to my attention many years ago when I was an undergraduate at St. Anselm College in

Manchester, New Hampshire. In this mystical experience I was drawn beyond myself into a "place" not of this world. I was taken into a transcendent ground where nothing was differentiated; everything was united with the divine one. There was no form or appearance in this realm, no structure, shapes, or colors, no objects of perception — only this vast openness of light, the source itself. I was not aware of myself as separate or distinct from it. I was only aware of the source, but my awareness was confined to a perception of its act of self-identity, that is, I was drawn up out of myself, and was resting in the divine self-identity. It was a triadic act of inner identity in which the divine proceeded into itself, received itself, and was unified by itself. This triadic *unmoving-movement* went on for eternity — for everything of God is in eternity, not in time — but then it reached a point where everything was summed up in an image. The image was of Christ. And from this image, which I interpret to be the Logos, the One through whom creation comes into being: trillions of galaxies, stars, planets, moons, species, people, civilizations, plants, trees, mountains, and oceans. Everything was there.

I saw it all, though I couldn't grasp the details. The mystical state of consciousness of the totality is one in which a person beholds but does not comprehend. It is a glimpse of how God perceives reality. Everything is present to him in one eternal *now*. One of the differences between God and us is that he understands the details — sees the connections, and perceives them all as one in himself. Nothing is or can be separate from him. The experience of the totality happens in the divine consciousness, which we access in a moment of ecstatic union. In such a rare moment of grace one also realizes that everything that one perceives of the totality has meaning, has a place, and exists for a reason. Everything takes its meaning from the source in its holding of the totality in itself. The higher up the cosmic ladder we go, the more integrated and simplified everything becomes as it rests in the one source. The totality and the universe are identified in this eternal moment of their arising in the divine. My experience of the totality was at once part of natural mysticism and the farther reaches of contemplative, ecstatic unitive awareness.

* The Spirituality of Pilgrimage

We also relate to the natural world by visiting sacred sites as pilgrims. Pilgrimage, which usually involves vigorous amounts of walking, climbing, chanting, and praying, is universal, found in every age and culture, even in very secular societies.⁴⁰

Among indigenous peoples — and this is true of pilgrims from many traditions — a pilgrimage is a serious commitment to visit some sacred space in the natural world. It may be a sacred rock, river, or tree, or it may be the Four Sacred Mountains of the American Southwest. Embarking on a pilgrimage puts us in direct relationship with these sacred places, in the midst of the splendors of nature. In those pilgrimage sites are special powers, especially of guidance, associated with the spirit guides and animals of that place.

All the world religions have their holy places, shrines that have special significance in their spiritual history. The Jews have the Holy Land, particularly Jerusalem and Mount Sinai. Moslems have Mecca and Medina. Of course, the Christians also have the Holy Land, while Catholics have Rome and all the shrines dedicated to Mary. The Orthodox have Mount Athos and other important centers. The Hindus have thousands of pilgrimage sites, but two of the most venerable are Varanasi, the holy city on the Ganges, and Gangotri, the source of the Ganges. Buddhists have all the places associated with the life of the Buddha, especially Lumpini in Nepal, where he was born, and Sarnath in Northeastern India, where he gave his famous teaching on the Four Noble Truths in the Deer Park.

The act of taking a pilgrimage, especially when done in a way that requires us to leave behind the comforts of home so that we may turn our attention to the needs of our spiritual life, puts the body in a direct relationship with sacred space and time, sacred geography, and the eternal rhythms of the natural environment. In pilgrimage we can dramatically feel our connection with the earth and the cosmos. We become more keenly aware that we are just pilgrims passing through this life. On pilgrimage our senses are all engaged in the mystery and joy of the journey. We encounter incredible sights, sounds, fragrances, and foods, and our emotions are awakened to feel things we may not have thought possible.

When we enter a pilgrimage that demands that we stretch ourselves — say one that involves living in the wilderness — we are opened to the cosmic revelation, which enters us through the overwhelming beauty of nature. The Hindu pilgrimage to Gongotri, to Mount Sinai for the Jews, to Athos in the Orthodox experience, to remote Catholic and Buddhist monasteries, to the holy mountain of Sri Pada in central Sri Lanka — cherished by *four* faiths — and to the sacral sites of indigenous peoples, all occasion an immersion into the mystery of the natural world and hence into the cosmic revelation.

Pilgrimage always involves a relationship to the land, to a place, and to nature. This relationship allows the body to engage with the mind and spirit in the pursuit of spiritual goals. Unlike reading a book, or even praying, which both don't require much of the body's attention, pilgrimage is an important way for us to integrate with the natural world around us, and so, to participate in creation.

✦ Nutrition and Spirituality

What we eat comes from our natural environment. Many religions bless the food they eat as a gift from God. Still, although we know that good nutrition is related to good health, the relationship of nutrition to spiritual development is more elusive.

In my understanding, what we eat affects the depth and quality of our inner lives, our contemplative experience of the natural world around us. In the Indian tradition, this connection has been understood for countless ages. The seers and yogis realized that certain foods work against their spiritual lives, while other foods enhance consciousness on their inner quest. The modern West is just beginning to address this relationship. The importance of this connection was reinforced for me by Asha Paul and her husband, Russill, both friends of mine, and long adherents of a sane and health-sustaining diet that also enhances spiritual attentiveness. As the intermystical approach takes root around the world, the Indian tradition again will have much to contribute on this important relationship of food and spiritual life.

✦ Yoga and the Martial Arts

Yoga and the martial arts allow us to experience our connection with the natural world directly and intimately by stimulating our awareness of the life energy that flows through us. This connection is very clear in hatha yoga, a most ancient and gentle but vigorous practice.

Yoga, which means *yoke,* aims at union with the divine reality. This goal is the same in all forms of yoga. Hatha yoga, as the path of physical discipline and exercise, prepares one for higher forms of yoga, particularly meditation. Yoga unites us within by integrating our bodies, minds, and spirits. It is also proven to be an excellent aid in maintaining and enhancing health. This is one reason why so many today perform daily hatha yoga.

Carefully performing yogic postures or *asanas* increases one's well-being in body and clarity in mind. Each asana has a special significance and benefits some part of the body. Like meditation, yoga is a spiritual practice. It takes enormous effort and commitment; indeed, it requires tremendous effort to keep the commitment! In the long run of the spiritual journey though, the practice of yoga places the person in a unique position to receive many insights and to access states of consciousness beyond the reach of most people.

The Martial Arts

Martial arts can also be spiritually effective. T'ai chi, Aikido, and capoeira are clearly spiritual in intention, though they are also excellent means of self-defense.

T'ai chi is the most meditational. It is really meditation in motion. To watch t'ai chi, as to do it, is to engage in another state of consciousness. The practice of this martial art, as of others, makes our awareness more subtle and deliberate and eventually changes our awareness of everything. T'ai chi is a way to integrate the energy *(chi)* present in nature, the cosmos, and all things. It flows through us, around us, beyond us, and back again. T'ai chi is both meditation and exercise, but it is also a way of integration.

T'ai chi looks very much like a gentle, slow dance. Movements are deliberate, unforced, and flowing, in harmony with the Tao. These movements do not exhaust chi, they create and direct it. The movements are essentially circular, uniting the yin and the yang, represented by the two sides of the body. The forces of yin and yang, the masculine and the feminine, the active and the passive, the still and the assertive, are complementary to each other. In t'ai chi they consciously interact through movement. In time, the practice of t'ai chi brings about a perfect coordination of the body and the mind, the aim of self-mastery. Obviously, to achieve this kind of perfection takes many years, and the person has to keep aware of the goal of this ancient path.

Aikido, the Way of Harmony, has many points in common with t'ai chi. Its basic movements are also circular, but it is more vigorous in its application. It is similarly a path of integrating the body and the mind through the Japanese *ki,* or energy of the universe (really the same as the *chi*), which is this harmony. This harmony is itself love, according to the founder of Aikido, the Japanese master Morihei Ueshiba, who began it in the 1920s as a corrective to other martial arts that were emphasizing ego and competition. In Aikido, the fundamental principle is to receive an attack by moving out of its way, while blending with it, and returning it through the energy, the ki, in the exercise of an appropriate movement. Ueshiba stressed that the ultimate purpose of Aikido is "victory over the self, or oneself," the same goal of self-mastery we see in t'ai chi. On a mystical level, Aikido is a path to realizing the harmony of love that is the divine in all things.

Capoeira is another martial art form with great potential as a spiritual discipline. It serves as a way to integrate the body and mind and then relate them to the natural world in an intimate, friendly, comfortable way. Capoeira is a unique Brazilian form that unites marital arts and dance. Those unfamiliar with this strikingly original form should view a a fascinating martial arts movie entitled *Only the Strong* starring Mark Dacascos. This movie makes very clear the potential of capoeria as a spiritual practice.

Yoga, t'ai chi, Aikido, and capoeira are spiritual practices that provide individuals who embrace them with the possibility of evolving into a much heightened awareness. When they do, they then achieve the potential of these ways to facilitate their own inner and outer growth.

✦ Toward a Holistic Spirituality

A viable interspirituality must leave nothing out. Christian mysticism has always rejected the body, as evidenced by the extreme asceticism of Francis of Assisi. Francis was merciless to his body, which he called "Brother Ass." He spent a good deal of time fasting, praying sometimes all night on his knees. His poor body was a victim of his piety! Contempt for the body and its denial of a role in the spiritual life can be discerned in a Medieval Trappist saying: "When you enter the monastery, you leave your body at the gate!"

The East has its equivalent ascetical hardships on the body, but has also managed to understand that the body can be beneficial to the spiritual journey. In embracing the middle path, the Buddha rejected the extremity of asceticism and its toll on the body. And Tantric Yoga has a wonderful aphorism that places the body in a more positive position: "That by which we fall is that by which we rise." We may fall through the body, but we can also rise with its assistance by redirecting its energy and passion.

A holistic spirituality incorporates the body in the process of our inner and outer development. It unites the body with the mind and spirit in prayer, meditation, chanting, liturgy, spiritual reading, yoga, some of the martial arts, and walking, hiking, or just being in the presence of nature. At the same time, a holistic spirituality provides for the input that art, music, and poetry can make to our spiritual lives. A complete spirituality will be nourished by these creative avenues, and it will also be in communion with the natural world. It will be at peace with all beings, no matter what their species. A holistic spirituality will also make available all the inner resources of the various schools of mysticism to the inner and outer development of persons. A holistic mysticism is meant to make us whole, or to realize the wholeness or integrity that is always there. Understanding various parts is important to ensure this wholeness. For this kind of spirituality to evolve in our lives we need to be open, to relax, and to surrender to the discipline necessary to live the spiritual journey. To do so brings rich rewards of discovery and genuine peace.

✦ Natural Meditation

Here, I want to quickly present a spiritual method for deepening our sense of relationship with nature and the cosmos. I call it the practice of nature, or natural meditation:

Go out in nature, either sitting or walking. Take a long, loving look at the natural world by focusing on an object in it: a tree, a flower, a bush, a mountain. As you take the object in, realize that just as you are aware of this object, you are essentially connected to it and with all of nature, the earth, and the cosmos. As you experience this connection, allow yourself to luxuriate in it. Then express a sense of deep gratitude to the object, to nature, to the universe, and to God.

Now, sit back, get completely relaxed, and then look at the sky.[41] You can even lay down on the ground. After a while, realize that your true nature, your consciousness, is as vast as the sky. Realize that you, the sky, the whole natural world, the earth, the cosmos, and all beings are one.

Applying your innate ability to read the Books of Creation and Life, inwardly activate your awareness that your consciousness is as vast as the sky. Then feel the gratitude and joy that accompanies that wisdom and union.

✦ Discourse of the Rose

All of nature is a revelation of the ultimate mystery. Natural contemplation is in touch with this cosmic revelation, and it is capable of perceiving the great masterpiece of creation; it grasps the intrinsic meanings present in existence, especially in the natural environment. I awoke to natural contemplation in childhood, but only reached the fullness of it, the ability to read the Books of Creation and Life, in my thirties. This ability was largely triggered by my daily encounter with a large rosebush in the front yard of my home in West Hartford, Connecticut. I began to see in a new way, to perceive what is really there in the natural world.

Thomas Keating has often spoken about contemplation's gift to see the essential. He presents this insight by way of analogy. He says, just as you can summarize volumes in one paragraph, you can then summarize the paragraph in a sentence, and the sentence in a word, but then the word can be conveyed with a look. That is what natural contemplation does in relation to the symbols embedded in the universe. A contemplative person perceives that "look" of the symbol present in the actual entity. The symbols are often images; for instance, certain trees symbolically suggest the whole cosmos. A spider's web also symbolically expresses the totality and the interconnectedness of all levels of reality. All are part of the web of life.

In terms of symbolism and how it operates, nature tells us a story about being. It reveals certain metaphysical and spiritual truths, principles, and insights just by being. In this sense, the natural world is revelational and sacramental. It is always unfolding the meaning of existence literally before our eyes, could we but see. And to see, we have only to really look.

The difficulty is in knowing *how* to look. In the English mystical tradition they speak of contemplation as "a long, loving look at the real," and that is surely where it must begin. Natural contemplation is something to be exercised. We must look with our heart, our inner vision, our intuition. The truth is the whole system of cosmos and reality, and everything always refers back to the source. Nature teaches us, through its intrinsic symbolic function of portraying reality, that to be in a sense means to signify, as everything naturally implies the source. All things have an individual being and a symbolic function.

The significance or meaning of existence is intrinsic to each being; to really know any one thing will result in a knowledge of the whole. For everything anticipates or adumbrates ultimate meaning, and cannot help but reflect the whole. This entire symbolic function of natural contemplation is actually a form of illumination, a different, extraordinary state of consciousness. Yet it is really as natural as breathing once it awakens in an individual.

Let us look at the rose by way of example. When we examine the rose with our intuition through a long, loving look, we find that it is pregnant, like all of creation, with meaning, hidden truths, and practical wisdom. It participates in the whole symbolic order of nature, which is itself a kind of divine algebra in which certain truths and mysteries are concretely embodied. Whereas mathematics concerns principles of structure and relationship, symbolism concerns ultimate meaning. When we awaken to this dimension of experience in nature, being, and life through a contemplative encounter with creation, or through a natural object like a rose, we enter into an illuminative state, and this state is natural contemplation. The rose, or any other natural entity, can trigger a stream of metaphysical and mystical illumination.

In the rose's development from a tiny seedling all the way to its ethereal bloom and beyond to death and decomposition, a very basic metaphysical truth is being portrayed: that reality, life, and truth are essentially invisible, intangible, and mysterious, yet are subtly revealed in a dynamic process of unfolding, a gradual manifestation over a period of time. We might ask: What is the rose? When is the rose a rose? Where does it begin and end? Is the rose the seedling? The shoot? The stem? Or perhaps it is the bud, the stamen, or the final bloom?

Actually, the rose is all of them, all of its stages, from seed to blossom and beyond. The growth and development of the rose suggests and reveals the essential principle that the mystery of life, reality, and being is a *process*, a process not fully actual in any one of its moments. The movement of reality, being, and life aims at totality, which is expressed in the rose's full form when its bloom opens. Reality, the secret of being itself, is hidden in the process, which is always moving toward a goal, like the flower striving toward the perfection of its full bloom.

The fragile beauty, fragrance, and symmetrical form of the rose, in its completed being, reveal as through an allegory that the progress of life is moving toward a definite purpose. Life has a goal, and this goal is thoroughly spiritual, a truth exemplified so eloquently in the compelling perfection of the rose's goal: the blossom. In the blossom, we see its petals arranged in perfect relation and harmony to one another, as if designed by an artist who is also a skilled mathematician. Nothing in the rose is haphazard; its form and structure are perfect. This perfection of form indicates a comprehensive purpose at work. It suggests a spiritual purpose to life, the truth that we are in transit on our earthly pilgrimage towards the source, the origin of that very perfection that the rose and all creation reflect.

And yet the exquisite beauty of the rose in its blossom gives way to decay as the petals fall one by one, and the rose succumbs to time. But this is not the end of the process. The death of the rose expresses that the rose is only a symbol of ultimate purpose and perfection, not the purpose and perfection itself. It thus bows to the mystery of the source, the divine drawing all things to itself first by the interconnectedness of everything, then through its cosmic symbolism, and finally through the communion and union of the mystical journey itself.

PART IV

GLOBAL MYSTICISM

Chapter 9

THE PROMISED LAND
OF THE
SPIRITUAL JOURNEY

The most beautiful and profound emotion we can experience is
the sensation of the mystical. It is the sower of all true science.
He (or she) to whom this emotion is a stranger,
who can no longer wonder and stand rapt in awe, is as good as dead.
— Albert Einstein

As I look back over the extraordinary moments in my own spiritual journey, I am fascinated to see how interspiritual it is. Although I am primarily a Christian, a Catholic contemplative, my heart and life are now totally open to wherever and whenever mystical graces take me. My experiences have ranged from pure, unitive elevations into the divine reality, to a painful plunge into the void in my early years as an undergraduate. They have included intense nondual moments with nature and its inhabitants — trees, flowers, mountains, birds, deer, raccoons, dogs, cats — even one sagelike turtle I encountered in Oklahoma. I have had the classic upanishadic realization, the overwhelming awareness that everything is within me and within everyone and everything else.

My inner life has been the drama of the divine mystery communicating its presence and love to me, and saturating my being. But it has been an essentially apophatic experience — one that cannot be grasped or described. The mystical life defies our categories of systemization. Its vividity, clarity, intensity, and transcendental nature overflow our finite categories. Bede Griffiths once said to me that ultimate realization is similar to sitting in a completely dark room. You seem to be alone, but then all of a sudden someone comes up and wraps his or her arms around you. You know someone is there, but you can't see a face. You know the divine is there because it loves you, holds on to you, elevates you to greater capacity, but it rarely removes its veil.

My encounters with God have been rich and variegated, encompassing all the possibilities. I am certain this reflects the infinite richness of the divine expressed in the differing spiritual experiences of the world's religions. My inner journey — what I have been given and shown — has prepared me to appreciate the importance and possibility of a *universal* approach to mysticism because only such an approach will yield a better understanding of spirituality. In the end, I am convinced that the religions complete one another's understanding of ultimate reality.

✦ An Intermystical Bridge: The Guidelines for Interreligious Understanding

The Guidelines for Interreligious Understanding formulated by Thomas Keating and the fifteen members of his Snowmass Conference provide a strong foundation for fruitful dialogue among all the faith traditions. These points of agreement have been reached in the context of spiritual practice. Each member of the Conference is a leader in a tradition of spiritual wisdom. Each is committed to an interspiritual approach. That means that they are passionately interested in the spiritual practices, insights, intuitions, and essential formulations of *all* the schools of spirituality. These fifteen people have become close friends over the years. During their annual week-long retreats they have shared the spiritual resources and treasures of their different approaches and have found much common ground.

The guidelines we will examine here concern their basic orientations to the ultimate reality; the rest of the guidelines deal with spiritual practice.[1]

The First Guideline

The first guideline acknowledges the place of the ultimate reality in all the religions of the world. It expresses this truth in the following words: "The world religions bear witness to the experience of Ultimate Reality to which they give various names: Brahman, Allah, (the) Absolute, God, Great Spirit."

This guideline emphasizes experience, not mere conception. The basis of all the religions lies in the actual experience of these traditions' founders and leaders, over the course of many centuries. The recognition of the primacy of Ultimate Reality is the result of the mystical process. All the religions accept the place and role of Ultimate Reality, although, because always ineffable, it cannot be sufficiently characterized. All our terms or words are useless in any attempt to "name" the ultimate source.

The Second Guideline

The second guideline conveys the above insight: "Ultimate Reality cannot be limited by any name or concept." Our words, no matter how technical, precise, or specialized, are incapable of holding or conveying the intense, total, and certain reality of the ultimate in its actual nature. It is completely beyond the capacity of language, thought, imagination, and life to grasp — in any truly meaningful way — what the Ultimate Reality actually is. Our life and being are coordinated with it.

The Third Guideline

Our mystical process depends on our relationship with or connection to the elusive mystery. Guideline three recognizes this experiential insight: "Ultimate Reality is the ground of infinite potentiality and actualization."

It is only by opening up to and integrating with the source that we awaken to who we actually are, which is hidden in the mystery of the source itself. The source, as the Ultimate Reality, holds the key to our becoming, our awakening to the expanded being of our deeper identity in it. All that we are and can become has its identity in the source, the Ultimate Reality in its ineffable mystery. We cannot actualize our infinite potentiality except in and through the source. Every other form of potentiality is finite and, so, impermanent.

The Fourth Guideline

If we would actualize our innate potential for infinite life and development, we need to follow the path of faith, regardless of our tradition All paths traverse some expression of faith's compelling power to lead us into actualization of our spiritual potential. The fourth guideline defines the nature of this experience of faith: "Faith is opening, accepting, and responding to Ultimate Reality. Faith in this sense precedes every belief system."

Faith is essentially the quality of openness, eagerness, and expectation we see in children and other enlightened souls. It is a basic attitude of trust in the ultimate mystery behind existence; it is a gesture and stand of pure openness. This attitude of trust precedes a system of belief or a tradition. It is a universal experience and requirement for the higher life; without it, the spiritual journey is impossible. In a certain sense, faith is also a willingness to relinquish control to the source. It is a capacity to trust the mystery of the ultimate.

The Fifth Guideline

We are all mystics by virtue of our birth. We are meant for something more. All the religions inform us of this truth, and their many forms of spirituality are ways for each one of us to nurture the awakening and steady growth of our inner realm of connection with the source. Guideline five addresses this point: "The potential for human wholeness — or in other frames of reference, enlightenment, salvation, transformation, blessedness, *nirvana* — is present in every human person."

We have — indeed, we *are* — this potential for unlimited being because this mystical dimension is part of what makes us human. Realizing our potential for wholeness, for the divine inner core of our nature, is the goal of life. We are beings in transit to this wholeness. That is precisely why we are here.

This world is a launching pad! We are sometimes restless because we are made for a permanent fulfillment. The character Auntie Mame reflects this insight when she says to her wide-eyed nephew: "Life is a banquet, but most suckers are starving!" The mystical life is the banquet. Anything short of this is just a cheese sandwich.

The Sixth Guideline

Everything is an avenue leading to the experience of Ultimate Reality. The divine communicates itself in all things. That there are infinite ways to encounter the source is the essential truth of the sixth guideline: "Ultimate Reality may be experienced not only through religious practices but also through nature, art, human relationships, and service of others."

The ultimate can be experienced in virtually anything. There is no place, no activity that restricts the divine. It is everywhere.

The Seventh Guideline

One chief characteristic of the age we live in is our willingness to explore other ways of looking at life. Recognizing this pattern is one of the assumptions of this book. We are beginning to feel comfortable experimenting with other traditions, particularly with alternative prayer forms, meditation, and yoga. We are hungry for the divine; we are striving for a breakthrough. Sooner or later, it *will* happen. If a person is really trying, and is devoting time for prayer or meditation each day — preferably twice a day — then, sooner or later, a breakthrough will occur.

One of the great problems of the contemporary world is the sense of isolation people feel — from the ultimate mystery, nature, other people, and our fellow creatures. This feeling of separation is a relative perspective growing out of a cultural milieu of human autonomy from the source and from one another. Such a perspective is, in the end, an illusion. The seventh guideline, and a further basis for interreligious conversation and cooperation, recognizes this danger of isolation and separation: "As long as the human condition is experienced as separate from Ultimate Reality, it is subject to ignorance, illusion, weakness and suffering."

When our life is divided against itself, it is out of touch with the way things really are: each person as part of a vast community of consciousness that embraces the totality. Bede Griffiths often said that sin is separation, referring to the false posture of autonomy so many people assume in their lives. Autonomy is illusion, and the paramount ignorance of our time. It has justified so much destructive behavior, in government, business, education, health care, and within families. But if we understand that we are intimately connected with the totality, and with all others, then our attitudes, habits, words, and actions will be measured, always seeking harmony.

The Eighth Guideline

Guideline eight turns to the issue of spiritual practice, emphasizing its utter importance in the mystical journey. Yet it also recognizes that spiritual practice alone will not achieve the transformation we desire. It is deeper than simply a matter of our own efforts at inner and outer change, regardless of how noble and heroic these are. Our transformation is based, rather, on the depth and quality of our relationship with Ultimate

Reality. It is this relationship that determines our elevation into higher awareness, compassionate being, and loving presence. The eighth guideline says: "Disciplined practice is essential to the spiritual life; yet spiritual attainment is not the result of one's own efforts, but the result of the experience of oneness (unity) with Ultimate Reality."

In other words, what transforms us is not what we do but our integration with what *is*. What we do in the way of our spiritual effort, our habits of prayer, meditation, compassion, and love are all important; but the cause of change is the inner mystical process of union with the source. That, and that alone, is what brings about inner change and carries us into the everlasting roots of our expanded identity in the divine.

Prayer Is Communion with Reality

The Snowmass Conference adopted further guidelines related to the practical dimension of the spiritual journey. We have covered similar territory in this book, so it isn't necessary to list them all here. One guideline in particular, however, about the direction of prayer is very helpful to our discussion: "Prayer is communion with Ultimate Reality, whether it is regarded as personal, impersonal (transpersonal), or beyond them both."

Prayer is an essential, absolute activity found in every culture and every time. It defines human nature in its highest sense, in its efforts at spiritual attainment, and inner change of heart, mind, and behavior. It is the fundamental and perennial method of scaling the heights and probing the depths of the real.

✦ The Summit of the Spiritual Life

Earlier, we explored the summit of the mystical journey in a number of the world's religions. Here, I want to further elaborate on the goal of the mystical journey, the summit of the spiritual life. The importance of this topic cannot be overemphasized; it defines the inner journey in large measure, staking out its contours and giving it direction.

All the great systems of the inner life have a clear understanding of the eventual goal of the spiritual journey. Is this goal the same in all the traditions? This is a difficult and slippery issue — difficult because of the different contexts in which the mystics of the various traditions have discovered the ultimate reality, and slippery because of the inevitable limitations of the language in which they housed their discoveries. In the end, we may be dealing with semantic differences, but we are a long way from a conclusive resolution of this question. We can, however, sketch out some of the archetypal mystical experiences in these traditions as they pertain to the ultimate mystery, and then relate them to one another.

The Hindu Tradition: Nonduality

Advaita, or nonduality, is the core unitive experience of the Hindu tradition. The vast majority of educated Hindus are *advaitins,* adherents to a very mystical understanding of the Sanatana Dharma. Advaita, or nonduality, is ancient. It is mentioned in the Vedas and developed in the Upanishads, especially in the Brihadaranyaka Upanishad.[2] It was then elaborated at length in the seventh century by Gauda Pada (640–690), the founder of the nondualist schools, and in the ninth century by his celebrated follower, Shankara, who greatly extended its influence in the Vedantic tradition.

One of the most significant modern examples of a pure advaitic teaching in twentieth-century India was Sri Ramana Maharshi, the silent sage of the holy mountain Arunachala, in Tamil Nadu, South India. Ramana had an enlightenment experience when he was only seventeen years old, an experience that centered around his own imagined death. It sparked a radical transformation of consciousness. He immediately left home — a course recommended by Hinduism when one has a mystical experience, particularly when so young — and went directly to Arunachala, where he remained until his death in 1950, fifty-four years later.

Ramana wrote a Tamil translation of one of Shankara's works that contains incisive passages on the nature of advaita. The following is an especially lucid example of advaita. Quoting Shankara, Ramana writes:

> The Jnani (a sage, self-realized being) who, through experience, has realized his Self (Atman) to be the Brahman as It really is, as Truth, Knowledge, endless Bliss, the Single Essence, eternal, boundless, pure, unattached, and impartible, not only does not return to bondage, but is that Brahman Itself, the Advaita. That is to say that knowledge of the identity of Brahman and Self is the prime cause of release from bondage. For him who aspires after Liberation (moksha) there is no other way of release from bondage but knowledge of the identity of Brahman and Self. Therefore you too, by your own experience, know

your Self as always "I am Brahman" *(aham brahmasmiti)*.... Since there
is nothing other than Brahman, It is the supreme Advaita.[3]

Advaita means coming to realize that you are God, the Brahman, with
whom you are so intimately united. To awaken into this consciousness is
to achieve liberation, or moksha; it is called brahmavidya and atmavidya:
the experiential realization of Brahman and Atman, that you are the
Brahman and the Atman, the eternal self.

Saccidananda is a further level of depth to this experience of the goal.
As we discussed earlier, in the context of Abhishiktananda's appropriation
of this central understanding of the ultimate reality in the Vedanta, saccidananda is the summit of contemplative consciousness in Hindu mysticism. Again, it is the inner awareness the divine has of itself: infinite
existence, in total, unbounded awareness, resting in boundless, inex-
haustible bliss. Saccidananda is the boundless bliss (ananda) of realizing
total and unlimited awareness (cit) of being infinite existence itself (sat).
Saccidananda is not primarily a concept but a mystical consciousness, an
experiential realization of the divine identity by being united with it
through the mystical experience of brahmavidya and atmavidya.

To enter into the consciousness of the Godhead in this manner of
infinite Existence-Awareness-Bliss requires considerable meditative skill.
The divine reality subsists in its transcendent mystery at a very subtle fre-
quency of vibration, which is the purity of consciousness in its infinity
and eternity. Through a rigorous meditation practice, one's consciousness
is made more subtle as well, and undergoes a radical change that allows
it to become sensitive to the divine's vibration.

When that happens, human and divine consciousness merge — or
rather, we become intensely engaged in the Brahman's awareness of itself
— so intimately that our human identity is overtaken by the divine reality. Our sense of identity is like a phantom in relation to the Brahman's
reality, and so, we can no longer distinguish ourselves from the Brahman.
Advaitic mysticism maintains that what we encounter in these states of
awareness is who we actually are and were all along, the deeper reality
of the supreme identity, in whom we subsist.

The Buddhist Tradition: Enlightenment

The summit of Buddhist practice is enlightenment. The term enlightenment derives from the Sanskrit word bodhi, which means awakening

— awakening into awareness of what is, what is real, and who we are. In the Zen tradition, the Japanese words satori and kensho express this meaning of awakening. There are degrees of bodhi, satori, or kensho, although the Buddha's awakening is regarded as perfect, hence ultimate.

In Buddhist thought, enlightenment presupposes the unity of all experience and reality; this unity is the essential, inescapable interrelatedness of all beings. As in Hindu mysticism, it is a nondual state of awareness. Awakening, the bursts of illumination, of intense clarity of insight into the nature of reality, always involves this condition of unity.

At the same time, this awakening is also an experience of the *emptiness* of everything, particularly the emptiness of all form, of all the things we can perceive on any level of perception — sensory, thought, feeling, emotions, imagination, dreams. To say that all things are empty, that they are bounded by shunyata, is to realize that nothing is permanent in this realm of becoming. All phenomena, beings, and entities are intrinsically empty. The reality of any being is related to its interconnection with all other beings or entities. So emptiness is the recognition that only the system of interbeing, as Thich Nhat Hanh calls it, is real and absolute. By *interbeing* he means "the Buddhist teaching that nothing can be by itself alone, that everything in the cosmos must 'interbe' with everything else."[4]

The fundamental problem in the West is our attachment to individual being as an absolute category of life and experience. We see its epitome in the American dream, which is predicated on the ultimate value of the individual project — our individual pursuit of happiness, rather than the happiness of all sentient beings. Buddhism sees the American dream as a supreme illusion because it leaves out reality — it ignores the welfare and the happiness of the whole.

The summit of contemplation, of the spiritual journey in the Buddhist understanding, is also the arrival into nirvana and nirvanic awareness. Nirvana is life and being beyond bondage to our desires. We only begin to see when we are free of desire, or craving. Our grasping for the objects of desire blind us to the real. Nirvana sets us free, and allows us to develop wisdom.

A statement attributed to the Buddha sums up the goal of the journey in the realization that "All is emptiness, and all is compassion." To really grasp what the Buddha is saying here requires us to set aside desire as a motivating focus of our will and action. Only if we are truly free of craving for what we want are we in a position to see reality as it is: empti-ness, the interconnectedness of everyone and everything. When we acti-vate that awareness, then we also understand that compassion is the virtue that binds us all together. Only when we comprehend shunyata can we experience the depths and heights of compassion for all sentient beings. That is the substance of all wisdom, and it's very near to the Christian view of love as an absolute.

The goal of the Buddhist spiritual vision of human existence is not union with a personal, loving deity, nor is it self-realization in the Hindu sense. Buddhism doesn't think in terms of a personal God, and it rejects the idea of a personal self or soul. Rather, it emphasizes realization of our ultimate nature as consciousness. The genuine and eternal nature of con-sciousness is beyond the rational mind; it transcends the ego, personali-ty, or claim to selfhood and soul. These will all pass away because they are impermanent. What is everlasting in us is consciousness itself. To access this awareness is the plenitude of enlightenment, the Buddha-mind or Buddha-nature. We are this Buddha-nature and we are this Buddha-mind: the vast, all-knowing, total consciousness of what is.

The Buddhist vision is the inner awakening and development of our own inherent divinity, our Buddha-mind. We must wake up and actualize the awareness in our consciousness that we are also "God" by nature, the immanent divine of consciousness. Buddhism is the spirituality of appro-priating our ultimate identity. It therefore has some similarity to advaitic perception of our ultimate divinity, but in an immanent rather than a transcendent sense.

The Christian, Sufi, and Jewish Traditions

The summit of mystical contemplation in Christian and Sufi spiritu-ality is a union and communion of love between the soul, or person, and God. The Jewish understanding, which is also the theological view of both Christianity and Islam, emphasizes the utter transcendence of God; but for Christianity and Islam this transcendent life of the divinity is balanced by God's nearness to us, his indwelling presence within the depths of our subjective experience.

Jewish mysticism preserves the transcendent focus, but it cultivates in the Kabbalah and the Hasidic schools a kind of intimacy with God from a distance. The archetype of this somewhat remote intimacy is Moses' relationship with God: He could never see God's face. The prophetic experience continues this kind of relationship. God is the goal of our lives and the inner process we pass through. Hebrew mysticism is filled with stories of the nearness of the divine to the human, and the human ascending, in mystical states, to Paradise or Heaven, and conversing with God in a transcendent communion. Although distance is always involved, it is essentially nondual.5

In Christian and Sufi mysticism, this distance is overcome by an intense unitive relationship with God. The predominant emphasis in both of these profoundly rich and vast traditions is on love mysticism: the permanent experience of a transforming union, in which a stability of relationship emerges. God remains transcendent, but it ceases to be an obstacle. It is overcome by God's immanent presence in the cosmos and within the deepest places of our hearts.

Ludovicus Blosius or Louis de Blois, an obscure sixteenth-century Christian mystic, was a Benedictine abbot and spiritual writer. In a work entitled *Speculum Spirituale,* the *Spiritual Mirror,* he maps out the inner journey. A powerful though brief chapter on mystical union succinctly sums up the whole ascent to God. The way he expresses his experience of mystical union suggests the Rhineland mystics, Eckhart and Ruysbroeck:

> It is a wonderful thing...to be united to God in the divine light by a mystical and denuded union. This occurs when a humble, pure and resigned soul, on fire with ardent charity, is elevated above itself by the grace of God...and totally fluid with love, and reduced to nothing, melts away into God. Then it is united to God without any medium, and becoming one spirit with Him, is transformed and changed into Him, as iron placed in the fire is changed into fire, without ceasing to be iron. Becoming one with God does not imply becoming the same substance and nature as God.6

Although only a brief passage, here Blosius veritably summarizes mystical theology in his time. Everything necessary to the spiritual journey is present: the methodology of the ascent (love and grace); moral conversion (growth in detachment, humility, and purity); psychological preparation (becoming nothing, or removing the obstacle of the false self in order to *become* God — a union allowing them to be of the same spirit, while retaining the metaphysical distinction between God and the soul).

This is quite a feat; it is a Christian form of advaita, for there is always a "between" in union, even when this "between" is barely felt. Blosius gives us a clear, highly nuanced, and yet mysterious glimpse of mystical union. It unites the various strands of the Christian mystical schools up until his time: the metaphysical mysticism of the Rhenish mystics like Eckhart, Ruysbroeck, Tauler, and Suso, with their propensity for the reflective; the speculative depth of Pseudo-Dionysius, the sixth-century Syrian monk; the affectivity, or emphasis on love of the Cistercians (Trappists) and the anonymous author of *The Cloud of Unknowing*.

The primacy of love at the summit of the spiritual journey is extremely important in the Christian and Sufi understandings. It is the defining characteristic of Christian contemplation, and is the very heart of mystical union: a union between God and the person in the intimacy of an intense and enlightened love, one that transcends all selfishness. The entire contemplative tradition rests on this insight.

The Spanish mystics of the sixteenth century, Teresa of Avila and John of the Cross, also conveyed their experience and its elaboration in terms of this love-mysticism. They drew heavily on the bridal images of the Cistercians, notably Bernard of Clairvaux in the twelfth century, who developed insights from his own contemplative experience in the rich framework and symbolism of the Song of Songs.

Teresa of Avila speaks at length about the degrees of mystical union. Her discourses on the nature of this union are usually related to love within the context of the degrees of contemplative or mystical prayer. Both she and John of the Cross detail the stable mystical union known as the spiritual marriage — an unbreakable bond of profound affection in which the soul as the bride and God as the bridegroom, the lover and the beloved, become inseparable.

To make this point clear, Teresa uses the metaphors of water and light streaming through windows — images common to John of the Cross as well:

> In the spiritual marriage, the union is like what we have when
> rain falls from the sky into a river or fount; all is water, for the rain that
> fell from heaven cannot be divided or separated from the water of the
> river. . . . Or, like the bright light entering a room through two different
> windows; although the streams of light are separate when entering the
> room, they become one.7

Teresa affirms that divine union overcomes all sense of separation —

a normal feeling in the human condition — by this perfect divine love, the love that Jesus taught his disciples, the binding force of his unity with them and with his Father. A union of love necessarily involves more than one; it means that at least two are so joined. Teresa also mentions the essential obscurity, hiddenness, and mystery of the mystical union: "This secret union takes place in the very interior center of the soul, which must be where God Himself is, and in my opinion there is no need of any door for Him to enter."[8] There, in that secret interior chamber, God is loving and giving himself to the person.

John of the Cross also defines contemplation in terms of this hidden love: "Contemplation is nothing else than a secret and peaceful and loving inflow of God, which if not hampered, fires the soul in the spirit of love."[9] Here he refers to infused contemplation, which is the beginning of the unitive life. It is very difficult to attain the spiritual or mystical marriage. Considerable suffering is endured, a suffering that purifies the self before a permanent state of union with God arrives. This suffering is what he calls the dark nights of sense and spirit, in which we are inwardly liberated by God from obtaining satisfaction from the sensory level of experience and our own former self-preoccupation. Alluding to this suffering and the difficulty of achieving divine union, he says: "One cannot reach this union without remarkable purity, and this purity is unattainable without vigorous mortification and nakedness regarding all creatures."[10] There must be total focus, a single-minded intention for the divine alone. That is true purity of heart.

No one who wishes to reach divine union can escape this mystical suffering. It is a death to the false self, the egocentric life. It is the abandoning of the falseness to which our society habituates us. The divine refashions us within. The mystical life is so much about this inner work of transmutation. The Sufis have also always understood the need for this death experience of the worldly, selfish identity. They understand, like the Christian mystics, the indispensable role of mystical suffering, of the dark nights on the journey. They refer to this death experience as *annihilation*, as *nonexistence*, expressed through the Arabic term *fana*. Without fana, or annihilation, there is no union, or reintegration with the divine. Union with God is called *subsistence*, or reintegration, and is conveyed in Arabic as *baqa*. We must be annihilated in the divine in order to reach our full potential in union with God.

The Persian mystic Rumi, one of the great Islamic poet sages, comments on the mystical death process and the resulting permanent life of union:

> No one will find his way to the Court of Magnificence (Paradise) until he is annihilated....You are your own shadow — become annihilated in the rays of the Sun (God)! How long will you look at your shadow? Look also at His Light....Come into the garden of annihilation and behold: paradise after paradise within the spirit of your own subsistence (union with the Divine). [11]

Another name for this fullness of the mystical life, or for the goal in the spiritual journey, is supernatural union because initiated by God. We must struggle to rid ourselves of all that hinders union, since only likeness to God through love opens the door to supernatural union. The dark nights of sense and spirit, in John of the Cross, reveal the way divine love operates by breaking down all the barriers or obstacles to this supernatural union. Perfect union only exists where there is a perfect conformity of wills, the human with the divine will. [12] It is God's ultimate will for us that we become totally transformed into love itself, like him. John says: "God communicates himself more to the soul more advanced in love, that is, more conformed to his will. A person who has reached complete conformity of will has attained total supernatural union and transformation in God." [13]

For all the mystics of the Christian tradition, as well as in Islam, or Sufism, Judaism, and even in most Eastern forms, some kind of inner suffering or purification is necessary in order to arrive at a more complete integration with the divine. This freedom from an ego-driven life, or the hold of the false self, is utterly necessary. Even in the heights of union, the self can intimate its own agenda. For that reason, Thomas Keating sees a need for greater interior purification: "Without a lot of purification our ways of relating to God continue to be influenced by the false self." [14] Purification is recognizing the obstacles within us, and then letting them go. If we continually surrender to the divine will, it will lead us inevitably through inner purification to transforming or supernatural union.

❧ Mystic Visitations: Personal Experience of the Summit

I have had many advaitic experiences, and ones that might be regarded as Buddhist in nature. But my primary and enduring understanding is informed by an intimate and personal unitive relationship with God.

During a brief period in 1966 when I attended the branch of the University of Connecticut in Hartford near my home, I met a bitter Vietnam vet. More than an atheist, his hatred of God really made him an antitheist. In our heated arguments about the existence of God, he shattered my childhood faith. I was a little Catholic kid from Hartford, Connecticut. Pious and innocent, my faith was simple, devout, and unquestioning. I was certainly ill-equipped to defend my convictions. He sowed seeds of doubt, propelling me into a period of agnosticism, confusion, and anxiety, which lasted three years. This period was really a very painful dark night of the soul for me.

In tandem with this unsolicited doubt came an intense confrontation with my mortality; the fear of death continually confronted me. My interior suffering was so great that life seemed pointless. My heart was exploding with sorrow. Indeed, it was a kind of death experience for me. Never wanting to disturb my family's strong but simple faith, I never told them about my questioning. I kept it all to myself. Through it all, however, my heart and my mind remained open.

I went on to study at a small Catholic college in Manchester, New Hampshire, run by the Benedictine order. There I majored in philosophy, partially as a way to negotiate myself out of agnosticism and to shed light on my predicament. It was during my college years that my first mystical experiences occurred.

At first, these experiences confused me. Should I welcome them, or shut myself off from them? It was Thomas Keating who wisely guided me through these early encounters. He urged me to surrender to them. "Receive them for the gift they are," he said, and I found myself accepting these gratuitously given experiences. As my acceptance grew, everything changed for me. The encounters became more frequent, and they shifted in intensity, duration, and extent. The divine completely took me over.

I could never predict either the time or the place these divine raptures would occur. I was often taken out of myself, my consciousness enlarged, and perceptions of everything altered from within. Space and time were suspended. My faculties were similarly suspended — I couldn't think, analyze, remember, imagine, or speak. I hovered between fear and awe, finally resolving into total openness and trust. I was thoroughly invaded by the divine presence, saturated by its incomparable love and mystery. The divine loved me, and all I could do was to assent to its presence within, around, and through me. Through this assent, fired with urgency and expectation, I gave myself to the divine.

In these unitive moments I often feel myself being transformed into divine love itself through my capacity to receive. My identity expands into the infinite reality of God. My identity seems like a shadow, insubstantial and unreal. This divine reality is a boundless, loving presence that surrounds me on every side and takes hold of my being, uniting it with itself.

For many years I have been intensely aware of the divine as a breathing presence that surrounds me, is within me, and takes me into itself. The breathing presence can be completely overwhelming, or as gentle as a summer's breeze in the cool of evening. Whenever I am aware of it, there is no mistaking it for something else. I immediately know who it is. At the end of his masterpiece, *The Living Flame of Love,* John of the Cross briefly mentions this state of contemplation in which the person is aware of the divine breathing within:

> It is a spiration which God produces in the soul, in which, by that awakening of lofty knowledge of the Godhead, He breathes the Holy Spirit in it in the same proportion as its knowledge and understanding of Him, absorbing it most profoundly in the Holy Spirit, rousing its love with divine excellence and delicacy according to what it beholds in Him.[15]

✦ Stations of the Mystical Summit

The unitive experience of the God-centered traditions of mysticism points to a strong sense of the person's distinct identity in relation to the divine. This experience is thus vastly different from the Hindu and Buddhist, although in all three of these approaches there is an awakening and enlargement of one's consciousness, identity, and potential. It is really a difference of emphasis, as Bede Griffiths wrote: "Perhaps the fundamental difference is this: that the heart of Christian mysticism is a mystery of love, whereas both in Hinduism and in Buddhism it is primarily a transformation of consciousness."[16] Although the ultimate goals are not identical, they are complementary. The religions need one another precisely because they complete one another! Together, they enlarge our understanding of the ultimate. This is what animates and characterizes interspirituality.

The religions are like the ten blind men trying to describe the nature of the elephant; it is only when they put all their experience together that a clearer understanding of the elephant emerges. Similarly, it is only when the religions various forms of mystical spirituality are related to one another in a larger context of truth that we will have a better idea of the shape of the absolute.

Interspirituality honors all the experience and insight of each tradition, and gathers these experiences together into an organic synthesis. We awaken to this synthesis when we walk the intermystical path with an open heart and a capacity to be transformed in our understanding and in our being. When we do that, we can utter, like Raimon Panikkar: "I am a Hindu, Christian, Buddhist," and more, "I am a Christian, Hindu, Buddhist, Jewish, Moslem!"

✦ Dreams: Channels of the Sacred

Dreams are vitally important in the spiritual journey. Their significance is attested to in every culture, religion, and age. In their highest function, dreams are a channel of access to the divine realm, or the more subtle levels of consciousness.[17] They are also a medium through which the numinous unfettered reality communicates to us directly. Dreams are also a transtemporal meeting place with deceased loved ones, for the dream state transcends the laws of physics and the distinction of past, present, and future. All events and persons, entities, angels, the divine itself are simultaneous, participating in the eternal now. And certain dreams take us to that place beyond time and space.

We find compelling insights into the nature and place of the dreaming mind in the New Testament and the Bible, in indigenous people's experience, in Hinduism, Tibetan Buddhism, Islam, and all other religions. Dreams make available to us a mine of psychological and spiritual treasures. They provide guidance vital to our journey, and they point to areas of ourselves where we need to work. In the West, we are actually only beginning to learn how to fathom the depth, height, and breadth of dream awareness, and the potential it has to contribute to our inner growth. Many of us sense that dreams are a source of great insight into existence, that they are a doorway to other worlds and even to the domain of the ultimate.

Depth psychology has discovered the importance of dreams in gauging the health and activity of the psyche. C. G. Jung did much to educate us in the nature, structure, types, and symbology of the dream state; in this he has taken our knowledge beyond the obvious limitations of Freud. He made possible the emergence of transpersonal psychology, thus creating a bridge to the wisdom traditions of the human family.

Tibetan Buddhism, in its teaching on dreams, is somewhat similar to the dream analysis popularized in therapy by Jung. The Tibetans have a form of meditation whose sole purpose is to develop the capacity to remain alert and aware in the dream state. Their purpose is to facilitate lucid dreaming as an aid in making decisions that affect our journey to final liberation. Interspirituality includes the dream state as a potentially beneficial tool in our spiritual lives. It is an area of discovery and research that each one of us needs to explore and integrate.

Something of profound significance happens to every one of us in dream consciousness. Often, we cannot grasp it; but when a dream is of this higher order, we sense it upon waking. It leaves an emotional afterglow and a wonderful feeling of peace. These are signs that the spirit has been at work in us. It is this work that is so elusive, even to those engaged in serious study of this phenomenon. I have been able only to briefly allude to this dimension of the inner life here, but in doing so, I want to emphasize its place in the future, a place long ago understand by the upanishadic seers.[18]

✦ Experimental Mysticism

I am asked from time to time during my lectures whether or not experiences brought on by psychoactive plants and chemicals are the same or similar to mystical states that occur without their use. I don't claim to have an easy answer to this important question, but I know it's one that cannot be avoided or ignored. Too many people are raising it everywhere. People have used mind-altering substances for millennia. Its use exists in most ancient cultures, certainly in India, China, Persia and Greece. And shamans in indigenous cultures, especially in South America, have been exploring other levels of consciousness for countless ages.

Thousands of scientists and thinkers are researching various aspects of this issue, particularly the possible relationship between drug experiences and mystical states. The Buddhist publication *Tricycle* devoted a

1996 issue to this very question, focusing on visionary substances and spiritual realization.[19]

Some Native Americans such as the Native American Church use peyote as a psychoactive sacrament in their religious ceremonies. They speak of it as a way to connect with the Great Spirit. Although the U.S. Congress in 1994 granted an exemption from the drug laws to permit the sacramental use of peyote by Native Americans, the broader issues around psychoactive sacraments are far from settled. Passion is strong on both sides of this question, and at times it seems that a rational discussion is not possible in our society.

A rational, scientific, philosophical debate within our broader culture is necessary. It's a question of pursuing truth. The truth is not always convenient, but we cannot dispense with it either. And so, we must also keep the door open to further research. Some advocate more than research. They suggest the use of psychoactives, or entheogens (facilitating God experience, or spiritual awareness). One organization promoting a sacral role for entheogens is the Council on Spiritual Practices, based in San Francisco.[20] It is committed to the possibility of using entheogens in a sacred context as tools of inner discovery. This group maintains good relations with the government, the academic community, and a circle of theologians. Its scientific work — conducted well within the bounds of the law — has the support of many influential figures within the religious community.

One of the most significant figures of our time in the area of comparative religion and spirituality is Huston Smith. In the 1960s he was at MIT with Aldous Huxley, a major thinker in entheogenic studies. Smith had many experiences with psychoactives during that time, and in subsequent years, wrote a number of articles for various journals on his experiences. He has since gathered these articles together in a book entitled *Cleansing the Doors of Perception: The Religious Significance of Entheogenic Plants and Chemicals.*[21] His book will certainly not settle the issue, but it may awaken our culture at last to an honest discussion.

Although it's certainly not possible at this point to give a conclusive answer to the question of entheogens in the spiritual life, a few points can be made. After much study, reflection, and conversations with spiritual teachers, psychologists, and researchers, I think that entheogens can play a positive role in spiritual development.[22] They can act as a catalyst to profound inner change and facilitate mystical insight, but I do not believe they are a substitute for the hard work of transformation through regular spiritual practice, the development of the virtues, and compassionate, loving service to others. At best they are a tool in the spiritual journey; they must never become a substitute for spiritual practice, and they cannot be relied upon to bring about permanent change. And yet, they do confirm the truth of mysticism, and so, are an indicator along the path.

✦ Reaching the Further Shore of the Spiritual Journey

All forms of spirituality prepare us for our eventual encounter with death and what follows, whether this is conceived and experienced as heaven or some form of paradise, transcendence of the human condition subject to samsara or rebirth, or some other ultimate state of realization.[23]

Enlightenment of our consciousness and transformation of our will, achieved through our own effort or through a delicate balancing act of human effort and divine grace, bring us to a state of readiness for the eternal. Clearly, what we do in this life will inevitably affect us after death, whether this be in subsequent lives or in postmortem existence. The mystical or spiritual journey directly bears on this crossover into ultimate mystery, that point on the horizon of existence that tests the mettle of our faith and practice.

I don't think these two outcomes of the spiritual journey — reincarnation and life after death in heaven — necessarily exclude each other. They may, in fact, complete each other. In the Catholic tradition, there is an intermediate state of the afterlife called purgatory.[24] This state is designed for those who need further development, who must pass through a purgation of their limiting qualities that obstructed their spiritual lives. Theologically, reincarnation is compatible with purgatory because it serves a similar function: preparing the individual for liberation and the higher life with God in eternal paradise.

None of us need any instruction in the reality and inevitability of death; but when it comes to the mystery of the afterlife, we all crave insight, hope, and vision. All the spiritual paths of humankind reveal something about this unknown, the understanding of which requires our direct personal participation in the death process and experience. Of course, only by passing through death will we ever have absolute certitude about the afterlife.

We do have, I am certain, a substantial clue and a glimpse in the phe-nomenon of near-death. These experiences, found in every society around the world, point to the truth the various religions and spirituali-ties present. The near-death phenomenon is perhaps the greatest gift to the human family in our time relating to the enormous questions of death and the afterlife.[25] This phenomenon, and the experience to which it corresponds, can no longer be ignored nor explained away. We must appreciate it with openness and welcoming. Only in this way will we understand its message for this age, an age that is slowly recovering from complete skepticism, the residue of the Enlightenment. The near-death experience sheds light on death, and so also on the summit or goal of the spiritual journey itself.[26] It therefore has a place of value in the Interspiritual Age, and acquires a serious position in third millennial intermystical spirituality.

✦ Becoming Cosmic in the Center

Thomas Merton attempted this kind of universal understanding in a chapter of his book *Contemplation in a World of Action* entitled "Final Integration." While he was not as overtly transpiritual as Panikkar, his appreciation of a more universal vision was very much developing at the time of his death in December 1968. Merton had read the work of Reza Arasteh, an Iranian psychotherapist, who grounded his methodology and aims in Sufism. This focus greatly interested Merton and deepened his appreciation of the Sufis. Arasteh presented his approach and findings in a volume entitled *Final Integration in the Adult Personality.*[27]

Merton found in Arasteh's understanding the insight that true or final integration requires one to become more universal and transcul-tural, rather than to remain stuck in one tradition to the exclusion of all others. This universal openness characterizes the inner awareness of the person who reaches his or her spiritual potential. Merton describes such a person:

> Final integration is a state of transcultural maturity far beyond mere social adjustment, which always implies partiality and compro-mise. The person who is "fully born" has an entirely "inner experience of life." Such a one apprehends his life fully and wholly from an inner ground that is at once more universal than the empirical ego and yet entirely his own. Such an individual is in a certain sense "cosmic" and

"universal person." ... He/she is in a certain sense identified with every-body....[28]

An individual who has arrived at final integration is a mystic. That person has found a deep inner freedom that permits him or her to reach out to all that is, affirming it as part of the inner experience. The unified man or woman is not afraid of diversity of views but welcomes them and makes them his or her own. The essential openness of such an individual makes the possibility of appreciating and identifying with the wisdom of all the traditions within reach. Merton continues:

> Again, the state of insight which is final integration implies an "openness," a "poverty" similar to those described in such detail not only by the Rhenish mystics, by St. John of the Cross, by the early Franciscans, but also by the Sufis, the early Taoist masters and Zen Buddhists. Final integration implies the void, poverty and nonaction which leave one entirely docile to the "Spirit" and hence a potential instrument for unusual creativity. The person who has attained final integration is no longer limited by the culture in which he has grown up.... He accepts not only his own community, his own society, his own friends, his own culture, but all humankind.... He has a unified vision and experience of the one truth shining out in all its various manifestations, some clearer than others, some more definite and more certain than others. He does not set these partial views up in opposition to each other, but unifies them in a dialectic or an insight of complementarity.[29]

Only the mystics can attain this final integration because all wisdom and insight is available to them. The perspective they gain is the result of their inner freedom, and this freedom leads them to a transcultural or universal understanding in which they can embrace all. Only the mystic can be truly interspiritual, since in the end it is a matter of spiritual practice. Depth seeks depth.

Mysticism generates inner freedom and outer perspective. Mystics hear the call to continue on the way; they are not content to settle down, but must press on to greater and greater discovery. This was clearly the case with figures like Ramakrishna, Bede Griffiths, Krishnamurti, and Thomas Merton. The fully formed mystic or contemplative is the new cultural hero who guides humankind to its maturity. Mystics are heralds of the Interspiritual Age, in which all of humankind's wisdom will be gathered up and shared as in a common tradition. This process never ends, but must be renewed in each century. By realizing that this diversity of tradition and approach is willed by God, the mystic becomes the guardian of interspirituality.

Chapter 10

OPENING THE HEART OF THE WORLD: TOWARD A UNIVERSAL MYSTICISM

I must be sun and paint with my own rays
the color-free Sea of total Godhead.
— *Angelius Silesius*

There was a time in my life when I would never have walked into a Protestant church, let alone a synagogue, a mosque, or a Hindu or Buddhist temple. Catholics at one time were forbidden to participate in the liturgical rites of other traditions, and they were discouraged from even entering the sacred spaces of other faiths. I never questioned this directive of my church; I was content to see everything through the perspective of Catholicism. Then, when I was a teenager, the Second Vatican Council opened the door to many changes, including the innovation of interreligious dialogue. Although I was still secure in my own tradition, I began to be curious about others.

I reached a turning point in June 1977, when Thomas Keating sent me to the Petersham Conference, an East-West monastic meeting in Petersham, Massachusetts. He said at the time that this would baptize me in interfaith encounter, particularly in the Asian traditions. I went willingly, learned a lot, and met some fascinating characters.

All throughout the time of the Vatican Council, during my college years, graduate school, and life in Catholic religious communities, I was focused on Rome as my spiritual anchor. Although this continues to be true, with the Petersham Conference I began to appreciate and value other traditions. I discovered that Hinduism, Buddhism, Taoism, Sufism, the Kabbalah, and Hasidism did not take me away from my faith, but augmented my deep commitment to Christian contemplation. I became impassioned in my interest in these traditions, and how they related to the Christian faith.

After Bede Griffiths invited me to Shantivanam in South India, I ended up living in India periodically for two years. One day, after returning from India, it hit me: "I've changed radically." The change proved to be decisive, a spiritual renaissance in which, standing on my own two feet, I took responsibility for my spiritual life. Bede had taught me to regard the structure and authority of the church with a more critical eye.

The spiritual journey evokes these huge shifts in our perspective. We mature in our faith and inner life. We can never return to our spiritual womb after we change; we must press on. These personal breakthroughs have happened to many people, and now entire communities and cultures are expanding their outlook.

Interspirituality, and the intermystical life it entails, recognizes the larger community of humankind in the mystical quest. It realizes that we all have a much greater heritage than simply our own tradition. It acknowledges the validity of all genuinely spiritual experience. Interspirituality honors the totality of human spiritual insight, whether or not it is God-centered. To leave out any spiritual experience is to impoverish humanity. Everything must be included, that is, everything that is authentic and genuine, that springs from contact with the divine, however we know or conceive of this.

✦ A Universal Communal Spirituality

The discovery and emergence of community between and among the religions and the various cultures around the planet are a vital component of interspirituality. The active commitment to this larger community is itself a new type of spirituality. All those who are working in this area of interspiritual community are actually — whether they realize it or not — engaged in developing this new form of spiritual life. Promoting the growth of the bonds of community is a necessary spiritual activity. Such an activity is an act of solidarity with all living beings, of selfless service, and of prophetic action. Breaking down the millennia-old barriers that separate the religions and spreading the spirit of acceptance, mutual trust, and understanding is a profoundly spiritual act, one that advances community in the world and lays the foundation for a universal mysticism.

We augment this community-building by our own personal commitment to the inner life. This creative relationship between community and personal spirituality can be clearly seen in the normal course of monastic life. In monasticism, one's personal inner journey is nourished and sustained by the community. Monastic spirituality is a spirituality of the community, and of the person in the communal matrix of life and well-being. The spiritual life of the person is often indistinguishable from that of the community — at least in terms of the person's social being as it operates in the communal dimension of prayer and liturgy. There is, of course, always the hidden personal reality of the monk's or nun's interior prayer, which is carried on in the utter privacy of the person's heart.

Religions at their best, in their moments of greatest authenticity, are communal forms of spirituality; but the weight of the centuries adds countless formal elements that often have little relevance to a living spiritual practice. These formal, perfunctory forms of religion distract their adherents from the pursuit of the more authentic forms of the spiritual life. All traditions suffer this tendency to formality.

Bede Griffiths often remarked that community was the salvation of humanity, and a few of us were able to join him in an experiment in small community living in Vermont in the early 1990s. Father Bede, Russill and Asha Paul D'Silva, and I explored the joys and challenges of life together as we shared contemplative prayer, meals, work, study, and conversation over a number of months. We grew to understand how natural and nourishing community can be, especially when it is predicated on love.

We all originate from the tribe. So many of our skills as a species were learned and perfected in this early formative experience of tribal community. Hunting, protecting, agriculture, and certain arts all developed during this long period. It is in community that compassion and love have a room to unfold and take root in individuals. It is in and through community that the human family will resolve the ecological crisis that has been at least partially caused by people living apart in nuclear families.

Just as interspirituality became possible with the rise of community in the interfaith movement, the emergence of a global spirituality is only feasible as a result of the openness, mutual trust, goodwill, and generosity of the members of the world's diverse traditions. The mystical life of the next thousand years and beyond will have these significant components: It will be contemplative, interspiritual, socially engaged, environmentally responsible, holistic, engaging of other media, and cosmically open.

It Will Be Contemplative

The coming spirituality will be contemplative because it represents the maturity of the inner experience. Every form of spirituality or the mysticism that reaches that height of maturity does so precisely because it is contemplative.

Contemplation is the capacity to know the divine and oneself in intimate relationship with it beyond the finite and the impermanent. The interiority of contemplative awareness is a process of simplification and clarification of the self that prepares the individual for union with God, integration with the absolute.

Contemplation is awareness beyond the need for thought; it is free of rational analysis. It achieves its perfection in the silence of resting in the divine presence.

It Will Be Interspiritual and Intermystical

Third millennial spirituality will also be interspiritual and intermystical. It will be an enhanced understanding of the inner life through assimilating the psychological, moral, aesthetic, spiritual, and literary treasures of the world's religions. Each tradition will define itself in relation to every other viable tradition of the inner life; each will take into account the totality of the spiritual journey — all the forms it assumes in human experience.

Interspirituality is a commitment to this enhanced vision. It is no longer content to embrace one tradition alone, no matter how admirable. Interspirituality, as intermysticism, seeks the larger understanding of spirituality itself and will not settle for anything less. Intermysticism is the realization that there is one universal tradition of the mystical life with many branches. All of them are relevant and have a perennial value. If we are truly *intermystics*, we are open to wisdom wherever we find it.

It Will Be Socially Engaged

The emerging spirituality of the third millennium is socially engaged — it is deeply concerned with the plight of all those who suffer, wherever they are. It does not turn its back on broken humanity by retreating into the private domain of solitude, disengaged from the trials and tribulations of the masses living in deplorable conditions — the millions who are homeless, malnourished, uneducated, and unemployed. This spirituality has a heart sensitive to the pain of the human family, and it seeks to relieve this pain.

Socially engaged spirituality is the inner life awakened to responsibility and love. It expresses itself in endless acts of compassion that seek to heal others, contributing to the transformation of the world and the building of a nonviolent, peace-loving culture that includes everyone.

It Will Be Environmentally Responsible

The new spirituality is also environmentally aware and committed. It is the pursuit of the inner journey with a keen sense of the value of the created order. Natural mysticism is an indispensable part of intermysticism. It follows a strict adherence to ecological justice, and is always searching for ways to deepen the harmony between the human species and the earth, our human family and all the other species of families.

Interspirituality does not exist at the expense of the natural world but in relation to it. This spirituality and those who are part of it understand that the earth, all of nature, and the cosmos itself have the highest priority for us. The natural world is the matrix of all value and concern. The earth is a spiritual reality, and the basis of our collective life and well-being. The natural world possesses intrinsic spiritual value in its own right, and nature mysticism encompasses and expresses this value. This concern is an absolute priority of spirituality, and we must be constantly reminded of it.

It Will Be Holistic

Universal spirituality is also holistic, integrating body with the mind, soul, consciousness, and spirit. Any system of spirituality that concentrates only on the mind and excludes the body and the spirit is inadequate. Forms of movement meditation, from yoga to walking, are ways of bringing the body into harmony with the mind, the spirit, and nature.

So many forms of spiritual life work only from the neck up, as if the body didn't exist. We need to find creative ways to include the body in the spiritual journey. Again, the West has had an unbalanced view of the place of the body in the spiritual journey. This lack of balance must be corrected. The body is sacred, and it has to be integrated positively into the mystical life.

It Will Engage Other Media

Intermysticism engages other media as integral parts of contemplative practice. It doesn't just depend on books or spiritual reading, but looks to art, music, and movies as a means to nourish contemplative life and the sacred.

No matter the culture, music and art are present; they are universal languages of vast sacred potential. Art and music have an enormous and virtually untapped potential to contribute to our spiritual development; they are able to awaken, deepen, and expand the contemplative dimension of human being.

Integrating music and art into contemplative practice, or making them practices in themselves, is another way of allowing spirituality to become more holistic — to affect the whole person, each one of us in our expanded integrity. Art and music have special qualities that permit us to soar to heights far beyond the range of intellect into intuitive and suprarational experience. In time, and with guidance, they can become precious means of accessing mystical dimensions previously little known or experienced.

It Will Be Cosmically Open

Interspirituality is cosmically open. It recognizes that we are part of a much larger community than simply the human and earth communities. We belong to many communities: the human, the earth, the solar system, our galaxy, and the universe itself. The locus of this cosmic community to which we each belong is consciousness itself.

In chapter 3 I alluded to this larger community of consciousness that interconnects us with all other beings who exist somewhere and at some time. All these beings, in all possible worlds, are our brothers and sisters, belonging to the larger sacred community of the cosmos. The community of consciousness also includes the divine, spirits, and other entities unknown to us. As time progresses in the third and subsequent millennia, we will no doubt encounter other species of intelligence, and we will have to relate to them creatively and peacefully. It is necessary for us to be prepared in our spiritual lives, our theology, religion, philosophy, and in our general cultural experience. We need to make room for mystery and discovery, to welcome those who may show up on the horizon of history.

It Will Aim for Integration

All these elements are factors in the spirituality of a mature human family. Together, they allow for dimensions of experience that are missing from the inner lives of most persons, especially in the West. India has integrated yoga and tantra into its spiritual life and development, and Chinese culture has for the most part integrated t'ai chi into daily life. All societies have some form of sacred art and music, but only a few (notably Indian and Christian culture) have integrated them into the spiritual journey. Sufism in particular has made a place for music in the spiritual life of its practitioners.

Each tradition of the inner experience must be open to all the others and derive benefit from one another. No tradition is exempt from the necessity of social engagement where justice is at stake; indeed, the work of justice is itself a spiritual practice.

All the forms of spirituality must incorporate the dimension of the natural world and the openness to the cosmic community. They must guide us into a harmonious relationship with the earth and the universe itself.

Each tradition of spirituality must evolve into a more holistic understanding. Each will find a larger identity of insight, wisdom, and practice in an interspiritual approach.

Each form of spirituality is a living social organism capable of infinite growth as it acquires new insights, methods, and ways of formulating the goal of the mystical journey. We need to trust the experience of other traditions so that we can make it our own. In the long run, each tradition of the spiritual life will come to the service of the whole of humanity.

◆ Beauty in the Intermystical Journey

During my college years, I made a number of retreats at St. Joseph's Abbey in Spencer, Massachusetts, where Thomas Keating had been abbot for some twenty years — an extraordinarily beautiful place. On one of my retreats, I was transfixed by the rose window in the abbey church, one of the most stunning churches anywhere. As I walked back to my seat during communion, I gazed up at the rose window and was suddenly absorbed into it. I was so drawn into the brilliant blue, red, and pink window, so totally absorbed into contemplating the unity of God, that I failed to see the marble platform of a protruding altar and I tripped and fell unceremoniously on the floor! The beauty and the glory of the rose window had caught my attention and wouldn't let go!

Every one of us is irresistibly drawn to the beautiful. We thrive on our encounters with beauty, and these times of encounter are precious beyond all calculation. Beauty is not a feeling or emotion; rather, it evokes feelings and emotions in us. Beauty inspires us, lifting us out of our inertia and calls us all in numerous ways. We are all sometimes overwhelmed by the glorious grandeur of the natural world, the rapturous quality of mountains, the hypnotic effect of the ebbing and flowing ocean, and immersed in awe at the boundless expanse of the stars and the heavens. We are delighted by the countless number of species, their boundless array of color, shape, presence, and character. In witnessing all of this, do we not often feel a deep spirituality in the natural world and the cosmos?

Men, women, and children are also beautiful. So often when I encounter beauty in its physical manifestation in another person, I feel that this beauty is a borrowed quality, that it doesn't really belong to the person we think or regard as beautiful. Beauty, in this borrowed sense, is an absolute attribute of the divine itself; it is the divine's way of forcing us to attend to life and the world.

There is also people's moral beauty, the saintly quality of men and women who have given their lives to God or to service of others. Their beauty is not physical, but of something deeper. It is a kind of surrender to the transforming power of divine love, a letting go of the false self so that we can and do love. This perfection of their beauty is the reality of holiness, which is itself the perfection of love. Holiness is simply the radiance of divine love shining forth from those who have surrendered to it, and who allow it to transform themselves.

❖ Discovering the Mystic Heart Together

It is in the power, depth, and ultimacy of mysticism and beauty that the human family's unity manifests itself. Liberation is expressed in the longing for the divine. Every person is a mystic. The call to the spiritual journey is always inviting us. We need only respond. In this summons, in the cave of the heart, we are all one.

Beauty, in its highest sense, is in service to this call. The natural world, the cosmos, knowledge, and religion are also vehicles of the call. The mystical life is the common thread running through all the traditions, and so it is an intermystical task. Intermysticism is the deepest expression of the religious dimension of human life. It is the actual *religion* of each one of us when we arrive at the point of spiritual maturity. Community is the basis of universal spirituality. It is where the inner life is nurtured.

The common ground of human identity is not soul, self, or the Atman; it is not a permanent being animated by these forms. Our identity has its being in consciousness itself. That is the identity we share with all other persons, and it is the bridge that links together all the traditions. Consciousness is also the medium through which we experience life — relationships, interpersonal love, friendship, learning, religion, work, and spirituality. It is through our awareness that we experience ultimate states of being, the divine, and higher states of consciousness, thought and intellect. Consciousness is thus an essential part of an intermystical vision. The divine itself is consciousness, however we may experience it.

Interspirituality includes all ways that lead to ultimate reality, and all names for that great mystery. It especially embraces the inner and outer ways, or introversion and extroversion. The intermystical life also accepts the wisdom of the Hindu tradition in its wise understanding of the four stages of life. This natural, organic view of human existence is an important achievement in the evolution of our spiritual consciousness. A universal spirituality also has a place for various approaches to transformation from self-interest to other-centeredness, love, compassion, mercy, and kindness. This labor of transformation is the work of the contemplative in all of us, and generously accepting that work permits us to cultivate our own mystic character. The mystic character grows out of humility of heart and simplicity of spirit, a radical openness to the real. The mystic heart is able to abandon the false self, the egoic life of the deluded self.

The mystic heart in its maturity reflects the essential elements, gifts, and genius of all the traditions of spiritual wisdom: an actual moral capacity, solidarity with all living beings, deep nonviolence, humility, spiritual practice, mature self-knowledge, simplicity of life, selfless service and compassionate action, and the prophetic voice. These are further refined through a series of capacities that result from the inner journey: openness, presence, listening, being, seeing, spontaneity, and joy.

Moral capacity is present in all traditions; the sense of our solidarity with all life is present in all, but emphasized by Jainism, Hinduism, Buddhism, and Christianity. The characteristic of deep nonviolence has its purest, most eloquent form in Jainism, while the necessity of spiritual practice is again present in all forms of mysticism and religion, but contemplative practice is highlighted in Hinduism, Buddhism, Sufism, the Kabbalah, contemplative Christianity, and shamanism.

Similarly, self-knowledge is found in all types of spirituality, and here we have vast resources to draw upon, with breathless psychological depth and accuracy.

Simplicity of life is a fundamental commitment of every form of the mystical life, though it is practiced more by Hindu renunciates, or sannyasis, some Buddhist monks and nuns, and some Christians monastics.

Selfless service, compassionate action, and prophetic witness and behavior are deeply imbedded in the Western faith traditions, although compassion is preeminent as a spiritual value in Buddhism, and engaged Buddhism is discovering the realm of action as a result of its encounter with the Christian gospel. The Western religions all emphasize the spirituality of service and action.

Intermysticism has an important place for nature mysticism, which embraces nature and the cosmos in all its wonder, variety, and grandeur. Native American and other indigenous forms of spirituality are immersed in this cosmic mysticism. It is a spirituality of creation, a vital component of the mystical way. It cannot be neglected, since it reconnects us with the natural world and all its other life forms, a reconnection that is vital to our prospects for survival.

Interspirituality is a holistic understanding of the contemplative experience. It has room for all kinds of experiences, insights, methods of prayer and transformation. It values the experience of totality, intellectual vision, the way of pilgrimage, and forms of movement. It realizes the relationship between good nutrition and healthy spirituality.

The intermystic is the person who experiences the final integration that we encountered in Thomas Merton's insightful description. Such a person is truly a universal being. The interspiritual vision of the mystical life also perceives the perennial value of dreams as channels of communication between the realm of spirit and our earthly domain. It is in touch with the ultimate meaning of death and near-death as the final crossing over to the further shore of eternity.

All of these elements, factors, and qualities are part of the universal mystical tradition that undergirds the religions and cultures of the world. Intermysticism sees hope on the horizon, especially with the young who must be educated in the ways of the spiritual journey. They are the heirs of the various spiritual traditions, but in a special way of the intermystical vision now emerging all over the world, they can lead our planet into a universal civilization.

✦ A Special Message to the Young

This book is addressed to the whole of humankind, but it has a special message to the young. The reason is simple: Young people, especially children, are naturally spiritual. They have a need, perhaps a passion, for meaning (or a passion for the infinite, as Soren Kierkegaard would express it). I offer the following to the younger generation, although most of this message applies to everyone.

You must stand up on your own two feet in the spiritual life. You are responsible for this process; it cannot be shifted to your parents, your friends, or your teachers. You have to embrace the spiritual journey, and you are the one who has to be transformed. Don't concern yourself with what others are doing. Most have run their lives long enough in that way. You must find your own way, and you must be faithful to the truth you know or discover.

As you look to your parents or friends for guidance, ask yourself: "Are they good examples of the spiritual life? Are they serious about their own development and transformation, or are they wasting time on activities that distract them from the work of life? If they are serious about the spiritual dimension of existence, learn what you can from them. If their commitment is to a religious tradition, then respect it; try to integrate it. But if it doesn't include authentic spirituality, and it isn't open to other traditions, then discover your own path and find your own spirituality.

Look to all the traditions of the spiritual life and adopt an attitude of interspirituality. Claim the wisdom dimension of all the traditions for yourself, and let wisdom guide you. If you find your parents' approach lacking, don't reject it; rather, build on it. If their position is wanting, approach them with compassion. Perhaps you can teach them something!

Bracket the negative influence of your culture in your attempt to gain perspective on life and ultimate meaning. Attempt to transcend the influences of culture in making free decisions about your own inner life. If you reduce the stimuli of the surrounding society, you will acquire precious perspective on this matter, and it will put you in a position to embrace a healthy and viable spiritual life that will transform you. Gaining perspective on the influences of the culture and persons in our lives is extremely important. It allows our inner values, voice, and vision to emerge into clarity. It is an essential step in our process of clarification.

Don't give in to the temptation of cynicism and despair, especially as you look around you and see so many reasons to capitulate. Cynicism and despair are diseases of the spirit. They reduce our inner freedom, plunging us into moral, intellectual, and spiritual inertia, freezing our development and any hope of discovering ultimate meaning, direction, and belonging in life.

Always leave the door of hope wide open. Cast off skepticism, and be a radiant presence of depth, compassion, love, and kindness to others. Dare to be different! Dare to be yourself! Be who you really are; be who you know yourself to be in your moments of greatest clarity; don't allow others to determine your identity for you. Don't give away your power of self-determination.

Cultivate a love of quiet; learn to appreciate it. Gravitate toward silence; rest in the stillness.[1] Avoid noise, confusion, chaos, and needless tension. Make time each day just to sit and listen to the quiet. It's restorative and revelatory. Develop this attitude of appreciation and desire for contact with stillness; it will awaken the capacity for contemplation in you, and lead you into awareness of the divine. In my contemplative experience, quietness, silence, and stillness are the entry points to awareness of the ultimate reality. The stillness, quiet, or silence is the divine presence itself; it is a summons, an invitation into ultimate realization. As you become more proficient with the stillness, let your spiritual practice revolve around it by adopting some form of meditation practice. Watch what will happen; it *will* transform you!

✦ The Church As Matrix of Interfaith Encounter

One of the most significant characteristics of Catholicism in its long and rich history is its capacity to adapt. In its early history, the Greek and Latin fathers demonstrated this genius through a slow and careful assimilation of Greek philosophy and Roman law and culture. It made the insights of these civilizations its own, putting them into service for the Gospel in the evolution of a Christian civilization. Bede Griffiths has made much of this capacity of the Church throughout the ages, often commenting on the need for Catholicism to do the same in our age and the ages to come.

Interreligious dialogue and other forms of interfaith encounter have been going on since the time of the first Parliament of the World's Religions in Chicago in 1893, and previously in ancient India. Nonetheless, the Second Vatican Council has greatly stimulated interest in the study of other traditions and in mutual collaborations between members of the Catholic tradition and other faiths. The Catholic Church's promulgation of Vatican II's councilar document *Nostra Aetate* has proved to be nothing less than a revolution in religious relations.[2] This document commits the Church to the recognition of truth existing in the other traditions and to a desire to explore a new relationship with them.

Since the publication of this teaching in the early 1960s, the Church has embarked on a cautious program of dialogue with Moslems, Jews, Hindus, and Buddhists, not to mention the members of other Christian churches. The relations with the Jews has been one of the highlights of this new openness of Catholicism. Since Vatican II, the Church has systematically dismantled the theological and cultural support for anti-Semitism. In a very real sense, the Church has created a special place for the Jewish people in the Church without actually altering her structure. Her relationship with Judaism is a model of what can be accomplished with members of the other religions.

If the Church is willing to trust the promptings of the spirit rather than listening to the sirens of fear, she can play a major role in bringing all the faiths together by providing a welcoming space for them within herself. To open the door to a deeper relationship with the other traditions does not mean that the Church must change her nature or teaching, nor lose her identity. Rather, it means that Catholicism has decided to offer itself as a bridge that allows the religions to discover the source of their common identity in community, the community of religions within the Church, and this community of religions is actually a community of communities. It will take enormous vision and courage to walk this path in history. It brings to mind Christ's words: "Unless a grain of wheat falls into the earth and dies, it remains only a single grain, but if it dies it yields a rich harvest."[3] In changing, the Church also becomes a matrix of intermysticism and the interspiritual life as all forms of the inner experience take root in its being, and the universal elements shine forth in all its sons and daughters.

✦ A Universal Order of Sannyasa

The Interspiritual Age will require institutions and structures to carry, express, and support it. I suggest that a fundamental institution should be an interspiritual order of monastics or contemplatives open to all people — men and women, married and single, young, middle-aged, and old, confused or clear, adherents or not, with faith or agnostic — united in their desire for a deeper, more meaningful life. This would be a truly universal society of *sannyasa*, an order that welcomes as members individuals from all the world's religions and even from no tradition at all.

The term sannyasa, meaning renunciation, refers to all those seers, sages, ascetics, and yogis over thousands of years who have renounced the world and who have populated India's remote mountain sanctuaries, river banks, forests, and deserts. The term refers to an extremely ancient state, probably considerably older than Hinduism itself. In Hindu tradition it has always been understood that sannyasa makes possible something beyond the comprehension of religion, something that transcends religion, because it is infinite and ineffable. It eludes the capacity of any concept or doctrine to express or contain it. Sannyasis transcend religion because they seek integration with the absolute, which is infinitely beyond our spiritual institutions and all our conceptual and theological formulations. Sannyasa is a call to the mystical life. What mysticism seeks cannot be encompassed by any religion, even though sannyasa remains part of Hinduism and is the fourth stage in the Hindu view of life.

A universal or intermystical order of sannyasa, of contemplatives or mystics, would act as a meeting point for all traditions. It would also democratize the spiritual life as a state in which people could help one another, sharing their insights and spiritual resources. Sannyasa would be an existential place of encounter, free of the doctrinal differences that divide the traditions. Sannyasis from the various religions could then join together in collaborative efforts to reverse the negative habits that produced the ecological crisis, countless wars, and the many forms of injustice, oppression, and inequity.

The interspiritual society of sannyasa would also provide a forum for the further exploration of the mystical journey in all traditions, and in the emerging universal tradition as well. Teachers could be trained in the order in a universal vision, formed in the commitment to interspiritual practice, and yet loyal to their own tradition of origin.

The role of the spiritual teacher is very valuable. We mustn't be discouraged when some teachers fall down, when they are discovered to be all too human. Genuine spiritual leadership is very much needed, and is a treasure in the crown of the mystical life. The genuine spiritual teacher or guide has a very special relationship to his or her disciple. There is no doubt of the contribution the teacher makes to the inner life of countless people. We need the spiritual teacher because we must be guided. The Interspiritual Age will have an honored place for the guru, and there will be plenty of work for them to do.

Spirituality is the very breath of the inner life. It is an essential resource in the transformation of consciousness on our planet, and it will be enormously beneficial in our attempts to build a new universal society. Spirituality, intermysticism, and interspirituality can clear a path for a return of the sacred in wider culture. This return is necessary if we are to create an alternative to what now exists. I believe there is a real possibility for a genuine renaissance of the sacred, and with its dawning comes the hope of a universal civilization with a compassionate, loving heart. If that compassionate, loving heart is cultivated in a large number of people, then the universal age will be born. It all depends on a intermysticism that is open to all.

Spirituality, finally, is awareness and sensitivity, and sensitivity is itself awareness-in-action. It is this quality that we most require in our time and in the ages to come, but it is a quality refined only in the mystic heart, in the steady cultivation of compassion and love that risks all for the sake of others. It is these resources that we desperately need as we build the civilization with a heart, a universal society capable of embracing all that is, putting it to service in the transformation of the world. May the mystics lead the way to this rebirth of the human community that will harmonize itself with the cosmos and finally make peace with all beings.

Chapter Notes

Introduction

1. Thomas Berry, *The Dream of the Earth* (San Francisco: Sierra Club Books, 1988), 36–49.
2. Anonymous, *Meditations on the Tarot: A Journey into Christian Hermeticism* (Rockport, MA: Element Books, 1985), 102. Hermeticism itself is "crystallized mysticism," or mystical union that is self-aware during the integration with the divine reality (p. 36).
3. For an exhaustive record of this event, see John H. Burrows, ed., *The World's Parliament of Religions*, 2 vols. (Chicago: Parliament Publishing Co., 1893), and Richard Hughes Seager, ed., *The Dawn of Religious Pluralism: Voices from the World's Parliament of Religions*, 1893 (La Salle, IL: Open Court, 1993).
4. See Cairns and Teasdale, *The Community of Religions: Voices and Images of the Parliament of the World's Religions* (New York: Continuum, 1996); for material on the interfaith movement, the religions, the critical issues, and the Parliament, see Beversluis, *A SourceBook for Earth's Community of Religions*.
5. Acts 17:28.

Chapter 1

1. *Dzogchen* means the great perfection of the mind. It is a nondual state of enlight-enment, of seeing, perceiving, and realizing everything through the unified awareness of the original, eternal condition of consciousness.
2. Naomi Burton, Patrick Hart, and James Laughlin, eds., *The Asian Journal of Thomas Merton* (New York: New Directions, 1975), 338.
3. John K. Ryan, trans., *The Confessions of St. Augustine* (Garden City, NY: Image-Doubleday, 1960), 43.
4. In the Catholic Church there are numerous religious orders of men and women, and they take their original inspiration from the monastic experience. Over the centuries, however, many of these orders arose to meet specific needs in the Christian community, such as teaching, running orphanages, operating hospitals, or caring for widows, migrants, and the poor. Persons in such religious orders, as well as those in monasteries, are referred to as *religious*, a canonical term that designates someone under vows in a community.
5. Evelyn Underhill, *Mysticism: The Development of Humankind's Spiritual Consciousness* (London: Bracken Books, 1995, rep.), 72.
6. See Tenzin Gyatso, the XIVth Dalai Lama, *The Global Community and the Need for Universal Responsibility* (Boston: Wisdom Publications, 1990).

Chapter 2

1. For a good example in relation to Zen, see Robert Kennedy, *Zen Spirit, Christian Spirit: The Place of Zen in Christian Life* (New York: Continuum, 1997).
2. The material from India that follows can be found in my book *Towards a Christian Vedanta: The Encounter of Hinduism and Christianity According to Bede Griffiths* (Bangalore: Asian Trading, 1987), 17–42.
3. Abhishiktananda, *Saccidananda: A Christian Approach to Advaitic Experience* (Delhi: ISPCK, 1974).
4. Abhishiktananda, *Saccidananda*, 178.
5. Some of these books include: *Christ in India: Essays towards a Hindu-Christian Dialogue* (New York: Charles Scribner's Sons, 1966); *Vedanta and Christian Faith* (Los Angeles: Dawn Horse, 1973); *Return to the Center* (Springfield, IL: Templegate, 1982); *The Marriage of East and West* (Springfield, IL: Templegate, 1982); and *A New Vision of Reality: Western Science, Eastern Mysticism, and Christian Faith* (Springfield, IL: 1989).
6. In a letter to the author dated April 1990.
7. Some of his forty or so books include: *The Vedic Experience* (Pondicherry, India: All India Books, 1983); *The Silence of God: The Answer of the Buddha. Faith Meets Faith Series*, trans. Robert R. Barr (Maryknoll, NY: Orbis Books, 1989), and *Invisible Harmony: Essays on Contemplation and Responsibility*, ed. Harry James

Cargas (Minneapolis: Fortress Press, 1995).

8. Burton, Hart, and Laughlin, *Asian Journal*, 233, 235–36.

9. *The Documents of Vatican II*, ed. Walter Abbott, et al. (New York: Guild Press, 1966), see *Declaration on the Relationship of the Church to Non-Christian Religions (Nostra Acetate)*, 660–668.

10. MID publishes a journal three times a year, *Bulletin of Monastic Interreligious Dialogue*. It is housed at Abbey of Gethsemani, Trappist, KY 40051.

11. See *The Gethsemani Encounter: A Dialogue on the Spiritual Life by Buddhist and Christian Monastics*, ed. Donald Mitchell and James Wiseman (New York: Continuum, 1997).

12. Thomas Keating's most important books are *Open Mind, Open Heart: The Contemplative Dimension of the Gospel* (Rockport, MA: Element Books, 1986); *Invitation to Love: The Way of Christian Contemplation* (Rockport, MA: Element Books, 1992); and his masterpiece, *Intimacy with God* (New York: Crossroad, 1994).

13. For more information about the work at Naropa, see *Speaking of Silence: Christians and Buddhists on the Contemplative Way*, ed. Susan Walker (New York: Paulist Press, 1987).

14. Walker, *Speaking of Silence*, 126–29.

15. Joel Beversluis, ed., *A Sourcebook for Earth's Community of Religions* (Grand Rapids: CoNexus Press, 1995), 171.

16. Beversluis, *A Sourcebook for Earth's Community of Religions*, 171.

17. This document is available from the Vatican by writing to the Vatican Press, Vatican City, Europe.

18. Rodger Kamenetz, *The Jew in the Lotus: A Poet's Rediscovery of Jewish Identity in Buddhist India* (San Francisco: HarperSanFrancisco, 1994). See also his *Stalking Elijah: Adventures with Today's Jewish Mystical Masters* (San Francisco: HarperSanFrancisco, 1997).

19. Thich Nhat Hanh, *Living Buddha, Living Christ* (New York: Riverhead Books/Penguin-Putnam, 1995).

20. *Meister Eckhart*, ed. Franz Pfeiffer, trans. C. de B. Evans (London: Watkins, 1947), Sermon LVI, "The Emanation and Return," 143.

Chapter 3

1. *Upanisads*, trans. Patrick Olivelle (New York: Oxford University Press, 1996), 187, Taittiriya Upanishad 2:5. It is rendered there *prajnanam brahma*.

2. Olivelle, *Upanisads*, 272, Mundaka Upanishad 2:2, 272.

3. Olivelle, *Upanisads*, 289, Mandukya Upanishad v. 2. It is expressed as *Ayam atma brahma*.

4. Olivelle, *Upanisads*, 152, Chandogya Upanishad 6:8:7. This is the celebrated *Tat tvam asi, or That art thou*.

5. Olivelle, *Upanisads,* 15, Brhadaranyaka Upanishad 1:4:10.

6. Olivelle, *Upanisads,* Svetasvatara Upanishad 3:8.

7. An important source text for advaita is Brhadaranyaka Upanashad 2:4–14, Olivelle, p. 30.

8. A good work on his life is Edward Thomas, *The Life of Buddha as Legend and History* (London: Routledge & Kegan Paul, 1969). Thomas draws on all the available sources in his volume.

9. There has not been the the equivalent of biblical critical scholarship done on Buddhist sacred texts, or *suttra* criticism, as has been done so exhaustively in the Bible and the New Testament. Nor, for that matter, has there been any vedic and upanishadic critical scholarship, or Koranic historical criticism. Eventually, this will happen, and it will bring changes in interpretation and understanding.

10. *Buddhist Texts Through the Ages,* ed. Edward Conze (New York: Harper Touchbooks, 1954), *Prajnaparamitra Sutra* 146, 152.

11. Edward Conze, *Buddhism: Its Essence and Development* (New York: Harper Torchbooks, 1959), 40.

12. In Christian mystics of this type, one of the most important is Pseudo-Dionysius. See *Pseudo-Dionysius: The Complete Works,* ed. Colm Luibheid, *The Classics of Western Spirituality,* ed. John Farina (New York: Paulist Press, 1987). Buddhism similarly slips into apophatic language when attempting to describe nirvana, particularly when it has exhausted the more traditional categories.

13. Genesis 1:24–26.

14. *The Collected Dialogues of Plato,* ed. Edith Hamilton and Huntington Cairns (New York: Pantheon Books, 1961), 364, Meno 81c-d..

15. *The Basic Works of Aristotle,* ed. Richard McKeon (New York: Random House, 1941), 555, *De Anima* (On the Soul), 412. 2. 1. 20–23.

16. McKeon, *The Basic Works of Aristotle,* 592, De Anima 429. 3. 5. 23-25

17. *Basic Writings of St. Thomas Aquinas,* ed. Anton C. Pegis (New York: Random House, 1945), 43–46, "Summa Contra Gentiles," ch. 25.

18. Pegis, *Basic Writings of St. Thomas Aquinas,* 111, ch. 63.

19. Pegis, *Basic Writings of St. Thomas Aquinas,* 112.

20. Jan van Ruysbroeck, *Werken,* ed. by the Ruusbroecgenootschap. 4 vols. (Mechelen: Het Kompas, 1932–1934) *Die gheestelike brulocht, Werken,* vol. 1, 246. For a fine translation of his major works, see *John Ruusbroec: The Spiritual Espousals and Other Works,* trans. James A. Wiseman (New York: Paulist Press, 1985).

21. An important study of this commonality between traditions is that of Arthur O. Lovejoy, *The Great Chain of Being: A Study of the History of an Idea* (Cambridge: Harvard University Press, 1976). An excellent book on the self in the Western sense, a primarily Christian view, is that of Louis Dupre in his *Transcendent Selfhood: The Loss and Rediscovery of the Inner Life* (New York: Crossroad, 1976).

22. See Ken Wilber, *Sex, Ecology, Spirituality: The Spirit of Evolution* (Boston: Shambhala, 1995), 8–9.

23. For more on the new cosmology see Brian Swimme and Thomas Berry, *The Universe Story: From the Primordial Flaring Forth to the Ecozoic Era* (San Francisco: HarperSanFrancisco, 1992).

24. See Ken Wilber's brilliant synthesis of the study of consciousness *The Spectrum of Consciousness* (Wheaton, IL: Quest Books, 1977).

25. See Peter Russell, *The Global Brain: Speculations on the Evolutionary Leap to Planetary Consciousness* (Los Angeles: J. P. Tarcher, 1983).

26. The history of physics is well developed by Albert Einstein and Leopold Infield, *The Evolution of Physics from Early Concepts to Relativity and Quanta* (New York: Simon & Schuster, 1966).

27. Amit Goswami, *The Self-Aware Universe: How Consciousness Creates the Material World* (New York: Tarcher/Putum, 1993). Another interesting book that presents a more popular approach to science and spirituality is Michael Talbot, *Mysticism and the New Physics* (New York: Penguin-Arkana, 1993).

28. Others are attempting to do the same. See Ken Wilber, *The Marriage of Sense and Soul: Integrating Science and Religion* (New York: Random House, 1998).

29. Goswami, *The Self-Aware Universe*, 204.

Chapter 4

1. *Upanisads*, trans. Patrick Olivelle (New York: Oxford University Press, 1996), 264, Svetasvatara Upanishad 6:12.

2. Olivelle, *Upanishads*, 240, Katha Upanishad 4:1.

3. Olivelle, *Upanishads*, 246, Katha Upanishad 6:11.

4. *The Upanishads*, trans. Juan Mascaro (New York: Penguin Books, 1971), 102, Maitri Upanishad 6:19.

5. *The Dhammapada: The Path of Perfection*, trans. Juan Mascaro (New York: Penguin Books, 1973), 38.

6. Bede Griffiths, *River of Compassion: A Christian Reading of the Bhagavad Gita* (Warwick, NY: Amity House, 1987), 124.

7. *Dark Night of the Soul, The Collected Works of St. John of the Cross*, trans. Kieran Kavanaugh and Otillio Rodriguez (Washington: ICS Publications, 1973), 297–329.

8. Mascaro, *Upanishads*, 101, Maitri Upanishad 6:19.

9. Acts 17:28.

10. Bede Griffiths, *River of Compassion: A Christian Reading of the Bhagavad Gita* (Warwick, NY: Amity House, 1987), 118.

11. For Koranic discussions of Paradise, see Koran 78, 13:19–35, 20:117–119, 2:38, 62, 74, 77, 112.

12. *The Cloud of Unknowing*, ed. James Walsh, *The Classics of Western Spirituality*

(New York: Paulist Press, 1981).

13. Anonymous, *Meditations on the Tarot: A Journey into Christian Hermeticism* (Rockport, MA: Element Books, 1985), 319–20.

14. For an excellent introduction to the asramas see Patrick Olivelle, *The Asrama System: The History and Hermeneutics of a Religious Institution* (New York: Oxford University Press, 1993). Sri Lankan scholar Olivelle points out that the classical system of the stages developed to reconcile the opposition between two competing systems, that of the householder and that of the renunciate, ascetic, or the acosmic mystic (p. 4).

15. See D. T. Suzuki, *Essays in Zen Buddhism* (New York: Grove Press, 1961), 92–93, and Philip Kapleau, *The Three Pillars of Zen: Teaching, Practice and Enlightenment,* (Boston: Beacon Press, 1967), 301–311.

16. Koran 50:16.

17. *Meister Eckhart: Teacher and Preacher,* trans. and ed. Bernard McGinn, in *The Classics of Western Spirituality* (New York: Paulist Press, 1986), 270.

Chapter 5

1. Thomas Keating, *Intimacy with God* (New York: Crossroad, 1994), 163.

2. In Taitetsu Uno, *River of Fire, River of Water* (New York: Doubleday, 1998), 202.

3. Joel Beversluis, ed., *A Sourcebook for Earth's Community of Religions* (Grand Rapids, MI: CoNexus Press, 1995), 131–37.

4. Matthew 25:40.

5. Fritjof Capra, *The Tao of Physics: An Exploration of the Parallels Between Modern Physics and Eastern Mysticism* (Berkeley, CA: Shambhala, 1975).

6. David Bohm, *Wholeness and the Implicate Order* (London: Routledge & Kegan Paul, 1981).

7. The *Seville Statement on Violence,* in Beversluis, *A Sourcebook for Earth's Community of Religions,* 281–82.

8. For the *Universal Declaration on Nonviolence: The Incompatibility of Religion and War,* see Beversluis, *A Sourcebook for Earth's Community of Religions,* 171. Two excellent books on nonharming are Nathaniel Altman's *Ahimsa: Dynamic Compassion* (Wheaton, IL: Quest Books, 1980), and his *The Nonviolent Revolution: A Comprehensive Guide to Ahimsa — The Philosophy of Dynamic Harmlessness* (Rockport, MA: Element Books, 1988).

9. Theophane Boyd, *Tales of the Magic Monastery* (New York: Crossroad, 1984), 54.

Chapter 6

1. *The Collected Works of St. John of the Cross,* trans. Kieran Kavanaugh and Otilio Rodriquez (Washington, DC: ISC Publications, 1973), 675, Maxims, 24.

2. *Tao Te Ching*, trans. Gia Fu Feng and Jane English (New York: Vintage Books, 1972), ch. 49.

3. For a very thoughtful and accurate account of the origin and nature of *lectio divina*, see Thelma Hall, *Too Deep for Words* (New York: Paulist Press, 1989); Thomas Keating, *Open Mind, Open Heart: The Contemplative Dimension of the Gospel* (Warwick, NY: Amity House, 1986), pages 19–31 for the history of contemplation and its connection with *lectio divina*; and his masterpiece, *Intimacy with God* (New York: Crossroad, 1994), 46–54, on the process of *lectio*.

4. Luke 2:19, 51.

5. Keating, *Intimacy with God*, 164.

6. It is also legitimate to speak of what I call *confused* contemplation to name those forms emanating from an inadequate understanding, as is common in some new age literature, or through the teachings of certain self-appointed gurus. There is a further distinction to make here: mention should be made to what I refer to as *refused* contemplation, and this is the situation where many simply reject the call of contemplation or the mystical process in their lives either because they are ignorant of it or too immature to appreciate its incomparable value.

7. In addition to his very useful and practical books — the fruit of his experience and teaching — he has made twenty-four hour-long videos on the spiritual journey. These are available through his movement, Contemplative Outreach. These videos reveal the depth of his understanding of the mystical life, and I have never met another figure in the Christian tradition whose practical wisdom equals his. Contemplative Outreach is located at 9 William Street, P.O. Box 737, Butler, NJ 07405. The phone number is (201) 838-3384.

8. In a very real sense there is only one, whole meditation, just as there is only one love, or love is a unity with different aspects. There are many approaches to meditation, but they are all doing the same thing: transforming us from within.

9. Keating, *Intimacy with God*, 76–79.

10. Keating, *Intimacy with God*, 75.

11. Laurence Freeman's organization, based in London, is called The World Community of Christian Meditation. Each year, usually in the summer, they host the John Main Seminar. Past seminars have been led by Bede Griffiths, Raimon Panikkar, the Dalai Lama, Thomas Keating, and Huston Smith. These are highly informative and intensely oriented toward meditation practice.

12. See William Hart, *The Art of Living: Vipassanā as Taught by S. N. Goenka* (San Francisco: Harper & Row, 1987), and Kevin Culligan, Mary Jo Meadow, and Daniel Chowning, *Purifying the Heart: Buddhist Insight Meditation for Christians* (New York: Crossroad, 1994). Goenka is one of the foremost masters of Vipassanā in the world, and has his main center in Bombay. *Purifying the Heart* details a wonderful example of interspirituality occurring between Christians and Buddhists around practice.

13. There are many good books on Dzogchen, including *Buddha Mind: An Anthology of Longchen Rabjam's Writings on Dzogpa Chenpo,* trans. Tulku Thondup Rinpoche, ed. Harold Talbot (Ithaca: Snow Lion, 1989); Chokyi Nyima Rinpoche, *Indisputable Truth* (Hong Kong: Rangjung Yeshe Pub., 1996); and Chokyi Nyima Rinpoche, *The Union of Mahamudra and Dzogchen* (Hong Kong: Rangjung Yeshe Pub., 1994).

14. The best book I know on the subject is Thomas Keating, *The Mystery of Christ: The Liturgy as Spiritual Experience* (Warwick, NY: Amity House, 1987).

15. Shaykh Fadhlalla Haeri, *The Journey of the Self: A Sufi Guide to Personality* (San Francisco: HarperSanFrancisco, 1989), 93. See especially chapters 1–3, pages 9–104.

Chapter 7

1. *Chuang Tzu,* xvii. 3, in *The Texts of Taoism,* trans. and ed. James Legge (New York: Dover, 1969).

2. St. John Climacus, *The Ladder of Divine Ascent,* trans. Archimandrite Lazarus Moore (Willits, CA: Eastern Orthodox Books, 1959), 187, step 24, 9.

3. Climacus, *The Ladder of Divine Ascent,* 188, 19.

4. Climacus, *The Ladder of Divine Ascent,* 188, 19.

5. Climacus, *The Ladder of Divine Ascent,* 189, 26.

6. *The Collected Works of St. Teresa of Avila,* 2 vols., ed. Otilio Rodriguez and Kieran Kavanaugh (Washington, DC: Institute of Carmelite Studies, 1976), Life, vol. 1, ch. 15, 8, 105.

7. See her autobiography, *The Long Loneliness* (San Francisco: HarperSanFrancisco, 1997), and the biography by Robert Coles, *Dorothy Day: A Radical Devotion* (Reddington, MA: Addison-Wesley, 1987).

8. The German Lutheran church hardly put up any resistance to the Nazis, besides individuals like Dietrich Bonhoeffer. Certain segments of the church actually collaborated with the Third Reich.

9. In any future program of reform of the Vatican, I believe it is necessary to carefully examine the origin, history, and culture of this church government. What most people do not realize — least of all popes and the curial officials, staff, and employees, let alone rank-and-file Catholics — is that this system is a product of the Roman Empire, that is, the culture of power that the Roman Empire produced. It is most curious how the empire and the church were at enmity for three hundred and twelve years, but eventually became intimate friends. A historic synthesis of the two occured at the time of Constantine in 312.

10. For more information consult their website, at www.worldtibetday.com, or call (561) 388-0699.

11. See Jean-Pierre de Caussade, *Abandonment to Divine Providence* (Garden City, NY: Image-Doubleday, 1975), ch. 2.

Chapter 8

1. It was the philosopher Leibniz who coined the term perennial philosophy, or *philosophia perennis* in recognition of a universal wisdom found in all cultures and undergirding all knowledge. See Aldous Huxley, *The Perennial Philosophy*, (New York: Harper & Row, 1945), and Seyyed Hossein Nasr, *Knowledge and the Sacred* (New York: Crossroad, 1981). S. H. Nasr is the world's leading exponent of the perennial philosophy.

2. Two excellent books on this subject are Jeanine Miller, *The Vision of the Cosmic Order in the Vedas* (London: Kegan Paul, 1985), and Bede Griffiths, *The Cosmic Revelation: The Hindu Way to God*, (Springfield, IL: Templegate, 1983).

3. Bede Griffiths, *The Marriage of East and West* (Springfield, IL: Templegate, 1982), 88.

4. Bede Griffiths, *The Cosmic Revelation: The Hindu Way to God* (Springfield, IL: Templegate, 1983), 41.

5. Griffiths, *Cosmic Revelation*, 89.

6. Jeanine Miller, *The Vision of the Cosmic Order in the Vedas* (London: Kegan Paul, 1985). This entire book approaches the cosmic revelation through its manifestation in *rta*.

7. Griffiths, *The Cosmic Revelation*, 51.

8. Wisdom 13:5.

9. Romans 1:20.

10. Bede Griffiths, *The Golden String* (Springfield, IL: Templegate, 1980), 10.

11. Griffiths, *The Golden String*, 28.

12. William Wordsworth, "Intimations of Immortality from Recollections of Early Childhood," *The Oxford Book of English Verse (1250–1900)*, ed. Arthur Quiller-Couch (Oxford: Clarendon Press, 1925), 609–616. For a good treatment of the child's natural ability for divine things, see Robert Coles, *The Spiritual Life of Children* (Boston: Houghton Mifflin, 1990).

13. Quiller-Couch, *The Oxford Book of English Verse*, 609, 616.

14. "Nature," *The Journals and Miscellaneous Notebooks of Ralph Waldo Emerson*, ed. William Gilman et al, 13 vols. (Cambridge, MA: Harvard University Press, 1960), 1043.

15. Forrest Reid, *Following Darkness* (London: publisher unknown, 1902), 42.

16. David Suzuki and Peter Knudtson, *Wisdom of the Elders: Sacred Native Stories of Nature* (New York: Bantam Books, 1992), 212.

17. Sam D. Gill, *Native American Traditions: Sources and Interpretations* (Belmont, CA: Wadsworth Publishing, 1983) 91.

18. Jacqueline Decter, *Nicholas Roerich: The Life of a Russian Master*, (Rochester, VT: Park Street Press, 1989). The Nicholas Roerich Museum, at 319 West 107th Street, New York, N.Y. 10025, is completely devoted to this figure. Most of his works can be viewed on their website: www.roerich.org.

19. See the documentary, *Peace Like a River: The 1993 Parliament of the World's Religions*. Chicago Sunday Evening Club.

20. Thomas Merton, *The Inner Experience: "Kinds of Contemplation"* (IV), *Cistercian Studies*, 18, 4, 1983, 298. *The Inner Experience* was an unpublished manuscript that was serialized in *Cistercian Studies* (vols. 18–19, 1983–84).

21. For a more detailed treatment of natural symbolism, see my "Symbolism as Theophany," *Monastic Studies*, 16, 1985.

22. Bernardo Aperribay et al, ed., *Orbas De San Buenaventura* (Madrid: Biblioteca de Autores Cristianos, 1948), tomo V, *Questiones Disputatae de Mysterio Trinitatis*, q. 1, a. 2, concl., 134.

23. Aperribay et al, ed., *Orbas De San Buenaventura*, 134.

24. Aperribay et al, ed., *Orbas De San Buenaventura*, 136–138.

25. Leon Amoras et al, ed., *Itinerarium Mentis in Deum, Orbas De San Buenaventura*. (Madrid: Biblioteca De Autores Cristianos, 1945), tomo I, *Itin*. 1, 2, 564.

26. Amoras et al, ed., *Itinerarium Mentis in Deum, Orbas De San Buenaventura*., 1, 7 and 1, 9, 568 and 570–72.

27. Nasr, *Knowledge and the Sacred*, 189.

28. Nasr, *Knowledge and the Sacred*, 191.

29. Nasr, *Knowledge and the Sacred*, 191

30. Nasr, *Knowledge and the Sacred*, 200.

31. Rudolf Otto, *The Idea of the Holy: An Inquiry into the Non-Rational Factor in the Idea of the Divine and Its Relation to the Rational,* trans. John W. Harvey (Oxford: Oxford University Press, 1923), 4–40.

32. Thomas Berry, *The Dream of the Earth*. (San Francisco: Sierra Club Books, 1998), 11.

33. Berry, *The Dream of the Earth*, 80–81.

34. Berry, *The Dream of the Earth*, 18–19, 21–22. See also James Lovelock, *Gaia: A New Look at Life on Earth* (London: Oxford University Press, 1979), and Peter Russell, *The Global Brain: Speculations on the Evolutionary Leap to Planetary Consciousness* (Los Angeles: Tarcher, 1983).

35. Berry, *The Dream of the Earth*, 81.

36. Berry, *The Dream of the Earth*, 81.

37. Berry, *The Dream of the Earth*, 81.

38. Berry, *The Dream of the Earth*, 111.

39. Berry, *The Dream of the Earth*, 132. For a solid theology and metaphysics of creation that uncovers the deep roots of a creation-centered spirituality, see Beatrice Bruteau, *God's Ecstasy: The Creation of a Self-Creating World* (New York: Crossroad, 1997).

40. See Henry David Thoreau, *Walking* (New York: Penguin, 1995).

41. This step in the practice of natural meditation, I am borrowing from the sky meditation of Dzogchen in Tibetan mysticism.

Chapter 9

1. See Thomas Keating, "Guidelines for Interreligious Understanding: Points of Agreement or Similarity," in Joel Beversluis, ed., *A Sourcebook for Earth's Community of Religions* (Grand Rapids, MI: CoNexus Press, 1995), 148; and Thomas Keating, *Speaking of Silence*, 126–29, which contains only the guidelines. For simplicity's sake, the later edition found in the *SourceBook* will be followed. It is a refinement, and in some respects a rewording of the original guidelines.

2. Brihadaranyaka Upanishad 2:4:14.

3. *Collected Works of Ramana Maharshi*, ed. Arthur Osborne (London: Rider, 1969), 146.

4. Thich Nhat Hanh, *Living Buddha, Living Christ*, (New York: Riverhead Books, 1995), 203. Interbeing is something he addresses in many of his books.

5. A wonderful book that illustrates this approach is by Howard Schwartz, ed., *Gabriel's Palace: Jewish Mystical Tales* (New York: Oxford University Presss, 1993).

6. Ludovicus Blosius, *Speculum Spirituale*, cap. xi.

7. *The Collected Works of St. Teresa of Avila*, trans. Kieran Kavanaugh and Otilio Rodriquez, 2 vols. (Washington, DC: ICS Pub., 1976), vol. 2, The Interior Castle, 434, 7: 2.

8. Kavanaugh and Rodriquez, *The Collected Works of St. Teresa of Avila*, 433.

9. *The Collected Works of St. John of the Cross*, trans. Kieran Kavanaugh and Otilio Rodriguez (Washington, DC: ICS Pub., 1973), The Dark Night of the Soul, bk. 1, 318, ch. 10, 6,

10. Kavanaugh and Rodriquez, *The Collected Works of St. John of the Cross*, bk. 2, 388, ch. 24, 49.

11. William C. Chittick, *The Sufi Path of Love: The Spiritual Teachings of Rumi* (Albany, NY: SUNY, 1983), 179, translations by Chittick.

12. *The Collected Works of St. John*, The Ascent of Mount Carmel, bk. 2, 116, ch. 7, 3.

13. *The Collected Works of St. John*, The Ascent of Mount Carmel, bk. 2, 116, ch. 7, 4.

14. Thomas Keating, *Intimacy with God*, 159.

15. *Collected Works of St. John*, Living Flame of Love, 17, 649.

16. Bede Griffiths. *A New Vision of Reality: Western Science, Eastern Mysticism and Christian Faith*, (Springfield, IL: Templegate, 1989), 253.

17. Two classic and very good books on this subject are John Sanford, *Dreams: God's Forgotten Language* (San Francisco: HarperSanFrancisco, 1989), and Morton Kelsey, *God, Dreams, and Revelation* (Minneapolis: Augsburg, 1991).

18. The Mandukya Upanishad discusses the sacred syllable OM, and in this context, the four states of consciousness or the self, two of which are dreaming and dreamless sleep. See Olivelle, Upanisads, Mandukya Upanishads, 289–90.

19. *Tricycle*, 6, 1, Fall 1996.

20. The Council on Spiritual Practices can be contacted by writing to Robert Jesse, Box 460820, San Francisco, CA 94146-0820, or through their website at

www.csp.org. See their *Entheogens and the Future of Religion*, ed. Robert Forte (San Francisco: Council on Spiritual Practices, 1997).

21. Huston Smith, *Cleansing the Doors of Perception: The Religious Significance of Entheogenic Plants and Chemicals* (New York: Penguin/Putnam, 2000, forthcoming). See his article "Do Drugs Have Religious Import?" *The Journal of Philosophy*, 61, 18, Oct. 1, 1964.

22. For a classical scientific article, see Walter N. Pahnke and William A. Richards, "Implications of LSD and Experimental Mysticism," *The Journal of Transpersonal Psychology*, 1, 2, Fall 1969.

23. A few fascinating books on the subject of heaven include Peter Kreeft, *Heaven: the Heart's Deepest Longing* (San Francisco: HarperSanFrancisco, 1980); Colleen McDannell and Bernhard Lang, *Heaven: A History* (New York: Vintage-Random House, 1988); and Morton Kellsey, *Afterlife: the Other Side of Dying* (New York: Crossroad, 1982). For something on the widespread belief in transmigration, see Joseph Head and S. L. Cranston, *Reincarnation: An East-West Anthology* (Wheaton, IL: Quest, 1968).

24. For a comprehensive view, see F. X. Shouppe, *Purgatory: Illustrated by the Lives and the Legends of the Saints* (Rockford, IL: Tan Books, 1973).

25. See Elisabeth Kübler-Ross, *Death: the Final Stage of Growth* (Englewood Cliffs, NJ: Prentice Hall, 1975); and Raymond Moody, *Life After Life* (Atlanta: Mockingbird Books, 1975). For a celebrated case study, see Dannion Brinkley's *Saved by the Light: The True Story of a Man who Died Twice and the Profound Revelations He Received* (New York: Villard Books, 1994).

26. For a very good book that deals with the scientific evidence for the near-death experience, see Patrick Glynn, *God: The Evidence: The Reconciliation of Faith and Reason in a Postsecular World* (Rocklin, CA: Prima, 1997), chapter 4, "Intimations of Immortality."

27. Reza Arasteh, *Final Integration in the Adult Personality* (Leiden: E. J. Brill, 1965).

28. Thomas Merton, *Contemplation in a World of Action* (New York: Doubleday, 1973), 225.

29. Merton, *Contemplation in a World of Action*, 225–26.

Chapter 10

1. This stillness is the inner stillness, the *quies*, or *hesychia* (stillness) of the Desert tradition of early monasticism in Sinai, Palestine, and Syria. See *hesychia* in The Philokalia, comp. *St. Nikodimos of the Holy Mountain and St. Makarios of Corinth*, 3 vols., trans. G. E. H. Palmer et al. (London: Faber & Faber, 1979–1984), 106–8. There are references to stillness (hesychia) in many places throughout the three volumes. Hesychia has the connotation of nondiscursive thought, or intuitive wisdom without the need of thought.

2. *The Documents of Vatican II*, ed. Walter Abbott, et al. (New York: Guild Press,

1966), see *Declaration on the Relationship of the Church to Non-Christian Religions (Nostra Acetate)*, 660–668.

3. John 12:24.

Glossary

Acquired Contemplation: In Christian mysticism, the active dimension of the inner process in which *the person* puts effort into his or her prayer and search for the divine. Also called active contemplation.

Action: Our sphere of efforts in the world; often seen in relation or opposition to contemplation.

Advaita: In Hindu mysticism, the experience of nonduality, or unitive consciousness.

Advaitic: Refering to any nondual awareness, experience, or knowledge.

Advaitin: A Hindu, nondualist mystic.

Affective Prayer: Prayer of the heart that engages the emotions in expressions of love toward God.

Affectivity: A contemplative form of prayer based on movements of love for the divine.

Ahimsa: The Jain understanding of nonharming or nonviolence, which includes reverence for life and love.

Aikido: A Japanese martial art like yoga or meditation in motion.

Allah: Islamic name for God taken from the Koran, and based on God's revelation to Mohammed through the Archangel Gabriel.

Ananda: The Hindu experience of bliss; an attribute of *Saccidananda,* the Godhead.

Asramas: The Hindu stages of life: student, householder, forest dweller, and renunciate.

Atmavidya: Mystical realization of the eternal self; inner awakening to the indwelling divine reality, the self.

Apophatic: Any approach to the divine that transcends reason's usual ways of knowing. It is a knowing by not knowing; the divine is actually experienced,

but   because
it is ineffable it cannot be expressed adequately in language. The apophatic
way approaches the ultimate without the use of concepts. It depends on acts
of love that focus the will in a steady attention to the divine.

Apophatism: The whole movement of the apophatic way as a method seeking
union with God by way of negation of the intellectual component, and
emphasizing contemplative rest in the divine presence in pure trust beyond
understanding.

Atman: In Hinduism, the eternal self, and also the human self. Both are immortal. The Atman is said to be one with the Brahman.

Beatitude: The life of all the elect in Heaven, in which they have the eternal vision
of God.

Bhagavad Gita: Meaning *Song of God,* it is one of the sacred texts of Hinduism,
and really a compendium of the whole tradition.

Bhajan: A devotional, often ecstatic song in Hindu spiritual practice.

Bhakti Yoga: One of the Hindu paths or *margas;* it stresses the way of love and
devotion to God.

Boddhisattva: The "one who has the courage to be awake." In Mahayana
Buddhism, a saintly sage who takes a vow not to enter liberation until all sentient beings are liberated from the cycle of rebirth, or samsara.

Bodhi: The Buddhist sanskrit word for enlightenment; a breakthrough experience of profound insight into the nature of reality as emptiness, or *shunyata.*

Book of Creation: The experience of all of nature, the cosmos, and life as revelational of the divine through a symbolic system of meanings present everywhere.

Book of Life: Life as possessing intrinsic meanings embedded in our experience
by the divine.

Book of Nature: The whole of nature as participating in an elaborate and intrinsic symbolic order of meanings available to the mystic who knows how to
contemplate or see these meanings.

Boundless Consciousness: The Buddhist notion of the absolute or ultimate state
of consciousness as essentially unlimited and free.

Brahman: The Godhead in Hinduism.

Brahmacarya: Studenthood in the Hindu *asramas,* or stages of life, usually from
twelve to twenty-four.

Brahmavidya: Direct mystical apprehension of the divine, or the brahman.

Brahmacari: The student in the stage of *brahmacaya.*

Buddha-Mind/Buddha-Nature: Enlightened awareness, who we really are.

Capoeira: A Brazilian martial art form that combines dance with basic moves.

Cave of the Heart: Also called the *guha,* the place of deepest interiority where we
are one with God. It is an Indian metaphor for contemplation.

Chit: Infinite consciousness as one of the attributes of the divine.

Cosmology: The study of the universe in astrophysics and philosophy.

Centering Prayer: A Christian form of prayer that facilitates the cultivation of contemplation by employing a *receptive* approach.

Christian Meditation: Similar to Centering Prayer except that it is a *concentrative*
method that depends on the constant repetition of the mantra, or prayer
word.

Christian Zen: The appropriation of *zazen* or sitting meditation by Christians.

Compassionate Action: An element of intermystical practice in which we incarnate our compassion and love in concrete situations — beyond simply maintaining an abstract notion of compassion.

Contemplation/Contemplatio/Contemplative: A mature form of prayer or spiritual practice in which the person has a longing for, awareness, and abiding experience of the divine reality beyond concepts. It is a *tasting* of God. A contemplative is a mystic who experiences the ultimate through this form of deep prayer.

Cosmic Revelation: The manifestation of the divine in the universe, the natural world, and in life.

Creation-Centered Spirituality: A kind of nature or natural mysticism committed to preserve and enhance the earth as the matrix of value for the human.

Dark Night of the Senses/Soul/Spirit: The periods of mystical suffering meant to purify the senses, the will, and the spirit in preparation for union with God.

de Broglie Wavelength: In physics, a measurement of the phenomenon of particles (photons) acting as waves, alternating back and forth as both waves and particles. The de Broglie Wavelength measures the length of the wave in relation to a particle in movement.

Deification: The early Christian insight of contemplation as a process of becoming like God, or the actual transformation into God, through a kind of participation in divine nature. One becomes God by participation, but not in a total way, as in Hinduism.

Dharma: The Way of Truth, or the teaching of Buddhism.

Divine Love: The inner reality of the divine as infinite love.

Divine Spiration/Breathing: An attribute of God through which God appears in a kind of breathing or spirating presence.

Divine Therapy: Thomas Keating's name for contemplation and the active living out of the Christian experience in a daily life of virtue and compassionate service.

Dualism: The notion of an absolute distinction between the divine and the human spheres, or between this realm of human life and the realm of the spirit. In Buddhism, the realm of relative truth.

Dzogchen: In Tibetan mysticism, the ultimate state of the perfected minded as essentially nondual, or unified, in a pristine awareness.

Ecological/Ecozoic Age: Thomas Berry's term for the present period of history in which we are becoming more conscious of the importance of the environment and establishing a harmonious, sustainable relationship with it.

Eco-Spirituality: A natural form of mysticism that regards the earth as a primary focus of value and spiritual insight.

Ego: The initial psychological identity that aids our process of individuation, or becoming mature persons; it is later seen as an obstacle to our human and spiritual maturity.

Evacuation: In Thomas Keating's view of Centering Prayer, the moment in each instance of practice when what comes up during the sitting, the unloading of raw contents from the unconscious, is released naturally and without effort.

Explicate Order: The view of David Bohm that the universe is the unfolding of a pre-existing reality called the implicate order.

Extroversion: The way or route to the divine through the external reality of the world, nature, and life.

False Self: The self-absorbed life of the immature person.

Forest Dweller: The third stage or *asrama* in the Hindu view of life, where one retires.

Geologian: A theologian for the earth itself.

Godhead: The transcendent source or ground of existence; the end and goal of life. It is both personal and impersonal.

Great Spirit: The experience of God in the Native American traditions.

Greater Vehicle: Mahayana Buddhism, with its commitment to compassion and service to the liberation of all sentient beings.

Grihastha: The second *asrama*, or stage of life in the Hindu view, that of the householder.

Guru: A spiritual teacher or master in the Hindu tradition.

Heart: A metaphor for the mystical organ of integration with the divine, or for ultimate realization. It is the subtle point of interiority beyond corruption, and totally available to the spiritual life.

Hermeticism: Crystallized mysticism, originating in ancient Egypt and medieval Europe.

Hinayana: Theravada Buddhism; also called the Lesser Vehicle as the earlier form of Buddhist practice, focused on self-transformation rather than on compassion toward other sentient beings.

Holistic Spirituality: A spiritual life that includes nature, art, spiritual practice, service to others, and the body.

Householder: The second *asrama* or stage of life in the Hindu approach that encompasses marriage, family, and work.

Hylomorphism/Hylomorphic: Aristotle's theory of reality as a combination of primary matter and substantial form as the basis of all existents here in this world.

Immanence: The presence of the divine, or ultimate awareness in all things.

Impersonal: The Buddhist understanding of the ultimate as not involving a personal God.

Implicate Order: In David Bohm's vision of cosmology, the implicit, undifferentiated seedling reality before its unfolding in the cosmos.

Inculturation: The practice of Christians expressing the Gospel, liturgical worship, and theology in the terms, categories, rites, and symbols of the cultures in which they find themselves.

Infused Contemplation: The state of passive receiving of the divine and special graces leading to union with God.

Intellectual Substance: The soul in St. Thomas Acquinas's view as an intellectual being related to vision of the divine reality, or God in Heaven.

Interbeing: The Budhhist idea of the interconnectedness of everyone and everything.

Interspiritual Age: The name for the age we are now entering, where people are no longer isolated within their home tradition but are exploring other traditions, finding what is useful to their own growth.

Interspirituality: The common heritage of humankind's spiritual wisdom; the sharing of mystical resources across traditions.

Introversion: The inner way of the mystical life.

Jesus Prayer: A contemplative practice centering on the repetition of this prayer: "Lord Jesus Christ, Son of the Living God, have mercy on me a sinner," the prayer of the publican in Luke's gospel.

Jnana Yoga: In the Hindu tradition, the path or *marga* of introspection; it involves an intellectual, philosophical character, but has a mystical component to it that directs its operation.

Jnani: One who follows the way of introspection, or the path of *jnana*. A *jnani* also has a degree of mystical understanding from direct experience.

Karma: The law of moral causality found in the Eastern religions, especially in Hinduism, Buddhism, Jainism, and Sikhism. The karmic law maintains that every action, thought, and word generates consequences. Good karma presents good results, while negative karma results in unpleasant and unwanted results. Both affect future lives, and even this life.

Karma Yoga: In Hinduism, the path or *marga* of selfless work. It is a way to God by dedicating one's action to the divine and ascribing the positive actions with their results to God.

Kavi: The saffron garb of a renunciate or *sannyasi*, which consists of two pieces of cloth, one a dhoti wrapped around the waist, the other a shawl put around the shoulders.

Kensho: In Zen, a sudden experience of enlightenment; also called satori.

Kindness: A sign of genuine spiritual attainment, where someone acts from genuine sensitivity to the sufferings and needs of others.

Koan: A little puzzle in Zen Buddhism meant to trip up the rational, analytical, philosophical mind, making room for satori or *kensho*.

Lectio Divina: A Christian monastic contemplative practice leading to the fullness of the mystical life. The first of the four moments is *lectio divina* or spiritual reading of a sacred text. This leads to *meditatio*, or reflection on the passage in question. This is followed by *oratio* or affective prayer, the movement of the heart. Finally, one reaches *contemplatio*, or rest in God.

Liberation: In the Eastern religions, final release from samsara, the cycle of rebirth.

Local Awareness/Consciousness: The consciousness or awareness of the human person in his or her normal state.

Mahavakyas: The Four Great Utterances or Sentences in the Hindu tradition that sum up upanishadic mysticism. These *mahavakyas* are: (1) Brahman is Consciousness, (2) Atman is Brahman, (3) That art Thou, and (4) I am Brahman.

Mahayana: The school of Buddhism of the Greater Vehicle, which produced the notion of the bodhisattva.

Mantric Meditation: A Hindu and Christian form of prayer that relies on the constant repetition of a word or mantra in order to bring the mind to inner quiet and receptivity to the divine presence.

Margas: In the Hindu view of life, the four paths to God: jnana, bhakti, karma, and raja yoga.

Maya: The Hindu notion of the relative or illusory status of the world that we perceive with our senses.

Meditatio: The second stage of *Lectio Divina* in the Chrsitian monastic tradition, in which one reflects on a sacred text in order to derive inspiration for prayer.

Meditation: A contemplative discipline involving sitting either in the lotus position, on a *seiza* bench or in a chair, with the purpose of stilling the mind in order to become more and more absorbed into the divine, or in Buddhism, to achieve insight into reality.

Moksha: In Hindu mysticism, liberation or release from samsara, the cycle of rebirth.

Mystic: Any individual with a direct experience and awareness of the absolute, the divine, or boundless consciousness.

Mystical Marriage: Mystical union in the Christian tradition of contemplation.

Mystical Totality: A rare contemplative state in which the person experiences everything in the divine unity, including the cosmos, nature, and all creatures in all worlds.

Mysticism: The desire for, awareness of, and insight into the ultimate reality, however this may be understood.

Nameless One: A term for the divine, the ultimate, or the absolute.

Natural Mysticism: The perception of the divine in the natural world and the cosmos.

Near-Death Experience: An experience of an after-death realm, in which people often experience subtle states of consciousness involving the divine, angelic beings, and deceased loved ones.

Nirvana: The ultimate state in Buddhism in which one is completely free of desire and understands the nature of reality.

Noetic: The element of knowledge in mystical consciousness, that this consciousness gives real knowledge of the ultimate.

Non-Dual: The *advaitic* or unitive consciousness.

Non-Judgment: The practice of suspending judgment on the motives and actions of others, and a sign of spiritual maturity in those who act with such restraint.

No-Self: The Buddhist notion that there is no permanent self, soul, or substance, though there is permanent consciousness.

Numinous: The presence of the divine in nature and the cosmos.

One (The): A name for God, the presence, or the Ultimate Reality.

Oratio: The third stage in the monastic contemplative practice of *Lectio Divina*, which expresses itself in affective prayer, or a loving movement in the heart toward God.

Oxherding Pictures: The ten Zen drawings that illustrate the process of awakening, enlightenment, and return to the world.

Panentheism: The mystical view found in Hinduism, Christianity, and Sufism that everything subsists in God.

Pantheism: The view that the divine is everything, and that it is exhausted in its immanence in everything.

Parinirvana: Ultimate, transcendent freedom in the state of boundless consciousness.

Participation: The Christian understanding of the ultimate nature of the person who is transformed in union with God as achieving a divine status: becoming God through participation in his nature.

Particle-Wave Function: In physics, the discovery that electromagnetic waves can act as particles, and particles can act as waves — their dual nature.

Passive Contemplation: An *infused* state of relationship with God in which the divine is doing all the work in the relationship, leading the person to union.

Pentecost: The experience of the Holy Spirit by the disciples of Jesus in the upper room after the crucifixtion of Christ. The Christian church traces its birth to this event recorded in Acts.

Perennial Philosophy: The primordial wisdom found in all traditions.

Personalist: An approach to the experience of the divine as a personal, loving being.

Planetary Consciousness (Gaia): The awareness the planet itself may have.

Pratitya Samutpada: The Buddhist metaphysical principle that views everyone and everything as bound together in a vast cosmic community of interconnectedness; the reality of interbeing.

Primary Matter: One of Aristotle's two principles in his cosmology; the other is substantial form. In his view, form shapes matter.

Primordial Revelation: The cosmic revelation and also natural mysticism.

Prophetic Action/Voice: One of the elements in a universal spirituality: the ability and courage to speak out and act in the face of injustice.

Puja: Temple sacrifice in the Hindu tradition. It is a rite performed in relation to a deity.

Purusha: In the upanishadic tradition, the Cosmic Lord, or Person. The personal manifestation of the divine reality.

Quantum Mechanics: The whole area of energy dynamics in contemporary physics, particularly as related to the properties of atoms and molecules, or the particle-wave duality.

Quantum/Quanta: In physics, energy and its interactions.

Raja Yoga: One of the paths or margas in Hindu spirituality. Called the royal way, it involves intense meditation and other psychospiritual activities in order to achieve integration with the ultimate.

Reading the Books of Creation/Nature/Life: The contemplative capacity to understand the intrinsic symbolism in nature, cosmos, being, and life.

Regional Awareness/Consciousness: The consciousness of human beings or any other intelligent species.

Renunciate: A *sannyasi* or monk in India.

Rinpoche: "Precious one" in Tibetan Buddhism, referring to any reincarnated lama (spiritual master).

Rishis/Rishic: The forest sages of Indian antiquity, and anything related to them.

Rta: In Hinduism, the cosmic and moral order.

Saccidananda: The absolute in the Vedanta. It is the Godhead as infinite existence, consciousness, and bliss: the bliss of being aware of being the fullness of existence itself.

Sacrament: A channel of divine grace manifested through nature and worship.

Sacramental: The capacity to be a channel of grace and the divine presence.

Sacred Word: A prayer word in Centering Prayer that symbolizes one's intention to surrender to the presence and action of God within one's being.

Samadhi: Contemplative ecstasy in Hindu mysticism; the state of empty mind in Buddhism.

Samsara: The cycle of rebirth.

Sanatana Dharma: The Eternal Religion, a name for Hinduism.

Sangha: The Buddhist (monastic) community.

Sannyasa: Hindu renunciate, or monk, and the fourth *asrama,* or stage of life.

Sannyasi: A person who embraces the state of *sannyasa.*

Sapiential: Wisdom, a characteristic of the mystical.

Sat: Pure existence in Hindu mysticism. It is part of *saccidananda.*

Satori: *Kensho* or enlightenment in Zen, in which one's sense of separation ceases.

Self-Subsistent Love: The inner nature of the divine in its Trinitarian identity.

Shoah: The Holocaust.

Shunyata: The Buddhist notion of emptiness, the interconnectedness of all beings, and the lack of intrinsic individual existence.

Soul: The view of many religions that each person, each living being has life because of a center of identity called the soul; it is the principle of life and will for that being. It is also a nonmaterial reality.

Spiration: Divine breathing through which God communicates himself to the person.

Spirituality: The whole inner movement of the heart to seek the divine. It is the commitment to the process of inner change, and a personal attachment to this way of life and the transformation it brings.

Spiritual Practice: A vital element in every valid form of the spiritual journey, which can take the form of prayer, contemplation, meditation, chanting, or liturgical devotion. Spiritual practice is always transformative, and in many ways, is the core means of inner change.

Stages: The four periods of life in the Hindu tradition: student, householder, forest dweller and renunciate.

Student: The one who is in the first stage of life in the Hindu view.

Substantial Form: In Aristotle's metaphysics and cosmology, the principle that gives structure to primary matter, or actualizes potentiality.

Sufi: An Islamic mystic.

Sufism: Islamic mysticism.

Symbol: An intrinsic meaning in the natural world, being, and life that reflects the source.

Synthesis: The highest act of the understanding in which views converge in a more adequate understanding.

T'ai Chi: A Chinese system of moving meditation.

Tanha: In Buddhism, selfish desire or craving, the cause of all suffering.

Tao: The Taoist understanding of the divine, often rendered, Way.

Theophany: Manifestation of the divine in the symbols or intrinsic meanings in nature, cosmos, being and life.

Theoria Physike: Natural contemplation.

Theosis: Deification, or becoming God through participation in him.

Transcendentalists: The American movement in the last century of mystic poets and writers who pursued a personal form of natural mysticism informed by Eastern mysticism, especially the Indian Vedanta.

Ummah: The Islamic commonwealth as a spiritual fellowship.

Unconscious: The realm of the hidden and unseen levels of identity.

Unified Field Theory: In physics, the view that there has to be something that integrates all the forces of the cosmos, especially the four chief ones: gravity, electromagetism, the strong and the weak nuclear forces.

Unloading: In Thomas Keating's vision of contemplation as the Divine Therapy, the third moment in Centering Prayer when past memories and raw emotions rise up and then are evacuated under the influence of the divine spirit.

Upanishads: The 108 sacred texts of the Hindu tradition. The essentially philosophical reflections on the Vedas, the earliest of the Hindu scriptures.

Upanishadic Mysticism: The *advaitic,* or unitive spirituality of the Vedanta.

Vajrayana: The Diamond tradition of Tibetan Buddhism.

Vanaprastha: The third *asrama* or stage in the Hindu view of life, that of the forest dweller.

Vedanta: Meaning, the end of the Vedas, or the goal of this ancient wisdom developed in the Upanishads.

Vedas: The four most ancient texts of the Hindu tradition containing the mystical utterances of the *rishis,* the forest sages of extreme Indian antiquity.

Vedic: Anything relating to the *rishis,* the Vedas, and the cosmic revelation found in the Vedas themselves.

Vipassanā: Insight meditation in Theravadan Buddhism.

Wakan Tanka: In Native American spirituality, the Great Spirit.

Yoga: The way of union or integration in India.

Zazen: Sitting meditation in Zen Buddhism.

Zen: A Mahayanan form of Buddhism that emphasizes meditation or *zazen* as the means to achieve enlightenment, satori, or kensho.

Recommended Reading

Abhishiktananda. *Hindu-Christian Meeting Point*. Delhi: ISPCK, 1969.

————. *Guru and Disciple*. Trans. Heather Sandeman. London: ISPCK, 1974.

————. *The Further Shore*. Delhi: ISPCK, 1975.

————. *Saccidananda: A Christian Approach to Advaitic Experience*. Delhi: ISPCK, 1984, rev.

Ajaya, Swami, ed. *Living with the Himalayan Masters: Spiritual Experiences of Swami Rama*. Hinsdale, PA: Himalayan International Institute of Yoga Science and Philosophy, 1980.

Anonymous. *Meditations on the Tarot: A Journey into Christian Hermeticism*. Rockport, MA: Element Books, 1985.

Arberry, A.J., ed. and trans. *Mystical Poems of Rumi*. Chicago: University of Chicago Press, 1968.

Attar, Farid Ud-Din. *The Conference of the Birds*. Trans. Afkham Darbandi and Dick Davis. New York: Penguin, 1984.

Berry, Thomas. *The Dream of the Earth*. San Francisco: Sierra Club Books, 1988.

————, and Swimme, Brian. *The Universe Story: From the Primordial Flaring Forth to the Ecozoic Era*. San Francisco: Harper SanFrancisco, 1992.

Beversluis, Joel. *A Sourcebook for Earth's Community of Religions*. Grand Rapids, MI: CoNexus Press, 1995.

Bly, Robert. *The Kabir Book: Forty-Four of the Ecstatic Poems of Kabir*. Boston: Beacon Press, 1977.

Borchert, Bruno. *Mysticism: Its History and Challenge*. York Beach, Maine: Samuel Weiser, 1994.

Bohm, David. *Wholeness and the Implicate Order*. London: Routledge & Kegan Paul, 1981.

Bruteau, Beatrice. *The Other Half of My Soul: Bede Griffiths and the Hindu-Christian Dialogue*. Wheaton, IL: Quest Books, 1996.

———. *God's Ecstasy: The Creation of a Self-Creating World*. New York: Crossroad, 1997.

Cairns, George and Teasdale, Wayne. *The Community of Religions: Voices and Images of the Parliament of the World's Religions*. New York: Continuum, 1996.

Capra, Fritjof. *The Tao of Physics: An Exploration of the Parallels Between Modern Physics and Eastern Mysticism*. Berkeley, CA: Shambhala, 1975.

———. *Ancient Wisdom and Modern Science*. Albany, NY: SUNY, 1984.

Carlson, Richard and Shield, Benjamin, eds. *For the Love of God: Handbook for the Spirit*. Novato, CA: New World Library, 1997.

Climacus, St. John. *Ladder of Divine Ascent*. Trans. Archmandrite Lazarus Moore. Willits, CA: Easter Orthodox Books, 1959.

Coles, Robert. *The Spiritual Life of Children*. Boston: Houghton Mifflin, 1990.

Colledge, Edmund and McGinn, Bernard, trans. *Meister Eckhart: The Essential Sermons, Commentaries, Treatises, and Defense*. Classics of Western Spirituality. New York: Paulist Press, 1981.

Conze, Edward. *Buddhist Texts Through the Ages*. New York/Touchbooks: Harper, 1954.

Corless, Roger and Knitter, Paul. F., eds. *Buddhist Emptiness and Christian Trinity: Essays and Explorations*. New York: Paulist Press, 1990.

Cousins, Ewert. *Bonaventure: The Soul's Journey into God, The Tree of Life, The Life of St. Francis*. Classics of Western Spirituality. New York: Paulist Press, 1978.

———. *Christ of the Twenty-First Century*. Rockport, MA: Element Books, 1992.

Culligan, Kevin et al. *Purifying the Heart: Buddhist Insight Meditation for Christians*. New York: Crossroad, 1994.

Davis, Wade. *Shadows in the Sun: Travels to Landscapes of Spirit and Desire*. Washington, DC: Island Press, 1998.

Decter, Jacqueline. *Nicholas Roerich: The Life and Art of a Russian Master*. Rochester, VT: Park Street Press, 1989.

du Boulay, Shirley. *Beyond the Darkness: A Biography of Bede Griffiths*. New York: Doubleday, 1998.

Eck, Diana L. *Encountering God: A Spiritual Journey from Bozeman to Banares*. Boston: Beacon Press, 1993.

Elkin, A.P. *Aboriginal Men of High Degree: Initiation and Sorcery in the World's Oldest Tradition*. Rochester, VT: Inner Traditions, 1994.

Fadiman, James and Frager, Robert. *Essential Sufism*. San Francisco: HarperSanFrancisco, 1997.

Feuerstein, Georg. *Yoga: The Technology of Ecstasy*. Los Angeles: Tarcher, 1989.

Fox, Matthew. *Original Blessing: A Primer in Creativion Spirituality*. Santa Fe: Bear, 1983.

———, and Sheldrake, Rupert. *The Physics of Angels: Exploring the Realm Where Science and Spirit Meet*. San Francisco: HarperCollins, 1996.

Fu-Feng, Gia and English, Jane, trans. *Tao Te Ching*. New York: Vintage, 1972.

Funk, Mary Margaret. *Thoughts Matter: The Practice of the Spiritual Life*. New York: Continuum, 1998.

Gardner, Jason. *The Sacred Earth: Writers on Nature and Spirit*. Novato, CA: New World Library, 1998.

Gellert, Michael. *Modern Mysticism*. York Beach, Maine: Nicolas-Hays, 1991.

Goswami, Amit. *The Self-Aware Universe: How Consciousness Creates the Material World*. New York: Tarcher/Putnam, 1995.

Griffiths, Bede. *Return to the Center*. Springfield, IL: Templegate, 1987.

———. *River of Compassion: A Christian Reading of the Bhagavad Gita*. New York: Continuum, 1987.

———. *A New Vision of Reality: Western Science, Eastern Mysticism and Christian Faith*. Springfield, IL: Templegate, 1989.

Haeri, Shaykh Fadhlalla. *The Journey of the Self: A Sufi Guide to Personality*. San Francisco: HarperSanFrancisco, 1989.

Hanh, Thich Nhat. *Living Buddha, Living Christ*. New York: Riverhead Books, 1995.

Happold, F. C. *Mysticism: A Study and an Anthology*. New York: Penguin, 1970.

Hart, Patrick, et al, eds. *The Asian Journal of Thomas Merton*. New York: New Directions, 1973.

Hart, William. *The Art of Living: Vipassanā as Taught by S. N. Goenka*. San Francisco: Harper and Row, 1987.

Harvey, Andrew. *The Essential Mystics*. San Francisco: HarperSanFrancisco, 1996.

Housden, Roger. *Travels Through Sacred India*. New Delhi: HarperCollins India, 1996.

Huxley, Aldous. *The Perennial Philosophy*. New York: Harper and Row, 1945.

Jacobs, Louis, ed. *The Schocken Book of Jewish Mystical Testimonies*. New York: Schocken Books, 1976.

Johnson, Willard. *Riding the Ox Home: A History of Meditation from Shamanism to Science*. Boston: Beacon Press, 1982.

Johnston, William. *The Inner Eye of Love: Mysticism and Religion*. San Francisco: Harper and Row, 1973.

———. *Mystical Theology: The Science of Love*. San Francisco: HarperCollins, 1996.

Kamenetz, Roger. *The Jew in the Lotus: A Poet's Rediscovery of Jewish Identity in Buddhist India*. San Francisco: HarperSanFrancisco, 1994.

———. *Stalking Elijah: Adventures with Today's Jewish Mystical Masters*. San Francisco: HarperSanFrancisco, 1997.

Kavanaugh, Kieran and Rodriguez, Otilio. *The Collected Works of St. John of the Cross*. Washington, DC: Institute of Carmelite Studies, 1973.

———. *The Collected Works of St. Teresa of Avila*. Washington, DC: Institute of

Carmelite Studies, 1976.

Keating, Thomas. *Open Mind, Open Heart: The Contemplative Dimension of the Gospel*. Rockport, MA: Element Books, 1992.

———. *The Mystery of Christ: The Liturgy as Spiritual Practice*. Rockport, MA: Element Books, 1992.

———. *Invitation to Love: The Way of Christian Contemplation*. Rockport, MA: Element, 1992.

———. *Intimacy with God*. New York: Crossroad, 1994.

Knudtson, Peter and Suzuki, David, eds. *Wisdom of the Elders: Sacred Native Stories of Nature*. New York: Bantam Books, 1992.

Kreeft, Peter J. *Heaven: The Heart's Deepest Longing*. San Francisco: Harper & Row, 1980.

Kriyananda, Swami (J. Donald Walsh). *The Hindu Way of Awakening: Its Revelation, Its Symbols*. Nevada City, CA: Crystal Clarity, 1998.

Kuhlewind, Georg. *Becoming Aware of the Logos: The Way of St. John the Evangelist*. Great Barrington, MA: Lindisfarne Press, 1985.

Lake, Medicine Grizzlybear. *Native Healer: Initiation into an Ancient Art*. Wheaton, IL: Quest Books, 1991.

Lopez, Donald S. and Rockefeller, Steven C. *The Christ and the Buddha*. Albany, NY: SUNY, 1987.

Lovelock, James. *Gaia: A New Look at Life on Earth*. London: Oxford University Press, 1979.

Maloney, George. *Uncreated Energy: A Journey into the Authentic Sources of Christian Faith*. Rockport, MA: Element, 1987.

———. *Why Not Become Totally Fire: The Power of Fiery Prayer*. New York: Paulist Press, 1989.

Mascaro, Juan, trans. *The Bhagavad Gita*. New York: Penguin, 1970.

———. *The Dhammapada: The Path of Perfection*. New York: Penguin, 1973.

McDannell, Coleen and Lang, Bernhard. *Heaven: A History*. New York: Vintage-Random House, 1988.

McGaa, Ed (Eagle Man). *Rainbow Tribe: Ordinary People Journeying on the Red Road*. San Francisco: HarperSanFrancisco, 1992.

McGinn, Bernard, trans. and ed. *Meister Eckhart: Teacher and Preacher. Classics of Western Spirituality*. New York: Paulist Press, 1986.

Merton, Thomas. *Mystics and Zen Masters*. New York: Farrar, Straus and Giroux, 1967.

———. *Zen and the Birds of Appetite*. New York: New Directions, 1968.

———. *The Way of Chuang Tzu*. New York: New Directions, 1969.

———. *Contemplation in a World of Action*. New York: Doubleday, 1973.

Mitchell, Donald and Wiseman, James, eds. *The Gethsemani Encounter: A Dailogue on the Spiritual Life by Buddhist and Christian Monastics*. New York: Continuum, 1997.

Moody, Raymond. *Life after Life*. Atlanta: Mockingbird Books, 1975.

Nasr, Seyyed Hosssein. *Knowledge and the Sacred*. New York: Crossroad, 1981.

Nugent, Christopher. *Mysticism, Death and Dying*. Albany, NY: SUNY, 1994.

Nyima, Chokyi Rinpoche. *The Union of Muhamudra and Dzogchen*. Hong Kong: Rangjung Yeshe Publications, 1994.

———. *Indisputable Truth: The Four Seals That Mark the Teachings of the Awakened Ones*. Hong Kong: Rangjung Yeshe Publications, 1996.

Olivelle, Patrick, trans. *Upanisads*. New York: Oxford University Press, 1996.

O'Murchu, Diarmuid. *Quantum Theology*. New York: Crossroad, 1997.

Osborne, Arthur, ed. *The Collected Works of Ramana Maharshi*. London: Rider, 1969.

Panikkar, Raimon. *The Vedic Experience*. Pondicherry: All India Books, 1983.

———. *Invisible Harmony: Essays on Contemplation and Responsibility*. Minneapolis: Fortress Press, 1995.

Ranade, R.D. *Mysticism in India: The Poet-Saints of Maharashtra*. Albany, NY: SUNY, 1983.

Ripinsky-Naxon, Michael. *The Nature of Shamanism: Substance and Function of a Religious Metaphor*. Albany, NY: SUNY, 1993.

Romano, Eugene L., ed. *In the Silence of Solitude: Contemporary Witnesses of the Desert*. New York: Alba House, 1995.

Russell, Peter. *The Global Brain: Speculations on the Evolutionary Leap to Planetary Consciousness*. Los Angeles: J. P. Tarcher, 1983.

Salwak, Dale, ed. *The Wonders of Solitude*. Novato, CA: New World Library, 1998.

Sanford, John A., *Dreams: God's Forgotten Language*. San Francisco: HarperSanFrancisco, 1989.

Schuon, Frithjof. *The Transcendent Unity of Religions*. Wheaton, IL: Quest Books, 1993.

———. *Stations of Wisdom*. Bloomington, IN: World Wisdom Books, 1995.

Schwartz, Howard, ed. *Gabriel's Palace: Jewish Mystical Tales*. New York: Oxford University Press, 1993.

Shah, Amina, ed. *The Tale of the Four Dervishes and Other Sufi Tales*. San Francisco: Harper and Row, 1981.

Singh, Jaideva, ed. and trans. *The Yoga of Vibration and Divine Pulsation: A Translation of the Spanda Karikas with Ksemaraja's Commentary, the Spanda Nirnaya*. Albany, NY: SUNY, 1992.

Suzuki, D.T. *Essays in Zen Buddhism*. New York: Grove Press, 1961.

Talbot, Michael. *Mysticism and the New Physics*. New York: Penguin-Arkana, 1993.

Theophane. *Tales of the Magic Monastery*. New York: Crossroad, 1984.

Torwesten, Hans. *Vedanta: Heart of Hinduism*. New York: Grove Press, 1991.

Walker, Susan, ed. *Speaking of Silence: Christians and Buddhists on the Contemplative Way*. New York: Paulist Press, 1987.

Walsh, James, ed. *The Cloud of Unknowing. The Classics of Western Spirituality*. New York: Paulist Press, 1981.

Wilber, Ken. *The Spectrum of Consciousness*. Wheaton, IL: Quest Books, 1982.

———, ed. *Quantum Questions: Mystical Writings of the World's Great Physicists*. Boulder: Shambhala, 1984.

————. *The Eye of Spirit: An Integral Vision for a World Gone Slightly Mad.* Boston: Shambhala, 1997.

————. *The Marriage of Sense and Soul: Integrating Science and Religion.* New York: Random House, 1998.

Winson, Robert and Sagan, Miriam. *Dirty Laundry: 100 Days in a Zen Monastery.* Novato, CA: New World Library, 1999.

Wiseman, James A., ed. and trans. *John Ruusbroec: The Spiritual Espousals and Other Works. Classics of Western Spirituality.* New York: Paulist Press, 1985.

Underhill, Evelyn. *Mysticism: The Development of Humankind's Spiritual Consciousness.* London: Bracken Books, 1995, rep.

RECOMMENDED DISCOGRAPHY

Chatterjee, Amit. *Colors of the Heart.* The Relaxation Co., 1997. ISBN 1-55961-424-2.

Dhar, Sheila. *Inde du Nord: Voyage interieur.* Ocora. Double CD, 1992. C560017-18.

Hykes, David, and the Harmonic Choir. *Hearing Solar Winds.* Ocora, 1989.

————. Atalyst, 1995. 09026-68347-2.

Gyume, Lama, and Rykiel, Jean-Philippe. *Lama's Chant: Songs of Awakening.* Sony, 1997.

Kalor, Kayhan, and Khan, Shujaat Husain. *Ghazal: As Night Falls on the Silk Road.* Shanachie, 1998.

Paul, Russill. *Nada Yoga: The Ancient Science of Sound.* Relaxation Co., 1999. ISBN 1-55961-514-1.

————. *The Yoga of Sound. Part I: Shabda.* Relaxation Co., 1999.

————. *Part II: Shakti, and Part III: Bhava.* Relaxation Co., 2000.

————. *Spirit Bridges.* Order through Russill Paul Music and Publishing at (510) 653-5368.

Von Bingen, Hildegard. *Vision: The Music of Hildegard von Bingen.* Angel, 1994. D106215.

Index

Fellowship of Reconciliation, 8
Fitzgerald, Father Paul, 123–24
forgiveness. *See* humility
Foucauld, Charles de, 149
Fox, Matthew, 198
Francis of Assisi, St., 113, 115, 140;
asceticism, 204; effect of prayer
on, 139; life of simplicity and
poverty, 148; and nature mysticism, 179–80, 193; vision of
Godhead, 199

G

Gandhi, Mahatma, 117, 148–49, 151
Gardner, Jason, 13
Genung, Jeff, 117–18
Gethsemani Encounter, 41
Gliberman, Rabbi, 49
Global Ethic, 112
global spirituality, emergence of a,
238
God: becoming like, 124, 144; belief
in, 45, 47; in Buddhism, 25, 26,
45, 47; communication with
humans, 101, 182–83; contemplation of, 63; distinction between
persons and, 87, 200; in Eastern
vs. Western thought, 87; everything is within, 83; experiencing,
23, 182; Hindu approach to, 34,
59, 80, 81; as infinite light, 75–76;
in the Koran, 86; nature of, 26;
realizing/finding, 80, 81, 182;
realizing that one is, 218, 220. *See
also* advaita; union and communion with, 20–21, 87, 134, 220–24
God-centered forms of mysticism,
127, 179, 226
Godhead, 48, 59, 218
Goswami, Amit, 74, 75
Great Spirit, 79
Greeks, 61–64
Green, Joyce. *See* Ma Jaya Sati
Bhagavati
Gregory the Great, St., 199
Griffiths, Bede, 11, 35–36, 79, 108,
113, 226; on Atman, 82; on
Catholic Church, 247; on commu-

nity, 237; on Dancing Shiva, 177;
and nature mysticism, 180–81;
reaction to the West, 166; *River of
Compassion,* 84; on separation,
215; spiritual practice, 139;
Teasdale's encounters with, 13, 15,
236, 237; on ultimate
revelation/realization, 176, 211–12;
on Vedic understanding of the
three worlds, 178
grihastha, 92–93
The Guidelines for Interreligious
Understanding, 42, 212–16

H

Haeri, Shaykh Fadhlalla, 142
happiness of others, as most important goal, xii
Hasidism, 96, 220
Hawking, Stephen, 3
health, 202
heart, 79; cave of the, 176–77; civilization with a, 5; dialogue of the,
29; humility of, 126–28; mystical,
242–45; open, 15; purity of, 223;
simplicity of, 150–52
Hegel, G. W. F., 46, 47
Heidegger, Martin, 36
hermetic understanding, 90–91
Hermeticism, 6, 90–91, 251n.2
hesychia, 262n.1
Hindu meditation, 53
Hindu mysticism, 52, 59, 182;
Buddhist and Christian mysticism
and, 35–36, 226; nonduality as
goal, 217–18
Hindu Vedantic tradition, 25
Hindu view of life, 91–95; similar
paths in other traditions, 96
Hinduism: approach to God, 34, 59,
80, 81; identity in, 55; and inner
path of contemplation, 80–81;
introversion *vs.* extroversion in,
80, 83; meeting of Christianity
and, 32–41; moral code, 110; personalist school. *See* Shaivism;
supreme identity in the
mahavakyas, 52–55. *See also specific*

O

oneness: sense of, xvii, 216. *See also* union; unity
openness, 3, 165, 232, 240, 241
oratio, 130
other-centered life, 68, 128
other-centeredness, 106, 122
others: ability to be present to, 165–66; happiness and well-being of, xii, xv–xvi. *See also* bodhisattva; honoring the humanity of, xv; moral responsibility to, 152; shifting from self to, 122
Otto, Rudolf, 195

P

Pada, Gauda, 217
pagan religious forms, 33
panentheism, 83, 183, 198–99
Panikkar, Raimon, 227
Panikkar, Raimundo, 36
pantheism, 83
paradise, 86–87
parents, following the spirituality of one's, 245
Parliament of the World's Religions, 7–10, 42–43, 164, 247
Paul, St., 178–79
peace, 119, 168. *See also* nonviolence
Pentecost, 9
perception, clear *vs.* distorted, 82–83
perennial philosophy, 65
Petersham Conference, 235
physics, 72–75, 115–16
pilgrimage, spirituality of, 200–202
Pius XII, Pope, 160, 161
Plato, 61, 62
Pontifical Council for Interreligious Dialogue, 40
Pontifical Council for Non-Christian Religions, 40
potential/potentiality, human, 213, 214
poverty: simplicity and, 148–50. *See also* homeless
power, yearning for, xv, xvi
prayer, 18, 125, 131–34; affective, 130; as communion with reality, 216;

contemplative, 24; conventional, 138, 139. *See also* Centering Prayer
presence, 165–66
present, 22
prophecy, history of, 158–59
prophetic voice, 157–64
prophetic witness, 244
purification, inner, 83; as necessary, 224
purity, 223
Purusha, 54

Q

quantum mechanics, 73–74, 115–16
quantum nonlocality, 74–75
quiet, 81, 246

R

raja yoga, 94–96
Ramana Maharshi, Sri, 217
Ratzinger, Joseph Cardinal, 45
real, the: seeking, 106
reality. *See* divine; Ultimate Reality
reflection, 130
Reid, Forrest, 183–84
reincarnation, 64, 230
relativity, theory of, 72–73
religion(s): added to *vs.* replacing each other, 49; changing one's, xii; community between, 236. *See also* interspiritual community; as completing each other, 212–16, 226–27; guidelines for bringing harmony among, xii; influence on each other, 6; neglect of mystical life, 11; origins, 11; similar potential among, xi; similar purpose among, xii
religious, being, 17
religious institutions, dependence on, 18
renunciation. *See* sannyasa
Resolution on Tibet, 42–43
respect, mutual, xvii
responsibility: to global community of the earth, 27; moral, 152
rest, 130, 133–34
resurrection, 64
revelation, 177–82; nature and,

About the Author

B rother Wayne Teasdale is a lay monk who combines the traditions of Christianity and Hinduism in the way of Christian Sannyasa. An activist and teacher in building common ground between religions, Teasdale serves on the board of trustees of the Parliament of the World's Religions. He is a member of the Monastic Interreligious Dialogue and helped draft their Universal Declaration on Nonviolence. He is an adjunct professor at DePaul University, Columbia College, and the Catholic Theological Union, and coordinator of the Bede Griffiths International Trust. He is co-editor of *The Community of Religions*, with George Cairns, and the author of two books and dozens of articles on mysticism and religion. He holds an M.A. in philosophy from St. Joseph College and a Ph.D. in theology from Fordham University. He lives at the Catholic Theological Union in Chicago. He is working on his forthcoming book, *A Monk in the World*.

New World Library is dedicated to
publishing books and audio products
that inspire and challenge us to improve
the quality of our lives and our world.

Our products are available
in bookstores everywhere.
For our catalog, please contact:

New World Library
14 Pamaron Way
Novato, California 94949

Phone: (415) 884-2100 or (800) 972-6657
Catalog requests: Ext. 50
Orders: Ext. 52
Fax: (415) 884-2199

Email: escort@newworldlibrary.com
Website: www.newworldlibrary.com